The
Butterfly
Mosque

THE
BUTTERFLY
MOSQUE

G. Willow Wilson

Atlantic Monthly Press
New York

ISBN-13: 978-0-8021-1887-5

Atlantic Monthly Press
an imprint of Grove/Atlantic, Inc.
841 Broadway
New York, NY 10003

Distributed by Publishers Group West

www.groveatlantic.com

10 11 12 13   6 5 4 3 2 1

for Amu Fakhry

with thanks to Warren Frazier and Elisabeth Schmitz

The
Butterfly
Mosque

Prologue

IN THE UPPER REACHES OF THE ZAGROS MOUNTAINS, THE AIR changed. The high altitude opened it, cleared it of the dust of the valleys, and made it sing a little in the lungs; low atmospheric pressure. It was a shift I recognized. We had been driving for hours, winding north along a wide dry basin between high peaks; then we turned west. Now the car, an old Peugot, struggled upward along switchbacks cut into the mountainside, past intersecting layers of rock laid down over geological ages.

For a moment I was reminded intensely of home. It had been almost a year since I had been back to Boulder, in the foothills of the Colorado Rockies. The snug valley where I had gone to high school, learned to drive, where my parents and sister still lived, could be seen as a tidy whole from this height in cliffs much like these. Looking down into the plain below, I felt as though I was seeing double, and that an hour's hike along the switchbacks would bring me to my own doorstep.

At the time, it was a sensation that seemed a little perverse. I had just flown into Iran from Egypt—this journey had begun thousands of miles from my own country. That a mountain and a change in the air in Iran should make me think of home in the spring of 2004, the spring of the War on Terror, the clash of civilizations, the jihad, the things that had made my quiet life almost unlivable, must be sheer perversity, I thought then. I didn't yet realize that the Zagros Mountains had no name when they were forced out of the ground millions of years ago, and neither did the Rockies, that the call of earth to earth might be something more real than the human divisions of Iran and America. I had faith, then; it was in the mountains that I first thought of divinity, and these mountains reminded me of that sensation. But I didn't yet have faith in faith—I didn't trust the connections I felt between mountains or memories, and if I had been a little more ambivalent, I could have allowed the Zagros to be foreign, and the memory to be coincidence.

Fortunately, I didn't.

Ahmad, my guide plus chaperone, pointed west over the receding peaks.

"If you kept driving that way, you would get to Iraq," he said. He was from Shiraz, and had silver hair and laugh lines. Before the revolution he flew planes for the Shah, whom he had hated, but not as much as he now hated the mullahs. During one of our conversations on the road from Shiraz to Isfahan, he told me he used to fast during Ramadan and pray with some regularity. In his eyes, though, the Islamic regime had so deformed his religion that he stopped. Thinking I would judge him for this lapse lest he provide a rationale (I was an American and a Sunni, and therefore unpredictable) he told me he didn't need to fast; fasting was meant to remind one of the hunger of the poor, and he helped the poor in other ways.

"Then why do the poor fast?" I asked him. The Ramadan fast was required of all Muslims, not just the wealthy. He looked at me out of the corner of his eye; evidently I was an American Sunni who discussed theology. Among the middle classes, theology had gone out of fashion in Iran. But I had just come from Egypt, where the reverse was true. Ahmad left the question floating in the air.

"Iraq?" I climbed on a rock near the edge of the promontory where we were standing, having parked the car on the shoulder of the road. My Nikes stuck out from under the hem of my black robe. I had overdressed. In Khatami's Tehran, chadors and manteaux had been replaced by short, tight housecoats and scarves that were barely larger than handkerchiefs. Knowing only that Iran was under a religious dictatorship, and Egypt was under a military one, I had dressed as conservatively as possible. I didn't realize that whatever the political reality, Egypt was far more socially conservative than Iran. The reasons for this would become clear to me only later: when a dictatorship claims absolute authority over an idea—in the case of Iran, Islam, in the case of Egypt, a hamfisted brand of socialism—frustrated citizens will run to the opposite ideological extreme. The Islamic Republic was secularizing Iran; in Egypt the short-robed fundamentalists multiplied and multiplied.

"Yes, Iraq. I think at night farther southwest you could maybe see the bombs falling. But far away; first the plain of

Karbala, then Baghdad." Ahmad came to stand next to
my rock, and pointed northwest. "Karbala is where Imam
Husayn is buried."

"We have his head," I said, thinking of the fasting argument. "In Cairo. There's a square named after him where
the shrine is."

"What?"

"His head," I repeated, wondering whether I should put
an honorific before *his*; Husayn ibn Ali was a grandson of
the Prophet and beloved by all Muslims, but particularly revered by Shi'ites. I didn't want to commit a faux pas. No
matter what Ahmad thought about fasting. I put one hand
to my back; the infection in my kidneys had manifested itself as a dull spreading pain there, and a touch of fever. Living in an industrial neighborhood in Cairo, not a clean city
to begin with, I had developed an unfortunate apathy toward my health.

"This is the first time I hear this about Imam Husayn,"
muttered Ahmad, and broke out into a laugh.

"It's true," I said. "The Fatimids brought him with them.
At least, that's what the *ulema* tell us; maybe it's all a lie and
the shrine is empty." A light wind ran down the channel of
the valley below. I took a breath and held it for a moment,
then let it out in a sigh. Ahmad smiled a little.

"Thank you," I said. "It's beautiful up here."

Later, in the car, Ahmad told me, "I think you are becoming a little bit Arab." He said so gently, but this is not a com-
pliment in Persia. On some level, I agreed with him—I was

so submerged in Cairo, so cut off from America, that something was bound to change. Yet I still felt like myself. I was disturbed because I had been told I should be disturbed; that the Arab way of doing things, being opposed to the American way of doing things, represented the betrayal of an American self. But I had discovered that I was not my habits. I was not the way I dressed or the things I did and didn't say. If I were all these things, then standing on that rock and looking west, I should have been someone else.

But I remained.

When the term "clash of civilizations" was coined, it was a myth; the interdependence of world cultures lay on the surface, supported by trade and the travel of ideas, the borrowing of words from language to language. But like so many ugly ideas, the clash becomes a little more real every time someone says the word. Today, it is a theory supported not only in the West, where it was invented, but also in the Muslim world, where plenty of people see Islam as irrevocably in conflict with western values. When threatened, both Muslims and westerners tend to toe their respective party lines, defending monolithic ideals that only exist as tools of opposition, ideals that crumble as soon as the opposing party has turned its back. The truth emerges. It is not through politics that we will be delivered from this conflict. It is not through pundits and analysts and experts. The war between Islam and the West is a human conflict, in which human experience is the only reliable guide. We are all standing on the mountaintop, and we must learn to look out at the world not through the medium of self-appointed authorities, but with our own eyes.

Kun

We say unto it: Be! And it is.

—*Quran 16:40*

IN A WAY, I WAS IN THE MARKET FOR A PHILOSOPHY. FIVE
months into my sophomore year of college at Boston University I was hospitalized, in the middle of the night, for a rare
and acute reaction to a Depo Provera injection I'd received
several days earlier. Up until then I'd been lucky enough
never to see the inside of an emergency room. The most dangerous things I'd ever done were take the Chinatown-to-
Chinatown bus from Boston to New York, walk home alone
late at night once or twice, and get my lower lip pierced at a
dimly lit shop in some basement off Commonwealth Avenue.
At the turn of the millennium, even rebellion was fairly sani-
tary. Landing in the hospital because of legal medication
seemed like a violation of the way things were supposed to
work.

For days I was in and out of doctors' offices with the
mostly untreatable symptoms of adrenal distress: heart pal-
pitations, sudden attacks of sweating and dizziness, and insomnia so severe that no amount of tranquilizer could keep
me asleep for more than four or five hours. In a blow to my
vanity, I was losing hair. Later I would learn that I was also

losing bone mass. At seventeen I was immortal; at eighteen I was a short and arbitrary series of events.

I wasn't very good with pain. And having always been the kind of person who could catnap at will, I wasn't very good with sleep deprivation, either. By chance, the three people who watched over me most diligently during the first days of my illness—a classmate, his mother, and a nurse—were all Iranian. Semidelirious, I took this as a sign. Addressing a God I had never spoken to in my life, I promised that if I recovered in three days, I would become a Muslim.

As it happened, the adrenal distress lasted a year and a half.

It was this unanswered prayer that sparked my interest in organized religion. I had been raised an atheist but was never very good at it. As a child I had precognitive dreams about mundane events like the deaths of pets, and I could not remember a time when I was not in love with whatever sat behind the world. Yet God was taboo in my parents' house; we were educated, and educated people don't believe in nonsense. Both of my parents came from conservative Protestant families. They left their churches during the Vietnam era, sick of the racist warmongering peddled from the pulpits. To them, God was a bigoted, vengeful white man. Refusing to believe in him was not just scientifically correct, it was morally imperative.

I learned to hide, deny, or dress up all experiences I could not explain. In high school a fatuous brand of neopaganism was popular, thanks to movies like *The Craft*; this gave my heretical impulses a temporary outlet. By the time

I was in my late teens I had adopted the anemic mantra "spiritual but not religious." I couldn't have told you what it meant.

Three days turned into three weeks. Doctors told me to sit tight—the Depo injection was effective for three months, and it might take another several months after that for my body to rebalance itself. I tired easily. Assignments that once took a few hours to complete now took days; walking from campus to my dorm left me exhausted. Twilight began to look bleak, the precursor of dark empty hours without sleep. Being eighteen and fortunate, it was a struggle to realize that this was not the end of everything. And, in fact, it wasn't. Since the big things were enough trouble, I began to let the small things slide. I went out without makeup. I stopped going to all the parties I didn't really care about. An alchemical process was taking place that I didn't quite understand. By small increments, my sense of humor and ability to cope were coming back, along with a new interest in the God who had not answered my prayers.

"I guess the Almighty doesn't bargain," I said one day to Elizabeth, who lived down the hall. We were on our way to Eli Wiesel's annual lecture on the Book of Job, about which we had to write a paper.

"Not with miserable sinners," she said cheerfully. She was Episcopalian.

"There is such a thing as respect, you know." Javad, whose steady supply of dining hall cookies and sympathy helped prompt my brush with Islam, appeared behind us with some other students from our section. "Even if God is only a hypothetical to you." He was a serious person, and smoked Djarum Blacks; he was not amused by my attitude toward the whole thing.

"I'm being respectful," I said. "I was serious. Hypothetically serious."

"So you feel like hypothetical God abandoned you?" He raised one eyebrow.

"No, I don't. But I'm having trouble understanding why that is."

"Of course you don't. You can't feel abandoned by a God you don't believe in," Elizabeth pointed out. I shook my head.

"I'm not sure it's that simple."

We found seats in the middle of the lecture hall just as Dr. Wiesel was being introduced. Since we were humanities students, the idea of listening to a lecture on Job was not all that terrifying. We had already faced Confucius, the Stoics, and the Bhagavad Gita and come through relatively unscathed. But as Dr. Wiesel talked about the role of suffering in God's covenant with the Jews, I began to feel uncomfortable.

"I don't think that's what it means," I muttered.

"What?" Elizabeth frowned at me.

"Job. I don't think that's what it's about. I think it's about—"

Someone several rows back made a shushing noise.

"I think it's about monotheism," I said, "the idea that faith in the God of mercy is also faith in the God of destruction. God causes Job's suffering, not the devil."

The shushing became more insistent. I slumped in my seat, dissatisfied.

When I made my desperate offer to trade faith for health, I had not read a word of the Quran. My otherwise exhaustive liberal education skipped right over it. The professors I queried said teaching the Quran as a work of literature angered Muslim students and put everybody at risk. I was skeptical of this answer. When we studied the Bible, it was as a work of *holy* literature, and there was a level of respect and suspension of disbelief in our discussions. If the Quran was afforded the same treatment, I had trouble believing Muslim students would be so ominously displeased. The few that I knew—Javad and one or two others—seemed benign enough. Through them, I had picked up some stray facts: I knew there were two major sects of Islam, and I knew not all Muslims were Arabs. But I knew almost nothing about what they believed, and even with a $30,000-a-year education, I had no idea Islam was the world's second-largest religion.

I began to investigate Islam on my own, and tried to understand the relationship of the three Abrahamic traditions. The beliefs of my religious friends, once a source of silent pity, were now fascinating: I wanted to know about the Trinity and the Eucharist and the Jewish concept of the afterlife. I discovered opinions I did not know I held.

"If there is one omniscient omnipotent God, why send a holy spirit to impregnate Mary? Why the extra step? Couldn't He just cause her to become spontaneously pregnant? Isn't that what omnipotence is? Why do people always point up when they talk about Heaven? If heaven is up there, where is it in China? Down? Where is it on the moon? How could there be such a thing as inherited sin? Isn't that a fundamentally unjust idea?" I was persistent, maybe even rude, and my questions were often met with ruffled silence. These are questions atheists often use to dismantle religion, but to me, they were urgent attempts to name what I was finding harder and harder to ignore.

I had been taught that it was weak minded to believe the world was created by an invisible man with superpowers. But what if God was not an invisible man with superpowers? Atheism had never taught me how to answer that question. It had only taught me to reject primitive little-g gods; anthropomorphized, local entities subject to the laws of time and space—it had taught me, in other words, to reject Zeus and the Keebler elves. And the God to whom I had prayed so desperately was not Zeus.

When I prayed, maybe I was trying to justify a belief I already held. Being ill had shaken something loose in my head. Sitting up at night under dark windows, my perceptions had altered. My body was no longer an infinite resource but a union of thousands of fragile things, chemicals and precursors and proteins, all in a balance that could easily be upset. That so many people were well—that I had been well for so long—seemed miraculous.

Illnesses usually bring people to religion through the front door; mine brought me through the back. I did not need to know if I was being punished or tested. Neither my health nor my illness was about me. The force that played havoc with the cortisol in my blood was the same force that helped my body recover; if I felt better one day and worse the next, it was unchanged. It chose no side. It gave the girl next to me in the hospital pneumonia; it also gave her white blood cells that would resist the infection. And the atoms in those cells, and the nuclei in those atoms, the same bits of carbon that were being spun into new planets in some corner of space without a name. My insignificance had become unspeakably beautiful to me.

That unified force was a God too massive, too inhuman, to resist with the atheism in which I had been brought up. I became a zealot without a religion. It was unclear to me whether there was a philosophy big enough for monotheism so adamant. It had to be a faith that didn't need to struggle to explain why bad things happen to good people, a faith in which it was understood that destruction is implicit in creation. I had a faint attraction to Buddhism, but Buddhism was not theist enough; the role of God was obscure or absent. I would have liked to be a Christian. My life would have been much easier if I could stomach the Trinity and inherited sin, or the idea that God had a son. Judaism was a near perfect fit, but it was created for a single tribe of people. Most practicing Jews I knew took a dim view of conversion. To them, membership in the historical community of Jews was as important as belief.

In Islam, which encouraged conversion, there were words for what I believed. *Tawhid,* the absolute unity of God. *Al Haq,* the truth so true it had no corresponding opposite, truth that encompassed both good and evil. There were no intermediary steps in the act of creation, God simply said, *Kun, fa yakun.* "Be, so it is." I began to have a feeling of déjà vu. It was as if my promise to become a Muslim was not a coincidence but a kind of inversion; a future self speaking through a former self.

It was a feeling that intensified as I stood in front of a vending machine in my Warren Towers dorm in the spring of my illness, on the verge of an epiphany. Another girl in a T-shirt and pajama bottoms stood in front of me with a deflated expression.

"Screw this," she said, punching the glass that divided her from the Almond Joy stuck inside, dangling by its wrapper. She sighed and turned away, muttering "Good luck," as she passed. Her T-shirt read, "Why does it always rain on *me*?" Apparently she had dressed for this moment of synchronicity.

I punched in the code for a Snickers. As it fell, it hit the trapped Almond Joy. When I pushed in the flap at the bottom of the machine I saw two candy bars, side by side. I looked around for the other girl, but she was gone.

"*Kun,*" I said to no one, and laughed. "*Kun fa yakun.*"

At that moment, the girl with the synchronous T-shirt was more upset about losing her candy bar than I was about having *osteopenia,* low bone mineral density. The moral microcosm of Warren Towers seemed profoundly balanced. What I had suffered was so slight compared to so many people; how appropriate that all I got for it was an Almond Joy.

I had just read a verse of the Quran about *rizq,* which translates as "sustenance," but has threads of destiny and fortune running through it. "Oh you who believe, partake of the good things We have provided for you as sustenance,

13

and give thanks to God, if it is truly Him that you worship."
With an infinitesimal shift in probability, an invisible wink,
a little *rizq* had been redistributed. The world seemed without contradiction. It was called into being, *kun,* with pain
and synchronicity and malfunctioning vending machines
already written on it. I was abandoning my ability to distinguish between the macrocosmic and the microcosmic.

At home in Colorado that summer, I got a new tattoo.
An artist named Fish inked *Al Haq* across my lower back in
Arabic calligraphy, talking to me as he worked to keep my
mind off the pain. I had signed up to take Arabic in the fall;
in the interim I taught myself part of the alphabet out of an
old textbook, to make sure I knew what I was putting on
my body. *Al Haq* joined another tattoo designed by a
kabbalist from Rhode Island, who gave me my first ink at
seventeen after I showed him a fake ID. He had told me
that nobody gets two tattoos—they either get one or they
get lots. I would get two more before I quit, making the
first in a series of difficult negotiations between art and
religious law. As it is in Judaism, tattooing is frowned upon
in mainstream Islam. The body is God's creation, and
therefore perfect; any medically unnecessary alteration is
seen as an affront. I'm glad I didn't know that when I decided to get this tattoo, because I'm not sure it would have
stopped me.

Al Haq was a note to myself that I could not erase. As I
got healthier, it would be easy to forget this part of my life,
to go back to thinking the world contained only me and
whatever I wanted at any given moment. Now I had a per-

manent physical reminder. One day I would work up the courage to convert. I wasn't ready yet—I still had chemical and social crutches, and it would take time to learn to live without them. When they were gone, though, I knew what I had to be.

The White Horse

Zuljanah walked forward a few steps and
stopped. Husayn stroked the horse's white
neck and said, "My faithful horse, I know
you are thirsty and tired. You have been
carrying me since morning. My faithful
horse, for the last time, take me to the
battlefield."

—Islamic folktale

BACK AT BU THREE WEEKS LATER, I WOKE UP TO A STRANGE
piece of news on the BBC World Service: Ahmad Shah
Massoud, the Afghani resistance leader who kept the
Taliban at bay in the north for almost two decades, had
been shot by men posing as journalists. I had been following his life for a class, and knew how important he was in
the Afghan struggle against the Taliban and its allies. I was
surprised that more attention was not paid to the cleverly
staged attack that brought about his death. In all probability, it had been carried out by his fundamentalist enemies.
The fact that they could come up with a plan so canny and
sophisticated was a little scary.

If working adults were graded on their knowledge of
current events the way college juniors are, we would live in
a very different world. I felt a kind of nausea that begins

between your eyes, like vertigo; the experience you have when you see a car skid across the center line and can picture the crash that is about to take place. Massoud's death was not the endgame; it couldn't be. He had been eliminated in preparation for something else.

It was September 11, 2001, at about eight thirty in the morning.

Boston is rarely part of the conversation about the attacks, but guilt was palpable in the streets afterward. The terrorists who hit the South Tower flew out of Logan Airport, the terrorists had been in Boston not two hours earlier, the terrorists *could have been stopped here*—people spoke as though they had been personally negligent. Then there was the paranoia: it was rumored that another terrorist cell was still in the city. We were to be quarantined, cut off from bridges and rail routes until the cell could be found. A few hysterical BU students rushed to South Station to catch trains home "before they shut everything down." There was no cell and no quarantine. But F-15s flew overhead, deafeningly low, and the sirens never stopped. My parents left a number of terrified messages on my phone, afraid I might have gone to New York to visit friends at NYU, as I sometimes did on weekends. I sent e-mails in return, begging them to obey the official request to stay off the phones.

With remarkable foresight, the chancellor of BU kept classes in session that day, becoming one of the first to argue that if we disrupted our way of life we would be helping the terrorists. And so, at three p.m., I went to the Arabic class I'd signed up for the previous spring, carrying a textbook whose title began with a big scarlet *A*.

17

The next evening I made dinner plans at the student union with Ben, another history major. I brought my Arabic homework, but lost interest as soon as I opened the book. I jumped when Ben tossed his bag on the chair opposite mine and sat down.

"I have a flask of gin in my coat," he said. "I say we get hammered and go see *Zoolander*. Apparently the movie theaters are open. I can't handle this anymore."

I sighed with relief. "Yes. Sure. That's the best idea I've heard all day."

We ate in silence and left, walking down a balmy and subdued Commonwealth Avenue toward the Fenway.

"What do you think is going to happen?" Ben asked without preamble, passing me the gin. It was cool and piney, like pool water and Christmas trees.

"I'm glad it's not my job to know," I said. I didn't want to think about it. My Arabic professor, a cheerful but permanently annoyed Egyptian man, had come to class looking exhausted. At that point, we assumed the retaliatory blow would fall on one of the countries whose citizens were responsible for the attacks.

"There will be a war," said Ben, in a curt voice he reserved for political predictions. "You were smart to start taking Arabic," he continued. "You could totally go into government intelligence."

"That's not why I'm taking it," I said with an involuntary twitch. "It's beautiful."

"It's useful."

"Well, why don't you learn it then?"

"I might." Ben was quiet for a moment and put his hands in his pockets. "I wish I understood what just happened," he said. "I woke up today and forgot what was wrong. It was just a feeling, a terrible feeling. It took me five minutes to attach the feeling to the event."

It didn't make any sense to anyone at that point. All we knew was that we were no longer living in a world divided into America, where things like this didn't happen, and Everywhere Else, where they did. The force of that realization brought people together. In line at the movie theater, people smiled at each other and started spontaneous conversations with strangers. I was struck by this—at such a time and in such a situation, our first instinct was tenderness.

I could not become a Muslim. Not after that. It would be a betrayal of the people I loved and an insult to what my country had suffered. When videos of angry men in beards flooded the airwaves, claiming their religion was incompatible with the decadent West, I believed them. It was my civilization they were insulting. Consciously and unconsciously, I began to resist Islam. I went back to the regular college diet of jello shots and wine in a box. I ate in front of my Muslim friends during the fasting month of Ramadan. In a logical backflip, I reasoned that becoming a Muslim would be anti-Islamic, because it would mean submitting to an institution rather than to God. About the religion itself I was aggressive and sarcastic. In arguments I defended Muslims in order to look liberal, but that defense was a

19

kind of domination: it allowed me to monopolize the subject, and cloaked in me the same sort of self-satisfied anger
of those who hated Islam more openly and more honestly.

I was desperate for the secular truth that seemed so self-
evident to other people. Fortunately, critics of Islam and
their books were in plentiful supply. I had high hopes that
The Satanic Verses would cure my religiosity, but I found the
book dense and unpalatable. On the other hand, I loved
Hanif Kureishi's urbane, subversive novels. *The Black Al-
bum* is still one of my favorite books, but even it did not
touch my belief in God. Nothing felt as right as what I had
seen in the Quran. I waited to be shaken by the great argument, the rejection of spiritual authority that had inspired
so many people to leave organized religion. No matter how
many iterations I read, I could not make it feel true. To me,
it seemed like the philosophers who argued that there is no
light had simply covered up the light switch.

Resisting the temptation to say the *shaheda*—there is no
God but God, and Muhammad is His prophet—became a
daily exercise. My dreams were suddenly cluttered with the
Old Testament images that are shared between all three
Abrahamic religions. In one, I saw Jacob's ladder. Instead
of running from Earth to Heaven, it ran between them, rung
after rung, cutting a swath parallel to the horizon. In another, I saw a wasteland of dry bones and felt a presence
behind me, like the shadow of a great bird, asking me questions. Upon waking, I couldn't identify it. Later that same
day, a professor read the story of Ezekiel and the valley of
bones in class, leaving me shaken and disturbed. Most
often, though, I dreamed of a white horse. It appeared in

nightmares, when I was threatened or hurt; I would climb on its back and without any prompting it would carry me out of danger.

Ben graduated the year before I did. At the same time, one of his professors retired and announced plans to return to her native Cairo to help run an English-language high school. Ben was at loose ends in an indifferent economy, so when she offered him a job, he accepted. He'd get his chance to learn Arabic after all. Our friends assumed I would follow suit once I was out of school. Inexpensive opportunities for Life Experience did not come along every day. When I came back, I'd have two of the most coveted job qualifications in post-9/11 America: Arabic language skills and knowledge of the Middle East. I could find no good reason not to go. With a history degree and no high ambitions, I had little reason to stay.

Still, I hedged and considered other options. I knew I would not go to Egypt to study and come back with a few good stories. I would go and convert. If I stayed in the United States, ordinary life would win out and help me forget about the Quran. I could move somewhere with a few friends, get a regular job, become fluent in car insurance and summer sublets. The idea of having a life I could plan— a life built on events I could predict, with people I knew— was attractive. For months I considered two very different futures.

The winter before my graduation, I came across a pack of Tarot cards on a friend's desk. I liked Tarot; as fortune-telling games go it was accurate enough. During high school I played regularly. While waiting for my friend to arrive, I shuffled the pack and laid out a standard seven-card cross. In the "past" position I drew the Queen of Wands—a very sensible and unsurprising card. In the future, though, was the Knight of Wands: a young man riding through the desert, past a group of pyramids. A young man on a white horse.

"No."

I looked at the ceiling, addressing empty space. It was the first time I had spoken to God verbally, without embarrassment or internal preamble.

"I won't do it," I said. "I'm not going."

It was the last time I would ever touch a Tarot deck. As a Muslim you waive your right to peek at the future. The people who tipped the scales were my parents, who thought I was crazy to turn down such an exciting opportunity abroad. If I had told them I was trying to save myself from a religious conversion, they might have felt differently. Resisting religion is a noble goal among secular liberals. But I didn't tell them—I didn't tell anyone.

On a warm August day in 2003, two weeks before my twenty-first birthday, I boarded a plane. It would take me to Frankfurt, and from there to Cairo. With me was Jo, a high school friend who was studying to be an artist. Restless in her degree program and looking for inspiration, she decided to take a year off and come with me to Egypt. We went with two suitcases of our most grandmotherly clothes, possessing no more sophisticated concept of modest dress. I also brought a box of Tampax. Ben's female roommate had warned me that there was none to be had in Egypt. I'm embarrassed to admit I believed this—if I had spared half a minute to think, I would have realized that even oppressed foreign women got their periods. Cairo, one of the largest cities on Earth, must accomodate them. Despite my supposed education, I was naive when it came to the Middle East. Being on the verge of a conversion to Islam did not give me any insight into the people who practiced it. I was, in many ways, as unprepared to live in Egypt as someone with no religious affinity for it.

I left my courage on the runway in Denver. Adrenaline buzzed in my head as soon as the plane was airborne. By the time we reached Frankfurt my palms were sweating, and when we took off for Cairo I panicked. When people ask me about the moment I converted, I usually find a way to dodge the question. I tell them I decided to convert during college, which is true. In another sense I feel I have always been Muslim, since I discovered in the Quran what I already believed. But if conversion is entering into the service of an ideal, then I converted on that plane. In the darkness over the Mediterranean, in no country, under no law, I made peace with God. I called Him Allah. I didn't know what waited for me in Egypt. I didn't know whether the clash of civilizations was real, or whether being an American Muslim was a contradiction. But for the first time in my life, I felt unified—that had to mean something. Cultural and political differences go bone deep, but there is something even deeper. I believed that. I had to believe it.

The Conqueress City

On the path between death and life, within
view of the watchful stars and within ear-
shot of beautiful, obscure anthems, a voice
told of the trials and joys promised.
—Naguib Mahfouz, *The Harafish*

I HAD BEEN IN CAIRO FOR LESS THAN TWENTY-FOUR HOURS
WHEN a man on the street asked me for a blow job. He was
in his thirties, skinny, with a mustache that drooped at the
edges. From the window of a taxi, I had asked him for
directions—Jo and I were lost in Maadi, the fashionable district where the apartment we inherited from Ben was lo-
cated. After pointing vaguely over one shoulder toward the
street we were looking for, he spat out his proposition, in
an accent so heavy that "blow job" sounded like bastard-
ized French.

"Did he just—?" I looked at Jo, barely comprehending.

Jo's pretty, aquiline features were twisted into a nauseated expression.

"Okay, just go," I said to the taxi driver, and slumped
back in my seat. My face felt hot. The driver looked over
his shoulder at me, frowning. To him, the address we gave
was an obscure jum-ble of numbers. Like most Cairene

taxi drivers, he navigated by landmarks—pass the white mosque, turn when you see a shop-keeper with a face like an angry rooster sitting in the shade. If we could not describe the landscape, he could not take us where we wanted to go.

"We can go," I said again, motioning with one hand. The taxi jerked forward.

We had arrived to find a city in a state of moral and financial collapse. Almost every man we encountered, from the taxi drivers who called to us in the airport parking lot to the umber-robed doorman who met us at our apartment, watched us with an expression of repressed sexual anger. Women were indifferent. The air was thick with the metallic smell of dust, a scent that invaded clothing and hair like perfume. This was the most pervasive quality of Cairo, I thought, this dust; even the palm and banana trees that rose from little walled gardens were more gray than green.

In the heart of the city, ancient mosques were crammed into the shadows of slapdash high-rises, some of which tilted precariously on their foundations. The crush of human traffic and the noise of machines were constant. Down the center of this metropolis snaked the Nile, coffee-dark and wide. From every direction, desert threatened to erode what was left of the river's rich floodplain; its seasonal glut of silt was bottled up behind a dam in Aswan. An ecologist might look at Cairo and see an omen of the future: a flat, burned, airless plain, the wreckage of too much civilization.

I loved it. I loved it obsessively, starting the minute I stepped out of the airport and into the fetid August heat. Confronted with this city, my anxieties seemed self-indulgent. The calm of some long-dormant survival instinct kicked in.

Meanwhile, I was a Muslim. Alone in my room, behind wooden-shuttered windows that looked out at a fringe of palms, I prayed. Prayer was difficult at first. I had never been taught to bow toward anything, or recite words when no one was around to hear them. The first time I prayed, I did not face Mecca—instead I faced west, toward home. It was there that I had first spoken to God. Mecca, on the other hand, was a place I had never seen, full of people I had never met. For a convert, I was unusually obstinate. Bowing—putting my forehead on the ground—felt embarrassing. At that time, if you had asked me what religion was, I would have answered that it was the expression of one's love for God. Years later, a Bohra Muslim friend would suggest something very different: God, he said, is the love between you and religion. Today, this makes profound sense to me. I quickly discovered that religion is an act of will. I assumed prayer would flow naturally from belief, but it didn't —it took practice. So I practiced, privately, without telling Jo or anyone else what had occurred.

For a week, Jo and I barely ate. We didn't understand how or where to buy real food. The apartment previously inhabited by Ben and his roommate sat on a side street lined with straggling hibiscus bushes. There was a series of little shops at the end of our block, but they made no sense to us. One sold finches and lovebirds in cages, another sold cell phones, a third displayed unmarked piles of computer parts on wooden tables. When we finally came across a tiny general store—a *duken,* we later learned to call it—we bought olives and bread. A donkey cart supplied us with mangoes. Programmed for supermarkets, we were bewildered that we couldn't buy meat or fish from the same place we bought milk.

One afternoon during this first proteinless week, the phone rang. Jo and I stared at it in dismay. The only other call we'd gotten was from the director of Language School, welcoming us to Cairo. Too late, I realized I had no idea how Egyptians greeted each other on the phone.

"You answer it," said Jo.

"Why?" I asked wildly.

"Because it might be someone speaking Arabic," she said. "Pick up, quick."

I did.

"Hello?"

"Is this Willow?" The voice was male and spoke in a pleasant Anglo-Egyptian accent. He introduced himself as Omar, whom I remembered from Ben's e-mails—he was a physics teacher at LS, as we called it, and one of Ben's closest friends in Egypt. Worried about all the trouble a couple of American girls could find in Cairo, Ben had asked him to keep an eye on us.

"I remembered today that you arrived on the fifteenth," he said. "I wanted to make sure everything was okay. Ben said you brought someone with you?"

"A friend," I said. "She's going to be working at LS as well."

"Oh good," he said politely. "Is there anything you need?"

I decided not to tell him about our state of enforced veganism. He apologized for not having called sooner—he had been in Sinai for the past few days.

"Can we invite you over for some tea?" I asked, grateful for his concern. "I have a book that Ben asked me to bring you."

"Sure," he said. "What time should I be there?"

He arrived an hour later and I opened the door to a tall, olive-skinned man in a button-down shirt and khakis. His expression was kind and curious, and faintly amused; he reached out to shake my hand when I hesitated, unsure of the polite way for an American woman to greet an Egyptian man.

"This room has changed since the last time I was here," he said as I ushered him inside. He stood in front of the coffee table and narrowed his eyes. The watercolor that hung in the living room while Ben lived there was gone, replaced by a framed print of the Ninety-Nine Names of God.

"Whose is that?" he asked, turning to me. "Not yours, surely."

"Actually, it is mine," I said.

"Really?" He raised his eyebrows.

"Yes." I excused myself and went to help Jo with the tea. I looked back at Omar from the doorway of the kitchen. He stood with his arms crossed, head tilted to one side, gazing at the calligraphic names. Light from the window glazed his cheek, turning it honey-colored. He smiled.

★ ★ ★

Omar must have noticed how little food we had in the house, perhaps because we had none to offer him. When he pressed us about what we were eating, we admitted that we mostly weren't. "Language School usually sends someone to look after the foreigners for the first week," he said. "You shouldn't be left alone like this."

"Are there supermarkets here that sell meat?" asked Jo.

"There are, but they're very expensive—only for rich people and those who get paid in dollars," said Omar.

"We can't do expensive," I responded.

Omar nodded. "*Khalas*. Tomorrow I'll show you the souk. That's where ordinary people shop. Okay?"

Too eager for protein to say no, we agreed.

Omar arrived promptly the next morning, bringing with him stewed fava beans and bread from a street vendor. When we'd finished eating and cleaned up, he led us out into a late morning mottled with glare and watery shadows. We took a cab a short distance to the underside of a bridge that ran over the Maadi metro stop. Here was the edge of the souk, an open marketplace that meandered through a series of cramped, unpaved alleys strung with tarps. Vendors sat behind piles of green and yellow mangoes, guavas, carrots, sweet potatoes, purple and white eggplants, and tomatoes as heavy as fists, all in dusty profusion. In stacked bamboo cages, chickens and ducks muttered to each other in the heat. Today the market was full: men and women wearing long robes and head cloths moved from stall to stall and called to their friends and neighbors.

"You get your meat from a butcher, like that one," said Omar, pointing at a reeking stone terrace, above which hung several carcasses that might once have been water buffalo. "But be very careful, especially in the summer—it's easy to get bad meat. When you find a butcher you like, stick with him."

Neither of us had an appropriately profound response.

"Chickens and ducks and doves come from poultry sellers," continued Omar. "Pick whichever bird you like and they'll kill it for you. Fruits and vegetables should be easy. For bread, go to any bakery. Most are fine. For cheese or oil or olives, anything like that, go to a *duken*." He pointed to a small shop similar to the deli near our building.

"Six stops for five food groups?" I muttered in Jo's ear. She giggled.

We wandered through the maze looking for fresh spearmint to use for tea. As we walked, I felt increasingly dizzy and nauseated, stifled under the long shirt and jeans I was wearing. Despite the sun beating down on my head, I began to shiver. I had a feeling that this was not a good sign.

"Are you okay?" Jo asked. "You look really pale all of a sudden."

Little points of light danced in front of my eyes. "I'm fine," I said, inwardly swearing not to faint in front of all these people. "But I should probably find some shade soon."

Jo turned and said something to Omar, who looked over her head at me, concerned. He spoke at a rapid tempo to a man crouched beside several boxes of greens. The man handed him a bundle of mint. Omar turned to me.

"Do you have fifty piastres?" he asked. "I have a pound but I'm out of change."

I didn't and neither did Jo. The man didn't have change for our twenty- and fifty-pound notes. He said something to Omar, who thanked him in a long-winded way I didn't fully understand.

"He says it's okay. You can give him the fifty piastres next time."

I looked at the man, swaying on my feet. He was grinning at me from under his turban, amused by my obvious discomfort, my out-of-placeness, maybe both.

"Thank you," I said in English, forgetting where I was. Jo took my arm and steered me away from the crowd, toward the shade of the tree-lined square opposite. Omar stood between me and the light like a sundial, casting a slim shadow across my face.

"Feeling a little better?" he asked.

"Yes. Just not used to the heat. I didn't sleep very well last night, either." At some point, the insomnia caused by adrenal exhaustion had become a physiological tic. Though I was healthy now, it sometimes cropped up again when I was stressed.

Omar quoted a few lines from Macbeth's sleep-no-more speech, smiling in a half-blithe, half-bitter way that I would come to associate with moments like this, when his considerable knowledge of western literature showed through. It was knowledge he did not particularly want. He had been educated in the British system, the last cultural and linguistic outpost of the colonial era. In order to learn more about his own society's literary history, he searched through the shelves of underpatronized Arabic bookstores and taught himself. This was the smile of a man who, like so many in the Middle East, wished his intellect could be put to better use.

Feeling a little cooler, I looked up and smiled back.

"When the hurly-burly's done."

"When the battle's lost, and won."

In the weeks that followed, I fell in love with the back of Omar's head. A family matter called Jo home briefly just before the start of the school year, leaving Omar and me to roam the city together. I can still hear his exasperated voice, in some dark vein of a crowded street, saying, "Please, Willow, walk in front of me or beside me but not behind me. I am nervous when I can't see you." I would inevitably lag behind, lost in thought and unable to navigate without following him. I couldn't take his arm; we touched only to shake hands. That is how I came to know Cairo: walking in his wake, he who had lived there all his life. He was tender with places, sensitive to the way the moods of Cairo changed from neighborhood to neighborhood. The city I was beginning to love had been a passion for him since childhood. Omar searched out the cafés and alleyways that remained undamaged by years of oppression and poverty, and shyly revealed them. The city was our interlocutor in the weeks before we could shut the door on her, when we were, for lack of a better word, friends.

We started with places where a young white woman would not attract attention.

"Naguib Mahfouz used to come here to write," said Omar one night, over a great deal of noise. We were at

Fishawi's, a crowded café inside one of Cairo's largest fine-goods bazaars. "He sat in that little space over there. There's a newspaper article framed above his seat."

I looked: in a warmly lit alcove behind us was a newsprint picture of Egypt's Nobel laureate.

"I loved *Children of the Alley,*" I said to Omar, my voice half-lost in the din.

"You've read it?" He seemed surprised.

"In translation. I did nothing but read depressing Arabic novels my last two years of college."

"Why?" Omar sounded so repulsed that I laughed.

"I was taking Arabic lit courses. I had to. Apparently there are no novels with happy endings in Arabic literature."

"That's why we don't read them," he said. "Real life is depressing enough. I can't stand Mahfouz."

I laughed again, thinking of my earnest Arabic literature professor. And it was true—of all the Egyptians I would ever meet, a scant handful read books for pleasure, and even fewer read fiction. Omar was in the small minority of readers for pleasure, and owned shelf after shelf of historical and philosophical and religious works, but I would never see a novel in his hand.

"I'm writing a novel," I said to him apologetically.

"Please don't be offended if I never read it."

"I won't be." I grinned, and realized I was flirting a little.

After we left the café, we went to walk along the Nile. The air was humid and thick, slightly sour. "Thank you, by the way," I said.

Omar made a dismissive gesture. "I enjoy showing you around Cairo," he said. "That's the easy part."

"What's the hard part?" I asked.

"Showing you the society of Cairo," he said. "That's very different."

It didn't occur to me then to wonder why he had said this. I wasn't used to innuendo. In Cairo interest and affection have to be inferred rather than spoken about directly. Among the middle classes, there is little "dating," and an offer of marriage must be made before a young man and woman are permitted to see each other alone. I was unaware that my friendship with Omar had already strayed into a gray area because we sometimes met by ourselves— always in public and always with a level of formality, but still unchaperoned.

In the beginning, he treated me like a beloved, naive younger sister. He patiently answered my questions about language, protocol, and the purpose of random objects— Ramadan lamps and horsehair tassels, God's eyes, dovecotes. He had much less curiosity about the United States, with the sole exception of music. He was the first to hear African rhythms in jazz and pentatonic scales in hip-hop, whenever either genre played on Nile FM. He loved musical cross-pollination, and talked about starting a rock band that included lutes and tablas.

"I used to play in a heavy metal band," he said with a grin, one night when we were at a concert of experimental music at the Opera House. We were in the open-air theater, a sunken courtyard surrounded by a veranda. "Before I gave up the West. I wore a lot of black and ankh necklaces."

I looked at him in disbelief. "So did I. God . . . you were a goth."

"What's a goth?"

"What you were. Someone who wears black and ankhs and listens to heavy metal."

He frowned. "But an ankh is an Egyptian symbol."

"That's why we thought it was so cool. Eternal life, mummies, vampires, that kind of thing."

"And you were like this?" He raised his eyebrows.

"Yes. By then heavy metal was dying out—we were into Nine Inch Nails and Front Line Assembly and Delirium. I dyed my hair about ten different colors."

"I have never heard of those bands. I listened to Black Sabbath."

I laughed. "When?" I asked.

He leaned back on his elbows. We were sitting on cushions at the edge of the theater, on steps that led up to the veranda. "In the early nineties. I was finishing high school. Maybe the first year or two of university."

"I started high school in '95. So we were goths at almost the same time." This delighted me.

"And now you're twenty-one? I'm seven years older than you are."

"That's not so much," I said defensively.

"Not so much for what?"

I flushed. "Not so much, generally."

"Ah." He smiled. "Okay."

When the concert was over, we shared a cab back to south Cairo, snaking along the Nile-side boulevard called the Corniche. Beyond the boulevard, in the water, the white sails of pleasure and fishing boats were visible. Somehow we strayed to the topic of love; Omar told me there were four different words for it in Arabic.

"*Hob* is love-love," he said quietly, so that the cab driver wouldn't overhear. He made a shape in the air with his hands, a transient gesture, attempting to communicate something too abstract to speak about in English. "*Hob* can be from anyone, for anything—you feel *hob* for your parents, your sister, for a good friend. For your favorite book or a very tasty mango. Or for the person you are in love with."

"*Habibi* comes from *hob*," I said, recognizing the link between *hob* and one of the first words every newcomer to Egypt learns: my beloved. *Habibi* showed up in the refrain of every popular song, and was used passionately to refer to close friends and patronizingly to refer to subordinates.

"Yes, *habibi* comes from *hob*," said Omar. "Exactly. Then there is *aishq*." The word began with the letter *ayn*, the same letter that began his name. It hesitated somewhere between a vowel and a consonant, and began in the very back of the throat. "*Aishq* knits two people together. They don't become one thing, but they make one thing." Again he raised his hands and laced his fingers together. "*Aishq* is what you feel for your spouse, what you feel for God. Well, sometimes. I don't know if what I'm saying makes sense in English."

"Perfect sense," I said.

The cab stopped at my apartment first. Omar stepped out to sit in front with the driver, as is the custom among men when there are no women to accompany. Before he got into the front seat he reached out to shake my hand, as he always did in parting. For a moment he pressed my hand between both of his. I found I couldn't look him in the eye. Then he disappeared into the cab, waving off my offer to split the fare. I brought my hand to my face and breathed in. Beneath the tang of dust I caught the faint sharp smell of soap.

Jo arrived back in Egypt just before our job training was due to begin. Language School had a large campus in Giza, within sight of the pyramids. From the outside it looked much like any suburban high school campus in the States— inside, however, it was a series of bare concrete classrooms without heat or air conditioning. Rows of desks faced dry-erase boards. The bathrooms were coated in grime and sported unsanitary bidets. Despite all this, LS was considered a cutting-edge school, and set tuition proportionately.

"If it was any barer, it would almost be like they were going for an ultramodern look on purpose," said Jo when we arrived for the first day of training.

"Don't judge." I gave her a condescending schoolmarm look.

Jo wrinkled her nose and giggled. Arriving at the school library, we brightened up at the sight of the other teachers. The faculty was evenly split between foreigners and Egyptians and roughly so between men and women. But while the word *foreigner* denoted the same thing throughout the room—we were all educated and middle class, dressed in the same ambiguous nonstyle of the expatriate—the word

Egyptian covered a much more diverse group. Some wore traditional clothes, but others wore Italian shoes and dark jeans, and spoke to each other in English. Of this group, the girls were especially friendly, and mingled with the expat teachers learning names and making introductions. Jo and I were swept up in the familial atmosphere as returning teachers wandered in and shouted greetings to each other, joking about weight gained and lost over the summer.

I looked around for Omar. He was sitting in the back of the room with a group of teachers who chatted quietly in Arabic. Many of the women wore head scarves and loose robes in green and ocher. The men were dressed in carefully pressed oxford shirts. There was something a little desperate in the razor-sharp creases of the fabric, as if it was very, very important for these men to make the right impression. When the vice principal called for our attention I sat hastily in the chair next to Jo's, troubled; I sensed that it would be inappropriate for me to approach Omar in this setting. There were two competing Egypts in the room: that of the westernized upper class and that of the traditionalist. As westerners, Jo and I were automatically considered part of the former group. I realized that for the past couple of weeks, Omar had been sneaking me into his Egypt—a place where I did not belong, and could not be sustained.

I kept looking over my shoulder at him, trying to read his expression. He listened attentively to the vice principal with his arms crossed, and leaned over every so often to comment to the man sitting next to him. I never caught him looking at me. I watched Jo as she took notes on her legal pad, and plotted my next move.

When we broke for lunch, I ambushed him.

"Hi, how are you," I said, trying to strike a true note between cheerfulness and reserve.

"Bored," said Omar, smiling. "None of what we are discussing can be applied in an Egyptian classroom. This training program was made for western teachers." His accent sounded heavier than I remembered.

"That isn't why it's boring," I said, and he laughed. There was a pause. "What are you doing after work?" I asked finally, and cursed myself in silence for sounding forward.

Omar shrugged. "I'll call you and Jo in the evening," he said.

"If you want. I mean if you're free. Don't feel obligated to find things for us to do." I could feel myself turning red, and felt childish.

"I don't," he said, and turned back to the lunch table.

Omar called that evening, inviting us to meet Nuri, one of his close friends. The four of us went to a café in Maadi. As soon as we ordered, Jo excused herself to go to the bathroom, with a glance in my direction that inspired me to do the same. When the door was shut behind us, she turned to me in alarm.

"It's two guys and two girls," she said. "Are we on a date?"

"Jesus," I whispered, and forced down a nervous giggle. She might be right: as far as I knew, most unmarried Egyptian girls didn't appear in public with men unless it was in large mixed groups. Ben accidentally dated a girl for weeks before figuring this out.

"What do we do?" asked Jo.

"I don't know," I said. "Maybe we should act really uptight, so they get the idea."

"Maybe." She tilted her head with a mischievous expression. "If it *is* a date, who's going out with who? Nuri sat down across from you and Omar sat down across from me."

I felt a stab of anxiety. If I was going to be tricked into a date, I didn't want it to be with the wrong person.

"Do you really think Omar would sell us out like this?" Jo's expression had turned serious.

"No, I don't think so," I said. "Let's just see what happens."

We went back out with primly downcast eyes. I planned to stay as quiet as possible, but Nuri was a lively conversationalist, and I was soon sucked in.

"I can't believe you're going to teach American history," he said to me over the rim of his coffee cup. His English was excellent, and lethal. "These kids don't even know their own history. This is exactly the kind of western cultural takeover Egypt is turning a blind eye on."

"I'd rather teach them their own history," I said, "but I didn't set my class schedule."

"When we try to teach our own interpretation of Middle East history, we get in trouble with the accreditation people," said Omar in my defense. "They watch what goes on in schools that use the American curriculum."

Nuri looked disgusted. "Perhaps, perhaps. But it's fashionable among Egyptian kids now to be illiterate in Arabic. Can you believe it?"

"That's an exaggeration," Omar scoffed.

Nuri grinned. "You used to be very concerned about the decay of the Arabic language *ya* Omar." He turned to us. "Did you know that he refused to speak English for almost seven years?"

"I got more moderate after that," Omar said sheepishly, then paused. "Now it's difficult—I have liberal friends and conservative friends, Egyptian friends, *khawagga* friends, this religion and that one. I have no frame of reference."

"To hell with your frame of reference!" said Nuri, tilting his coffee cup up to drain it. "We must make up our own. We must be good people before we are anything else."

"It's isolating," said Omar quietly. "Without a viewpoint that is even a little mainstream, it's isolating."

I looked up at him, surprised.

"I know exactly what you mean," I said.

Later, when Omar dropped Jo and me off at our apartment, Jo found a delicate way to ask whether we had, in fact, just been on a date.

"No!" said Omar, and laughed. "I brought Nuri because he is one of the only men I know who can see women as friends. So I trusted him. No, that was not a date."

"Oh good!" Jo laughed, too. "We didn't think you'd do that to us, but we had to check."

As Omar's cab disappeared into the dust, I felt less relief than regret. Jo and I kicked off our shoes at the door and went into the kitchen to eat mangoes. I lay my head on the chilly granite counter.

"I have a crush," I said.

Jo's eyes went wide. "Really?"

"Yeah."

"How bad is it?"

"Pretty bad. Very bad."

She paused with a mango in her hands. "Is that a good idea?"

"I'm almost sure it's a terrible idea."

"What are you going to do?" Jo slid a knife under the mango's skin, releasing a flowery scent into the air.

"Maybe nothing." I lifted my head and pouted at her. "It's too complicated." It was, I thought, the politest way to say what I was thinking. In my mind, the idea that Middle Eastern men were dangerous misogynists was an established fact. I had been told as much on television and in newspapers and on film. My experiences being ogled and propositioned in Cairo confirmed it. All that kept me from articulating this was a thin veneer of liberal education, and even that provided no counterargument—only the tepid belief that it was bad manners to generalize.

"You're not going to tell him?" asked Jo.

"If he doesn't feel the same way, we would probably have to stop seeing each other. That seems like the kind of noble thing he would insist on. Anyway, there would be too many cultural barriers." I watched her, hoping this politically correct hint would save me from having to be explicit. "Right?"

Jo smiled. "Of course there would be barriers. But Omar's not just some guy off the street. He's smart and sensitive and he's awfully attached to you."

"Ugh." I slumped back down on the counter, feeling guilty. "You're right. I'm being an idiot." It disturbed me that I couldn't unlump Omar from the faceless mass of Middle Eastern men I had been taught to fear. In the back of my mind was a lesson I'd learned watching the movie *Not Without My Daughter* and reading horror stories in women's magazines: they always *seem* like nice guys. It's only after you've gotten involved that you discover the honor-killing wife-imprisoning fundamentalist reality beneath the facade. Were there layers of Omar's personality I couldn't see? The possibility made me hesitant.

"I'm very comfortable," I said to Jo, holding out my hand for a slice of mango. "That's the problem. I'm very comfortable not dealing with this. Denial is a river in Egypt. I'm so there. I can see it out the window."

Jo laughed. Unconsciously, I had diagnosed myself: I *was* very comfortable. I liked having the luxury to avoid messy cross-cultural entanglements. I liked being a non-Muslim so much that I kept my new religion a secret and prayed alone behind a locked door. Even the person I most wanted to tell, the person I couldn't stop thinking about, knew nothing about my conversion. To the rest of the world, I was an upper-middle-class American white girl with bland politics and polite beliefs, and in this coveted social stratum I was happy. The status quo had been good to me. I was reluctant to abandon it—even for love, even for God.

Road Nine at Twilight

I am not to speak to you—I am to think of
   you when I sit alone, or wake at night
   alone,
I am to wait—I do not doubt I am to meet
   you again,
I am to see to it that I do not lose you.
        —Walt Whitman, "To a Stranger"

WE FOUND EXCUSES TO SPEND TIME TOGETHER. ALL ER-
rands, great and small, required each other's company: on
this we silently agreed. I turned down invitations to dinners
and parties at expat watering holes in order to go with Omar
to souks, tailors, or gritty outdoor cafés where I was the only
westerner. I began to anticipate his phone calls in the hours
after school, when Jo and I made little meals of bread and
olives and stood on our balcony to watch the hazy landscape. At night, Jo often went out with our coworkers; I did
nothing that did not include Omar.

One evening he called, sounding depressed.

"I have to see the dentist," he said, "there's no use putting it off. I wanted to call to say good night first since I
won't see you until tomorrow."

"You don't like going to the dentist?" I asked with mock
surprise.

"I hate it. I'm afraid of him, to tell the truth." He laughed at himself.

"Would it help to have company? I'll come if you want."

"You *would*?" This was a step beyond our cheerful codependence.

"Sure."

He arrived at the apartment half an hour later.

"You don't have to do this, you know," he said. "I don't want you to get bored."

"Don't be silly." I pulled a galibayya tunic over my T-shirt as we left the apartment. The evening was still new, and a wet, dewy scent had settled over Maadi. We walked through the dust to Road Nine, a genteel tree-lined street where old and new wealth mingled. Though antiaristocratic in most things, Omar was picky about dentists.

"It's the third part of a root canal," he explained to me as we walked. "I had the second part just before you arrived."

"You must have been in pain."

"I was."

"I couldn't tell."

"I didn't want you to think I was a weakling." He grinned. I held back a smile, happy at this small sign that he cared what I thought of him.

Since Omar and I weren't married, engaged, or related, deciding how to arrange ourselves in the dentist's waiting room was an interesting thought experiment. First, I sat down on a couch across the coffee table from Omar. This, I thought, was appropriately ambiguous. Spotting a man who looked inclined to chat me up, I got off the couch and sat down next to Omar instead. I felt a little thrill of vindication when he turned toward me protectively.

"You look nervous," I said.

He shook his head, mouth set in a grim expression. "It's like a phobia," he muttered. "A dentist phobia."

"You know what I've found helps in situations like these?" I asked.

"What?"

"Playing word games. You know, like I name a celebrity, then you name another one whose first name begins with the first letter of the first celebrity's last name. It takes your mind off things."

"I don't get it."

"Oh, you know, I say Gary Oldman and you say—"

"Omar Sharif?"

I paused. "There is no letter 'sheen' in English. I can see the bilingual element is going to cause problems."

"Whatever. This isn't helping."

I hid a grin with my hand. An assistant called Omar's name and he followed her into the examination room, shooting me a pained look over his shoulder. As soon as he was gone I felt isolated, shifting under the open stares of the other patients in the waiting room. Hoping to look busy, I flipped through a couple of Egyptian beauty magazines that lay on the coffee table. Somewhere in the bowels of the office a drill started up. I tried not to giggle as I thought of Omar, so collected and dignified, submitting meekly to the dreaded dentist. This was, by far, the weirdest nondate of my life.

Four years ago—no, two years ago—I could not have envisioned this, I thought. I could not have guessed that I would *stop* drinking at twenty-one, or that a dentist's office could become the scene of a clandestine romance. I had come to Islam and to Egypt without plans or expectations. I did not know who I was going to become, having made choices that steered me so dramatically off the path I was raised to walk. Everything from 9/11 to the Arab bad guys in action movies made me worry that those choices would lead to tragedy. Instead, they had led me to someone who was familiar from the moment he appeared on my doorstep, someone who cared enough to translate this confounding new reality into a language I understood.

Omar emerged an hour later looking shaken but relieved. "*Yalla?*" He held the door open for me and smiled when I looked back at him.

"This is—" He trailed off, following me outside into the damp heat. "I'm really glad you came. Thank you."

I could feel his hand hovering over my shoulder. Part of me wanted to stop suddenly and collide with his outstretched fingers, so he could touch me without feeling at fault. But this was not the way. I kept walking, and made a decision.

During a break in training the next day, I asked Omar if I could talk to him in private after work. I kept my voice and my posture carefully neutral; if we were overheard there would be scandal. For a moment Omar looked startled. Recovering, he agreed in an identical tone. Only his eyes betrayed anxiety, and, I thought, hope. For the rest of the day he kept me within sight, if not within arm's reach, though we did not speak to each other again.

After work, when Jo left to make posters with her co-teacher, Omar came over to the apartment. There was a moment of awkwardness when he stepped through the door —though we had gone all over the city together we had never been alone in private. The simple intimacy of standing with him in a closed room was almost frightening. I was used to having Cairo as a chaperone.

"I love you," I said in a rush. "And I know what that is going to mean. I mean, I know that's not a small thing to say, especially since—" I ran out of air and swallowed. "But I had to say something. I'm sorry." I grimaced. This wasn't meant to come out in such a graceless, forward mess.

A smile played over Omar's face and disappeared, then returned, like the sun between patches of cloud. "Give me your hand," he said, reaching out with his. This was a proposal. In Egypt, acknowledged love and an offer of marriage are the same thing, so for us, marriage came like love; an emotion and not a decision. Until the day we made it official, we would ask each other "Will you marry me?" almost whenever there was a lull in conversation but the real proposal was put forth and accepted that afternoon when he put out his hand and I took it. We had never been on a real date. We had never kissed. We had known each other for just over a month.

"There's another thing," I said, hesitating. Omar looked at me expectantly. I forced the words to arrange themselves on my tongue. "I'm a Muslim," I said.

Omar slumped forward with an expression of profound relief. "Thank God," he said. "Thank God. That makes so many things easier."

"You're not that surprised," I said, laughing.

"You're right." Omar sat up and grinned at me. "I guess it's because I've never become this spiritually close to a non-Muslim. There has always been a, similarity, between us, in that way. No, I'm not surprised." He put his arm around my shoulders and folded me against him. "I'm just very, very happy."

The texture of the shirt and the warmth of the shoulder I lay against unknotted my anxiety. Once you discover that the world rewards reckless faith, no lesser world is worth contemplating. Omar touched my hair, laughed, and said he had no word for its color. He wound a strand around his finger and kissed it. There were so many things, he said, so many things he had been waiting to tell me since before he had seen my face or knew my name.

Omar lived with his divorced mother and younger brother on the border of Tura, an industrial district just south of Maadi. Jo and I had been to their apartment once, briefly, and said quick hellos to his mother Sohair, a striking woman in her fifties with eyes rimmed in heavy kohl. I was surprised that Omar still lived with his family at twenty-eight. In Egypt, though, this is normal—most Egyptians stay with their parents until marriage. Interdependence is valued over independence; living alone and hoarding one's resources is seen as antisocial. Until I learned that all of my unmarried colleagues and friends still lived with their families, it was difficult for me to process.

The fact that Omar disappeared every day to visit an

American girl had not gone unnoticed. The evening after we got engaged, Omar called to tell me that he had announced our intentions to his family. His tone was matter-of-fact, as if we were discussing plans for a dinner or a day trip to the pyramids.

"You just told them? Just like that?" I bit my nails.

"Just like that," he said. His voice was firm and cheerful.

"And they didn't freak out?"

"No. They have concerns, of course, but they're happy for us. They want you to come over for lunch so we can all talk."

Though Omar's divorced mother and father were both nontraditional—they had been secular leftists in the wake of the revolution—it was still shocking for a young man to get engaged without first asking his parents' permission. Omar was not afraid of appearing eccentric. When his generation became religious, defying the westernized, socialist tendencies of their parents, he forged his own unorthodox path. He defended his music against the fundamentalists, and his piety against the secularists, at a time when people were pressured to choose a side. By simply announcing that he would marry me—without fanfare or apology—he was saying that he would tolerate no opposition.

The day of the lunch, I spent half an hour trying to decide what to wear. I was still getting ready when Omar arrived to pick me up.

"I feel like we're doing something wrong," I fretted as I put on my shoes. "I don't like just showing up like this. 'Hi, I'm your white American in-the-closet-convert future daughter-in-law. I've brought you some flowers and a catastrophe.'"

Omar shook his head. "We're not doing anything wrong. This is our decision." He smiled. "Everyone is going to like you."

"Everyone?" I looked up at him flirtatiously.

"Yes, everyone." He squeezed my hand. "I love you."

When we arrived at their apartment, I paid closer attention than I had the other time I'd visited. It was a snug space: two tiny bedrooms and a kitchen leading off of a main room that served as the living and dining area. Spread throughout the apartment was a great quantity of books. On almost every wall there were shelves lined with philosophies and histories in Arabic, novels in English and French. They competed for space with a few houseplants and a framed picture of Gamal Abdel Nasser, leader of the Egyptian revolution. On a wide couch in the main room lay two of Omar's ouds—ancestors of the lute—and an electric guitar.

Omar's mother, Sohair, came out to greet us. I let out a breath when I saw she was smiling.

"Hello, my dear," she said, kissing me on both cheeks. "Come sit down, please. Will you take tea?"

Another head poked around the corner from the hall: it was Ibrahim, Omar's younger brother. He came into the room with bright, wide eyes, holding out his hand. He was fairer than either Sohair or Omar—as a child he had been red-headed, a characteristic of his father's family, who hailed from the Nile Delta. He was six years younger than Omar, a year older than me.

"*Ahlan*," he said, shaking my hand. "Do you know *ahlan*? It means welcome."

"I know *ahlan*," I said, feeling suddenly shy.

"She took Arabic in college," Omar chimed in. "She knows a lot of words."

"Not really. I've found out everything I know is useless. I can tell you the new secretary is Lebanese, but I can't ask for directions."

Ibrahim laughed. "That's all right. We will teach you whatever you want to know."

As the four of us sat together and talked, I began to relax. Sohair and Ibrahim asked about my history and expectations, always kindly and without judgment. Despite the unorthodoxy of our sudden announcement, it was clear they were happy and a little relieved that Omar had found someone he wanted to marry. He had, I gathered, been fussy about potential mates in the past. It was unusual for a pious person to have interests as diverse and artistic as Omar's, which made looking for a wife more than usually difficult. When Omar insisted he would only marry a woman who was both religious and intellectually independent, his mother told him to be realistic. He was in his late twenties, an age when Egyptian men are expected to choose a wife and leave the family home. It was time, she thought, for him to make a decision.

Sohair was a revolutionary. Though Nasser's dream of a democratic, industrial Egypt had never come to pass, she held on to hope. Her energy and idealism were formidable: at my age she socialized with leftist politicos, earning her translator's diploma while pregnant with Omar. She and her sons' father divorced when Omar was in high school. Afterward, she had educated and provided for her children on her own, refusing help from relatives and friends. In recent years her job as a translator had taken her across Europe and West Africa; in a few more years she would travel to the source of the Nile with a group of backpackers half her age. The hardships she had faced as a young woman seemed barely to register—she had boundless optimism, and was more fearless at fifty than I was at twenty-one.

"Do you have a good relationship with your parents?" she asked me at one point during that first lunch together.

"I do," I said, running one finger nervously around the rim of my teacup. "And I don't want to keep secrets from them. I just think it makes more sense to tell them in person, after they've had a chance to meet Omar."

"When are they coming?"

"December, for Christmas. It's just another couple of months, so—" I trailed off and fiddled with my teacup again. A couple of months was not a long time, but it was long enough to make me feel guilty for concealing something so important.

"It's your choice," said Sohair, patting my hand. "If you think this way is best, then this is what we will do."

We sat down to a traditional meal of ground meat baked in filo dough, with rice and cucumber salad. Ibrahim talked about '70s power ballads and his fear of scorpions. I laughed when he and Omar argued over heavy metal bands. Ibrahim would later tell their extended family, "My heart is open to her," calming the fears they might have had about Omar's American fiancée. I felt safe sitting in the bright living room with Omar and the people who knew him best. At the same time, I wondered if Sohair's confidence in me was misplaced

—I wondered if I knew what was best. I wondered if I knew what I was doing at all.

Omar's father was an artist and lived alone on another floor of that same apartment building in Tura, in a flat littered comfortably with evidence of his craft: brushes in jars of turpentine, palettes left drying on newspapers, canvases leaning against the walls.

"My dear Willow," he said when Omar introduced us, enunciating each word. "For so you must become: precious." His name was Fakhry, but to me he was always Amu Fakhry, the word for *uncle* conveying my respect for him as an elder. He was in his early sixties and had a heart condition that made him tire easily, but his expressive eyes were youthful.

"I'm glad to meet you," I said, and kissed him on the cheek. I handed him the bouquet of flowers I had picked out at a local shop. He smiled, delighted.

"They are beautiful," he said, putting them in a green glass vase. "The color, everything is good. I pay attention to these things because I am a painter. I search for details."

We looked at some of his paintings. He was a devotee of Picasso, and had copied several of his paintings. A canvas based on "The Frugal Repast" caught my eye.

"This is amazing," I said.

"You like it?" Amu Fakhry seemed pleased. "Then when it is finished, I will give it to you."

"I would hate to take it away from you—"

"No, you must have it," said Amu Fakhry. "Art is not for the artist. Art is for other people."

We smiled at each other in silent agreement. From that moment, we were allies and coconspirators. The painting I admired would arrive wrapped at my doorstep several weeks later, with one addition: the bouquet of flowers I gave Amu Fakhry had appeared on the table near the subject's elbow, picked out in daubs of pink and green.

It's very easy to keep secrets from people who live thousands of miles away. It's much less easy to keep them from your roommate. I wanted to talk to Jo about my news, but I was a little afraid of her reaction. If I told her about the engagement, I'd have to tell her about my conversion as well, and that was a conversation I was not yet prepared to have with anyone whose opinions about religion were as strong as hers.

"Every time I see the word *God,* my brain shuts down," she told me one afternoon as we were walking in Maadi. After the news of a death in Jo's family, a colleague at school had given her a book of inspirational essays and sayings. She had read it dutifully, but it didn't stick. "It makes me suspicious of the whole book, even the parts I like. There were some beautiful ideas in there. But I just can't see God, God, God, and take them seriously."

"Why not?" I asked. We were walking along a street we'd named Dead Cat Road, in honor of the bloated tabby carcass that had been lying in the median for weeks. We stepped into the street to avoid him.

"The word doesn't mean anything positive to me," Jo said. "I'm not religious, and I feel like God is forced on me in a way that seems dishonest and manipulative."

"Not everyone thinks of God as a big white guy who floats on the ceiling of the Sistine Chapel pointing at people," I said irritably. "You could think of Him as something more pervasive and universal."

This got a smile. "I could," she said, "but that forces me to work too hard as a reader, which means the book isn't written well enough to catch my attention without using the word *God* as a crutch."

"*What?*" I squeaked. A *boab* in the doorway of a nearby apartment building stared at me. I ignored him. "Are you saying that if a book contains the word *God,* it's *badly written?*"

"Yes," she said. "That's what I'm saying."

I took a breath, caught a yeasty lungful of cat, and began coughing. We continued down the road in philosophical silence.

A few days later, Omar invited us to observe a lesson at Beyt al Oud, the music school where he studied with Iraqi lute maestro Naseer Shamma. The school operated out of an eighteenth-century house built in the traditional Arab style —there was an open courtyard called a *salamlek,* where concerts and group lessons were held, and above it a screened series of rooms used for practice, formerly the harem. While Omar chatted with Naseer and his students, Jo and I explored the house, admiring the high, painted ceilings and narrow stone stairs, and the latticework balcony where women of the house would sit to observe the men, centuries ago. We were lingering in the balcony when I told Jo that Omar and I were engaged. A lesson was in progress below us in the *salamlek,* and little melodies drifted up one by one, playful and sad. Omar chatted with Master Naseer near a dry tile fountain. Secluded behind the lattice, we could see everything without being seen. Jo squeezed my hand and said nothing. We listened to the music for a few more minutes before heading downstairs arm in arm.

When we were alone back at the apartment, the questions began.

"What about all the religion stuff? Don't you think that's going to cause problems between you?"

"I'm a Muslim."

Jo immediately looked worried. "You converted for him?"

"No, I converted before we ever said anything to each other. He had no idea I was a Muslim until we had the getting-married discussion."

"You converted before?" Worry became surprise. "When? Can I ask why?"

A gnawing sensation began in my stomach. I felt like I was back in fifth grade health class, when they separated the boys from the girls and taught us the Latin names for our anatomy and the mechanics of sex, all with a grim detachment that seemed Kafkaesque in retrospect. I could never quite shake this reaction to the question "Why religion?" To me it would forever feel like health class; like condensing something ineffable into a series of *events.* I knew, also, that I wasn't really being asked to explain my conversion, I was being asked to defend it. It was this that unsettled me most.

"I tried to be an atheist," I said plaintively. "It didn't work."

"Okay, yeah, but why Islam?"

"I discovered I was a monotheist. Believe me, I was as unhappy about it as you are. That rules out polytheism. I also have a problem with authority, which rules out any religion with a priesthood or a leader who claims to be God's representative on earth. And I cannot believe that having given us these bodies, God thinks we should be virgins unless we desperately feel a need to reproduce. That rules out any religion that's against family planning or sex for fun rather than for procreation. Islam is antiauthoritarian sex-positive monotheism."

"*Islam is sex-positive?* Come on."

I fought back my frustration. "In Islam, celibacy is considered unhealthy and unnatural. The best way for a Muslim adult to live is in a committed, sexually joyful relationship with another Muslim adult. That sounds about right to me."

"You see the way women are treated here. You walk in the streets. It's like being a hunted animal! If that's sex-positive I'm the freaking pope."

"I'm not arguing with that. It's disgusting and hypocritical and wrong. And I don't think there's a single Muslim cleric out there who'd disagree with you. This is not Islam. This is a society in freefall. This place is a *mess*. Egypt is at a lower point today, *today,* than it has been in its entire history." Tirade over, I realized my hands were clenched.

Jo looked out the window, into the street where we were harassed on a daily basis. Cairo was crawling with unemployed, furious, infantilized men who were still sleeping in their childhood beds and taking orders from their mothers. Parents of girls were demanding more and more in bridal settlements and real estate, putting marriage—and therefore adulthood—out of reach for many in this poverty-stricken generation. As the middle class shrank, marital expectations rose; by marrying well, a working-class girl could help her family climb back into a "respectable" social stratum. There was no higher goal than being *ibn i'nas* or *bint i'nas,* the son or daughter of genteel people. The stress this put on working-class men was almost unfathomable. These were the men who hunted us and hated us. In their eyes, they had been betrayed by female social mercenaries and denied their dignity by a class-obsessed society. I was marrying into a country on the verge of a meltdown.

Jo turned back from the window and studied me, sunlight illuminating her thick blonde hair. "Are you happy?" she asked.

"I'm happy," I said. It was a lie; I was terrified. There are few things more overwhelming than love in hostile territory. Despite my anxieties, I couldn't show any hesitation. My confidence was the only thing that would convince my friends and family that this was a good idea. I had to be disciplined about my own anxieties and focus on calming the fears of others.

Ramadan

And know that victory comes with pa-
tience, relief with affliction, and ease with
hardship.

—Prophet Muhammad

I TOLD JO ABOUT MY CONVERSION JUST IN TIME: THAT YEAR,
THE fasting month of Ramadan began in October. She
would have been dismayed—and maybe insulted—to discover me eating at sunset after refusing food all day. On the
twenty-ninth day of Sha'aban, Omar, Jo, and I were having
tea in our living room when Omar held up his hand for silence. The evening call to prayer had just gone up from the
city's thousand mosques. He was waiting for the special
chant that would announce the start of the holy month.

"Why don't they know when it is yet?" Jo was perched
on the couch sorting through our CDs, bemused by Omar's
restlessness.

"It's not an exact date—they have to see the crescent
moon." Omar shifted out of the darkened porch doorway
and came to sit in the living room with Jo and me. "If they
see it tonight, we start fasting tomorrow; if not, we start the
next day."

There was an electricity in the air I was used to associat-
ing with Christmas. "I think it's going to be tonight," I said.

"Do you?" Omar smiled. "I imagine it will be then."

A minute later we heard voices swell up from the mosques and fill the empty space between the noises in the street.

"Is that it?" I asked.

"That's it," Omar answered, cheerful now and pulling on his shoes. "Come on, let's go shopping for *sa'hoor*." *Sa'hoor* is the "late meal" eaten just before sunrise during Ramadan. In Egypt, that usually means stewed fava beans and yogurt, along with a licorice drink that helps the body retain fluids. And, for an untried westerner like me, lots and lots of water.

We went by cab to Souk el Maadi. It was crammed with shoppers carrying bags of vegetables and flatbread in their hands and on their heads. "From now until next month, Cairo will not sleep," Omar said. "A lot of these people will just stay up until dawn tonight, sleep all day tomorrow, and then get up for *iftar* and party. They're out buying food for *sa'hoor*, like us."

We stopped at a tiny general store to buy white cheese and bread.

"Remember to drink water tonight. Don't wait until dawn," Omar said in the cab on the way back. He came inside the apartment long enough to kiss me, promising to be back first thing in the morning. I went to bed with the holiday feeling lingering in my mind.

At 3:45 a.m. I woke to the sound of a man singing out in the street, accompanied by a drum. "*Sa'hoor, sa'hoor*, wake, oh, sleeper!" went his chant, echoing between the silent apartment blocks. I stumbled to the window and peered out, seeing a galibayya-clad man bathed in neon from the street lamp overhead. He swayed down the block, trailed by one of the local cats.

"Who wakes *you* up?" I asked as though he could hear me. The muffled clank of cooking pots could be heard from the flat upstairs. I went into the kitchen, feeling resolved; I drank a liter of water. This left almost no room for food, but it was the idea of going without liquid that made me nervous. Feeling slightly hypotonic, I went back to bed and slept.

I woke up again around ten a.m., dry-mouthed.

"It will pass," said Omar, who had appeared like a mirage in the living room. Both he and Jo were irritatingly awake and fresh-looking.

"How do you feel?" asked Jo, clearing away traces of her breakfast.

"Kind of jet-lagged, actually. Like I'm trying to adjust to a new time zone."

"The first day is like that," said Omar, smiling with encouragement. "After that it gets easier."

The rest of the day had a trancelike quality—sometimes I felt sleepy and sore, sometimes unusually alert. We watched *The Lord of the Rings: The Two Towers.* I drifted off again halfway through, cocooned between Omar and Jo, both of whom seemed at least partially convinced that fasting was incompatible with my Anglo-Saxon physiology. Much later, the sound of Omar's voice prompted me awake. He was reading Al Jabbar in English. "And I take *Al Haq*, the Truth, as my birthright; as a creature I am transitory. And He said, 'Veil this symbol, and know it, and be satisfied.'"

"I can see why we do this," I said.

When the sun began to drop into the Nile, Jo and Omar and I took a cab to Sohair's flat for *iftar,* the meal eaten to break the daily fast. According to prophetic tradition, *iftar* should be a modest meal of dates and milk. Egyptians ignore this. Syrup-coated butter pastries round out nightly feasts of stuffed eggplant, mutton, and rice spiced with cinnamon and fat raisins; despite a day's worth of dehydration, thick apricot nectar is the drink of choice.

"Sugar for energy, and salt to retain fluids," Ibrahim reasoned as we set the table. Jo helped Sohair in the kitchen; I heard her laugh. Outside, the call for sunset prayer rang out.

"They've started," said Omar, handing me a glass. "*Ramadan karim!*"

"*Allahu akram,*" I said, repeating the traditional response I'd learned just that morning. Ramadan is generous; God is the most generous. I raised the glass to my lips to take a polite sip.

It was the best glass of anything, ever. My senses, muted all day, clamored to be heard again, to taste and be full. The jumbled euphoria of fast-breaking—part chemical, part spiritual—was unlike any other sensation I could name. I slumped in my chair and let my head roll back.

"Oh *God,*" I said.

They all laughed. Jo poked me in the ribs and winked. I was happy with everything: the people sitting around Sohair's tiny wooden table; the drowsy, flushed desert

outside the window. I was happy, also, with myself. I had
lived up to my choices. If I could fast one day, I could fast
another twenty-eight—I could do it all again the next year.
And the year after. For the first time since I converted, I saw
a satisfying little glimmer of what the future might look like.
Choosing the way you live is choosing *to* live. From that
night onward, Ramadan to me was about having gratitude
—for revelation, for prophesy, for the sheer joy of being
human in the world.

After the food was eaten and the leftovers cleared away, we
lingered over tea. Omar took out his oud and played Arabic folksongs full of quarter-tones that do not exist in western music: fleeting, wry sounds. Ibrahim showed Jo and me
his electric guitar, explaining all the knobs and buttons the
nonmusical have trouble understanding.

"I would like to learn to play the piano as well. I started,
but," here he gestured at an old Casio keyboard sitting on a
shelf, "that thing is not very inspiring. I would like a real
piano."

"I wish there was such a thing as teleportation," I said.

"*Aeda?*"

"Making things disappear magically from one place and
reappear in another."

"Ah." He smiled. "Why?"

"At my parents' house in Colorado, we have a huge old
piano that no one can play. You would love it."

"Perhaps if I come visit you one day."

"You should. I want you to see our mountains."

He grinned, then looked away with a pensive expression. "I have met many Americans and they are all friendly and open-minded. I don't understand, then, why—" I'm not sure if he finished the sentence. "I try to remember this every time I see what the United States is doing to the Middle East or I watch your news—which is very depressing—but it is hard not to be angry. To become closed. There is so much lying."

In situations like this I always want to defend my country, and every rational way I might do so evaporates.

"The American media is much more radical than the American people," I said weakly. This was something I couldn't control but I still felt guilty. I could see Ibrahim standing in his living room with his prayer beads in one hand and his electric guitar slung over the opposite shoulder, and think, *He proves the world isn't so bad yet.* Yet there was still Afghanistan, and Iraq, and the net closing around Iran, and the encroaching disaster in Israel-Palestine. When such ugly conflicts were so close by, who in Egypt could feel entirely safe? Looking at Ibrahim, I thought, this Middle East is either being born or dying, and which it will be depends largely on people who will never see him play his guitar.

"It would make more sense if you saw it." I said. "If you saw America itself."

"Someday *in sha'Allah.*"

"*In sha'Allah.*"

In order to be understood, feelings that are universal—love, mourning, joy—must be expressed in a mutually comprehensible way. This should be easy. If the feelings are universal, their expression should be as well. In reality, they aren't. In the beginning, Omar was more conscious of this than I was; he saw that the only customs we had in common were Islam and rock music, and that these intangibles had to be cobbled together into the foundation of a third culture. Religion and art aren't terrible tools to start with, when it comes to creating a peace for two in the midst of a war. But even with them, the struggle for that peace would be painful and exhausting. Sometimes it felt like I was being asked to unstring my bones and pass through the eye of a needle. The image was constantly in my mind. Everything we thought, everything we did or said or wore or espoused unthinkingly, had to be brought forth and reconciled. In the process, old symbols were given a new vocabulary. That vocabulary would become the language we spoke in the culture we created for ourselves.

It began with the symbols I had etched into my skin.

"Ben told me you have an interesting tattoo," Omar said one night not long after we were engaged. "Is it true?"

I knew which one he meant. "Yes. Does it bother you?"

Omar was smiling. "No. But can I see it?"

I turned away from him and lifted the hem of my shirt so that he could see the lower part of my back. I wondered if the tattoo would shock him, or whether he would be able to read my good intentions in the ink. He was silent for a moment.

"It's beautiful," he said finally. I let out a breath. "Did an American do this? No."

"Yes, actually."

"But the style is very good. You didn't write it yourself?"

"No, no. I found it online."

"Why *Al Haq?*" He touched the first line, the letter *alif*, where the skin was smooth but raised like a scar. I closed my eyes as he traced the word with his index finger.

"I like *Al Haq*," I murmured. "Truth without untruth, truth without opposite. The real that encompasses even the unreal, the most-real. And it comes next to *Ash-Shahid*, the Witness, which I also like." I opened one eye. "But *Ash-Shahid* has more letters so it would've hurt more."

He smiled. "When you got this tattoo—were you a Muslim then?"

"No," I answered. "This is over two years old. I got it when I knew I would convert someday. I wasn't ready then, but I had the tattoo done to remind me."

"Amazing," he said, shaking his head. "I had no idea such a story was possible in America."

"Neither does anyone else back home, I'm sure. You were the first person I told."

He looked surprised. "Really?"

"Yes. People at home think I have a cultural or academic interest in Islam. I have six Qurans, not one of which I bought for myself, and at least as many books of Sufi poetry, which were also all gifts, but if I told the people who gave them to me that I've converted, they would all be horrified."

Omar's face darkened. "Is it so unacceptable?"

"Oh, yes."

He touched the back of my hand. "I hope you know that this is going to be very, very hard," he said.

"I know," I said. "I know."

★   ★   ★

A simple team-building exercise given to the staff at Language School showed us what we were up against. The principal was an Egyptian woman who had taught for years in the United States. It's safe to assume, then, that when she gave us this exercise she knew exactly what she was doing. We were given a handout with a short scenario: a woman whose husband is always away on business goes out at night to meet a lover. A known madman is on the loose. At the end of the evening the woman asks her lover to escort her home in case the madman appears. The lover refuses. The woman goes to a friend's house nearby and asks her friend to walk with her; hearing the reason why the woman is out so late, the friend refuses. The woman goes on alone. At the river separating her neighborhood from her lover's, she asks a ferryman to take her across. Because she has no money to pay him, the ferryman refuses. As a result, the woman is trapped on the wrong side of the river and killed by the madman.

"Who," said the principal, her eyes twinkling, "is responsible for her death? Rank the characters by the order of their guilt."

After a few moments of silence, like a communally gathered breath, the room erupted into shouting. The westerners all came down on the same side: obviously, the madman was number one, because he had committed the murder. After that, the friend, lover, ferryman, and wife came in various orders, and the husband, that gray absent figure, floated at the bottom of the list.

The Egyptians were aghast at this interpretation. Clearly, the wife was number one, as she was the one who decided to have an affair and leave her house late at night in the first place. The madman, they said, was insane, and could not be held fully accountable for his actions. Most of them put him at number six. Hearing this, all the Western women— including me—nearly went crazy ourselves. Our feminist principles had been insulted and we argued, patronized, and went red in the face to defend them. Some of the women looked shaken to the point of tears. Here was Arab culture, as chauvinist as everyone had warned us it was, staring us in the face after we had so generously assumed that beneath the differences in language and custom there were westerners waiting to emerge.

I looked at Omar; he held my eyes for a moment and then shook his head, as if to say, *The bridge you want to cross doesn't exist.* We could do no more than look; our engagement was not public knowledge. I felt it wouldn't be fair to my family if strangers knew about my engagement before they did. Here was another river that couldn't be crossed except by telling small lies.

I was pulled aside by Hanan, an Arabic teacher, who seemed eager to explain why the Egyptians thought as they did. The wife was the only one directly responsible for her actions, she said. No one forced her to have an affair, and emphatically, no one forced her to leave the house when she knew a madman was loose. Next to her in accountability was the husband. He had failed in his duty to his wife and should be ashamed of himself for neglecting her and, by doing so, indirectly causing her death. This startled me. It was a common thread in the argument being made by my Egyptian colleagues, both men and women: most of them had ranked the husband at number two and spoke of him with as much disgust as if he had been a real person. The westerners, on the other hand, had no idea where to put him, and usually stuck him between four and six.

While the westerners were arguing literal responsibility —who wielded the knife and who could have helped the woman but didn't—the Egyptians were arguing moral responsibility. Morally, the madman was like a force of nature; he couldn't distinguish between right and wrong and his actions were indiscriminate. The woman could distinguish between right and wrong, and had chosen to put her own life in danger for an inadequate reason. If her husband, who was responsible for her physical and emotional happiness, had neglected her, then he was at fault for encouraging his wife to seek happiness elsewhere.

I realized why the Egyptian teachers were so bewildered by our western anger: in their eyes we were arguing that cheating on one's spouse is not wrong and that a husband has no emotional responsibility to his wife. But our argument was about personal rights, not social responsibilities. To us, both the husband and wife had the right to make their own decisions. If the husband decided his career took priority over his marriage, that was his prerogative; if the wife looked for emotional fulfillment elsewhere, that was hers. Spousal responsibility never entered the argument.

In the end we settled on a compromise. The madman was slotted at number one for wielding the knife, the wife at number two for knowingly endangering her own life, the husband at number three for encouraging her to do so, the lover at number four for being a general bastard, the ferryman at number five for being uncharitable (a sin in Islam), and the friend, whose motives were questionable, at number six. We had argued as though the characters in question were waiting outside the door for our verdict. I was surprised that it took so little to divide a group of intelligent people straight down the middle, precisely along cultural lines, without exception. While everybody laughed about it afterward, and talked about the incident for weeks ("The ferryman! The ferryman!" was a standard greeting for a while), it was clear we were all unsettled. Everyone knew this compromise was not limited to the hypothetical.

This was not the last time Omar and I would look at each other from across a bewildering gap. It would open up suddenly, beneath our feet. Alone, our origins didn't seem to matter, but as soon as we found ourselves in a group he became an Egyptian and I became an American. It was automatic. Aside from love—which made us more sensitive to cultural differences, not less—there was nothing we could take for granted. When I talk about those early months, most people still make the optimistic assumption: surely there were things to build on. Surely at some point the expectations of two cultures must intersect. And I am forced to say: no. There was nothing. Violently, utterly nothing.

Jo was often the only one who understood what it was like to navigate this interworld, the little fissures between East and West where no clear common values held sway. As the weeks passed, we developed the shared rituals of outsiders. The most hallowed of these was Punch Fundie.

It was a game modeled on Punch Buggy—wherein you slug the person next to you if you spot a VW Bug while you're driving—but modified to fit the more common roadside appearance of a fundamentalist. According to the rules, a fundamentalist was anyone with the telltale beard but no mustache and a galibayya that stopped short of his ankles, or a woman who wore the all-encompassing black *niqab*, leaving only her eyes visible. All car rides were fair game. One smoggy day in a cab downtown, I felt two hard punches slam into my right arm just above the elbow.

"What the *hell*?" I turned to glare at Jo. Her eyes were wide. She pointed out my window.

"Punch Fundie *and* Punch Buggy," she said in an awed voice. I looked: sure enough, cruising alongside us was a fundamentalist driving a yellow VW Bug. He frowned into the oncoming traffic, sporting a calloused prayer bruise and an unkempt beard that crept up his cheeks like Spanish moss. We gaped out the window, unable to speak. When the car pulled away we pressed our hands over our mouths to keep from laughing, tears rolling down our cheeks. The whole thing—the city, the great world, the conflicts we faced —could not be mortally serious as long as there were fundamentalists in hippie cars. Jo and I spent the rest of the night breaking into spontaneous grins, confident, for once, that things were going to turn out all right.

The Bowl of Fire

He gave me a bowl and I saw then with
  great insight
Oh Shams and sunlight both, come to
  my aid
for I am divided from myself, and yet
  myself.
—Rumi

ON MY OWN, IN SMALL, QUIET INCREMENTS, I BEGAN TO
inhabit Islam. Once I wrestled my ego into obedience and
faced Mecca, I began to understand the reason for "organized" worship, in which ritual innovation is discouraged.
When you join an organized religion, you do not worship
in isolation, even when you are alone. In Islam, prayer is a
full-body experience: you stand, bow, stand, kneel with
your forehead to the ground, and stand again, repeating a
variation of this cycle several times. You become part of a
mathematical algorithm linking earthly and heavenly bodies. Your calendar is based on the phases of the moon, your
daily prayers on the movement of the sun across the sky.
Mecca becomes an idea with a location. You orient yourself toward it not with a compass, but with a Great Circle,
calculating the shortest distance between the spot where

you stand and the Kaaba, the shrine in Mecca believed to be built by Abraham. In most parts of the United States, you face north, over the frozen pole.

Festivals and fasts are unhinged, traveling backward at a rate of ten days per year, attached to no season. Even Laylat ul Qadr, the holiest night of Ramadan, drifts—its precise date is unknown. The iconoclasm laid down by Muhammad was absolute: you must resist attachment not only to painted images, but to natural ones. Ramadan, Muharram, the Eids; you associate no religious event with the tang of snow in the air, or spring thaw, or the advent of summer. God permeates these things—as the saying goes, Allah is beautiful, and He loves beauty—but they are transient. Forced to concentrate on the eternal, you begin to see, or think you see, the bones and sinews of the world beneath its seasonal flesh. The sun and moon become formidable clockwork. They are transient also, but hint at the dark planes that stretch beyond the earth in every direction, full of stars and dust, toward a retreating, incomprehensible edge.

There are hundreds of metaphors about the effect of religion on the religious. Religious experience is so abstract that drawing concrete parallels is often the only way to explain it. To me, religion was like a pill: once swallowed, it began to work in ways I could neither control nor anticipate, nor unswallow. If I left Islam tomorrow, I would remain chemically altered by it. Rituals that seem arbitrary to the irreligious—the precise wording and physical attitudes of prayer, the process of ablution—are carefully formulated tonics. Almost unconsciously, I was being changed by them.

The change manifested first in my dream life. Dreams have always been important to me—since childhood I've remembered mine almost every night. Together, they form a kind of parallel personal history or unconscious narrative. Dream symbols figured largely in the events leading up to my conversion. As more and more Muslim rituals became habit, the character and content of my dreams began to alter. There was less clutter, fewer indecipherable gibberish images. What was left came into focus.

A few weeks after Ramadan, I dreamed of a massive desert. Running through it was a highway, empty: no cars or trucks traveled along it, no people or animals. I walked along it alone, carrying a bowl of perfumed oil. I had to take the bowl to a Shi'ite friend in New York, and I was confident the highway would lead me there. I arrived to meet my friend at an ancient-looking stone building in a small park. When I offered her the bowl of oil, my friend refused, and asked me to keep it safe for awhile. Turning away, I dropped a lit match into the bowl. It burst into flame. In the fire I saw the face of Imam Husayn, the Prophet's warrior-poet grandson, who was martyred at Karbala in the seventh century. I don't know how I knew it was him—in Sunni Islam, we make no pictures of holy figures.

"He started to speak to me," I told Omar and Ibrahim later, "but I don't remember what he said. I think I woke up in the middle."

"You don't *remember*?" Omar looked crestfallen. "But that might be the most important part!"

I shrugged helplessly. "Maybe he was speaking Fus'ha," I said, using the term for classical Arabic.

"What did he look like?" Ibrahim asked.

"He had a rectangular face—not handsome, but strong. Pale skin and dark, almost black eyes. A dark beard. His head was shaved. He looked very intelligent and very sad."

Omar nodded. "That fits the way he's described. It was a true dream."

In Islam, dreams are divided into three categories: ordinary dreams, which are the internal ramblings of the unconscious mind; satanic dreams, which are nightmares; and "true" dreams or visions, believed to be inspired by God. A true dream is religiously provable, containing elements of Islamic history or scripture with which the dreamer may or may not be familiar.

It was not at all strange to Omar or Ibrahim that I dreamed of Husayn without ever having heard him described. They saw no boundary between the explicable and the inexplicable. To talk about such an experience without fear of judgment or skepticism was a profound relief. I was not strange or abnormal: I was experiencing the world as people had experienced it for thousands of years. This was what religion was to me. When I stumbled into Islam, I wasn't looking for a radical new moral or social system. I wasn't angry at society. I was looking for words, *the* words, ones that would match what I had seen and felt but could not explain. Like my dream. Faith, to me, is not a leap but an affirmation of personal experience. With Islam I gave myself permission to live in the world as I saw it, not as I was told to see it.

After dreaming of the bowl of fire, I was curious about Imam Husayn, and decided to visit the mosque named in his honor. Masgid al Husayn, as the mosque is known, makes up one side of a large square in Old Cairo. Beside it is the entrance to Khan al Khalili, a medieval bazaar made up of a hundred tiny alleyways, one of which houses Fishawi's café. The neighborhood is collectively called Husayn. It was one of my favorite parts of the city, but I had never been inside the mosque.

The shrine within the mosque was rumored to contain Imam Husayn's head. The claim is not unusual; Cairo is full of the bones of saints. To Sunnis, these holy figures occupy uncertain ground—praying *to* a saint is considered idolatrous, but seeking spiritual blessing at his tomb is acceptable. Hard-liners frown even on this practice, and many Wahhabis—puritanical Muslims—have called for the shrines and burial places of saints to be torn down, but the average Cairene can still tell the difference between loving reverence and outright worship, so the shrines remain. The Imam's official tomb is at Karbala in Iraq, and every Shi'ite I've ever spoken to is mortified by the suggestion that his head might be elsewhere. Still, most Cairenes believe that some physical remnant of the Imam is locked inside the shrine at Masgid al Husayn.

I went during the middle of the day, between the noon prayer and the midafternoon prayer. When I arrived, the women's side of the mosque was only half-full. I walked barefoot across the carpet, falling under a series of curious stares and smiles. In Egypt, visiting shrines is a habit most prevalent among the poor, whose mystical folk tradition is more resistant to Wahhabism than the pensive, rationalist faith of the middle classes. Most of the women I saw were working-class, and wore plain black or brown robes that left only their faces and feet exposed. A dozen stood clustered around the shrine on one side of the prayer space, abutting the men's section. The shrine was a cube of pure silver eight or nine feet high, decorated with ornate calligraphy and latticework. Men and women faced each other across it—a rare occurrence in a mosque; necessary, in this case, to provide both genders with equal access to the imam.

Finding a spot near the shrine, I cupped my hands in front of my face and whispered the Fatiha, the first words of the Quran. A woman squeezed beside me and greeted the imam with *as-salaamu alaykum,* as naturally as if he was a beloved uncle or family sheikh standing there in the flesh. Unsettled, I began to forget that I was looking at a silver box. I thought of a hike I'd taken once through the foothills in Colorado, when I saw a bear and momentarily mistook it for a person. There was nothing human about the bear, but its awareness and intelligence were so tangible that my brain tried to make it look like one. For an instant I saw an enormous, shaggy man bent over and hurrying through the grass. At the shrine, I felt the same disorientation: I was in the presence of an imam, and had mistaken him for a silver box. The sense of a definite personality, full of grace and sadness, permeated the room—whether it arose from the worshippers who greeted the imam, or from the silver box that may or may not contain his bones, didn't matter. Something pressed against all the knowable objects in the room, a reminder, strange and luminous, of all we could not see.

★　★　★

It was during this period that I learned to trust my religion, because it became one of the central arbiters of my daily life. More often than not, Egyptian culture and American culture demanded opposite things. American men kiss women on the cheek in greeting, for example, but not other men. In Egypt the opposite is true. Each side claims that a kiss on the cheek is not sexual, which raises a question: Why, then, should Egyptian men refrain from kissing women, or American men be afraid to kiss other men? This conflict, and others like it, exposed an exasperating truth: cultural habits are by and large irrational, emerge irrationally, and are practiced irrationally. They are independent of the intellect, and trying to fit them into a logical pattern is fruitless; they can be respected or discarded, but not debated. The question, *If a kiss isn't sexual, why kiss one sex but not the other?* is as rhetorical and inconclusive as searching for the practical function of a bow tie, or arguing the logistical merits of doorknobs (which are common in the United States) versus door handles (which are common in the Middle East). Culture belongs to the imagination; to judge it rationally is to misunderstand its function.

Omar and I turned to Islam, which was neither Egyptian nor American and often contradicted both, to arbitrate between us. It was an ethos we had both chosen and seemed the fairest way to resolve our disputes. Whenever we disagreed about something, out came the Quran and the books of hadith, or sayings of the Prophet. What we disagreed about nearly always had something to do with either gender or freedom of movement. Private life, with its ritualized and prescribed relationships, forms the axis of Egyptian society, but I was used to living my life publicly and independently. I paid little attention to the gender of this friend or that and what it might mean.

I was surprised by how often Islam, in its purely textual form, took my side. There is no religious limit on the public spaces that women can inhabit; nothing prevents them from running businesses or driving cars, there is no reason they must walk behind men or cover their faces. A woman's role is not defined by the kitchen and the nursery.

I discovered, as Omar and I patiently constructed the intermediate cultural space in which we would live, that Muslim women were in some respects freer in the seventh century than they are today. The Prophet's first wife, Khadijah, one of the most beloved women in Islamic history, ran her own successful business. Muhammad spent much of his early life working as her employee; they were married after she proposed to him. She was almost fifteen years his senior. Her death plunged the Prophet into mourning so intense that it is known even today as the Year of Sorrow. The Virgin Mary, known to Muslims as Maryam, is mentioned more times in the Quran than she is in the Bible, and raises her miraculous son entirely on her own; Joseph is not present in the Islamic version of her story. Asia, the wife of Pharaoh, is revered by Muslims for having disobeyed her husband in defense of Moses. A powerful entrepreneur, a single mother, and a rebellious wife: all three women are revered as the embodiment of perfect faith.

I didn't realize how much internalized prejudice I still had against Islam. I was surprised by the evenhandedness of the bulk of Shari'a law—and then embarrassed that I was surprised. Spiritual impulses aside, part of me unconsciously believed that I had done something shameful by converting to Islam. Religion was taboo in my family, and Islam was taboo in my society—these pressures are not easily shaken off, and I sometimes felt as guilty as if I had committed a crime. I would never have admitted it, but on some level I believed that Bin Laden's Islam was the real Islam—that barbarism was waiting on the next page of the Quran or in the next hadith, that someday soon I would turn a page and be horrified. There were parts of Shari'a law that were premodern and problematic, but no more so than the Old Testament. Islam had all the hang-ups, along with all the potential for resolution, of any ancient faith.

Some aspects of the law were actually more liberal than their counterparts in other Abrahamic faiths. In Egypt, I discovered, liberal Islamic divorce law is frequently the reason for conversion among local Christians who, under Coptic law, are prevented from divorcing their spouses except in extreme and often unprovable circumstances. In 2005, a scandal would break out when the unhappy wife of a Coptic patriarch converted to Islam in order to divorce him.

My initial impression of Shari'a law, based on western news reports, conservative pundits and Saudi propaganda, was actually an impression of Wahhabi law—an angry, violent tradition propagated by the nomadic raiders of the Arabian Peninsula. The sayings of the Prophet contain warnings that the people of Najd—the birthplace of Wahhabism—would try to corrupt the faith: warnings the Wahhabis, in their supposed piety and unstinting legalism, have chosen to ignore.

Those first few months were made up of conflict punctuated by calm. Looking back I am amazed by the trust and discipline it took to work so tirelessly for the sake of a relationship so new; there was no guarantee that we wouldn't drift apart for all the usual reasons. We had potential, not history, and yet that potential had to be protected with a kind of confidence that usually only comes after years of intimacy. There were moments—days, weeks—when I felt Omar was disappearing in a blind spot in my vision; that in creating a space in my life where he could exist culturally, I had lost sight of him as an individual. He also suffered from these moments: in certain social situations or about certain ideas, I would become unrecognizably American, and the intersection of personality and background would blur. It would sink us both into anxiety and doubt—though we were careful never to say it, I think we were both afraid it was possible we could never really know one another.

This came up again and again when we tried to go out with other American expatriates. Our Egyptian acquaintances were much more forgiving of my strangeness than our American acquaintances were of Omar's, and were affectionate and protective of me even when they disagreed with what I said or did. The Americans we knew, on the other hand, expected a certain amount of cultural submission almost as a matter of course. If someone didn't hold the right views about things like homosexuality and drinking, or couldn't adjust to their level of casual familiarity between men and women, the atmosphere would get strained and contemptuous. This was not always true, of course, and may have had a lot to do with age. Older and better-traveled expats tended to have more humility and a tougher sense of humor. The younger jet set—recent college graduates who wanted the same clubbing and boozing they had back home, but in a more exotic environment—could be poisonous.

One of these, a flamboyant college classmate, showed up shortly after Ramadan. He was traveling and hoping to find work abroad; my enthusiastic e-mails about Egypt convinced him to pass through the country. I agreed to meet him at a café in Maadi, where we sat down at a street-side table with cups of Turkish coffee. Our conversation was full of pauses. He wanted to pick up where we'd left off as freshmen in college, when we were irreverent and chemically fortified; for obvious reasons I found it difficult to speak in that key anymore. After an hour of stilted talk, we left, and he escorted me back to Omar's. Omar was sitting in the living room with his friend Khaled, a Bedouin whose tribe was settled less than fifty years ago, after Cairo began to encroach on their traditional campgrounds. After introducing himself and saying hello, my friend turned to leave—and as he did, cheerfully blew me a kiss. I stared after him, amazed.

"I hope Khaled didn't see that," said Omar afterward, with mild amusement. When it came to women, the Bedouin were one of the most conservative peoples in Egypt, though blowing a kiss at an engaged woman in front of her fiancé and a strange man was bizarre even by Cairene standards. It would take many more such incidents —voluble monologues about my ex-boyfriend, snide remarks about religion— before I realized that a lot of people I knew who visited Egypt were simply not interested in respecting local boundaries, and thought it was edgy and sophisticated to trample over them.

At first I tolerated these lapses in manners, or tried creatively to gloss over them. Omar was always surprised that I didn't simply call people out for their behavior. The intelligence he admired and cultivated was classically Islamic and essentially judicial: the facility to remember and assimilate huge numbers of facts for the purpose of determining right from wrong. The inventive way I had been taught to think—American public schools, with all their drawbacks, make use of one of the only education systems in the world that recognizes the necessity of the imagination—was alien to him. If a conversation took a bad turn, to his thinking I should end it, rather than manipulating it so that it limped along to a quiet and natural death. Personality, that compromise between one's culture and one's soul, was sometimes invisible; around other westerners, I was an American and he was an Egyptian.

"Then let's not think about it now," he would say to comfort me when we were confronted by this division. "Let's just stay here for a little while with what we already know."

A Tree in Heaven

Say 'in the name of God' to find your true
name.
—Rumi

IN EGYPT, THE MARRIAGE OF TWO PEOPLE IS REALLY THE
marriage of two families. Omar's was not limited to his parents and brother: there was a clan of aunts, uncles, cousins,
and second cousins, all living in different parts of Cairo.
Some of them I met at a cousin's engagement party. Most
of the family, however, was still a mystery.

They gathered together every Thursday evening at the
family flat in Doqqi, a district on the other side of the Nile.
Even in a country full of family-oriented people, this kind
of dedication stood out. They were, as Omar put it, a tribe.
Worried I would be overwhelmed by the crowd and the
Arabic—aside from Sohair and Ibrahim, no one else in the
family spoke fluent English—Omar kept postponing my in-
troduction, pushing it back by incremental Thursdays. But
a Thursday came when the meeting could no longer be
postponed: Sohair's father, the family patriarch, had passed
away quietly in the evening after saying his prayers.

"This is going to be intense," Omar said on the way to
the wake, taking my hand despite the curious glance of the
cab driver. "Will you be okay? Don't be afraid if the women

get very emotional." He looked tired, his face pale above the deep black he wore in mourning. I worried that I was a burden in an already stressful time.

"I'll be fine," I said, unconvinced. It felt awkward to intrude on the grief of people I didn't know, but it would have been insulting not to pay my respects. Grief is different in Egypt—there is no embarrassment attached to it. Funerals are public, open to all who want to mourn the dead or console the living. I was used to thinking of death as something deeply private. Worried I would do or say something wrong, I hung back as we got out of the cab and headed down a dark side street on foot.

The family flat was situated in an alley, in the classical Arabic sense of the word: a narrow street teeming with activity. There were grocers and peddlers, a "doctor," an ironing man, and a dressmaker, all packed precariously beside and on top of one another. Until very recently, it was not uncommon for people to be born, work, marry, and die in the same district. Omar's grandmother had lived in this alley for her entire married life. Sohair and her seven siblings had grown up in the very apartment we were visiting: boys sleeping in one room, girls in another, meals together in the middle. With the arrival of her first great-grandchildren, Omar's grandmother had seen four generations pass through her doors in the span of eighty-odd years.

As we walked down the alley I became aware of the color of my skin. Many of the people who lived here were East African, tall and slender and blue-black. I attracted appraising stares, as if I had arrived from another world. I almost felt like I had. This was a place where the raw facts of life—birth, survival, procreation, death—were so power-fully condensed that there was room for little else. Up until now, I'd lived my life in the space wealth creates between those forces, space where art and education and ambition can exist. Here, that life felt superfluous.

Omar opened a door and ushered me into a fluorescent-lit room with high ceilings. It was full of people: men with beards, women in head scarves, younger girls who were bare-headed, and young boys who squabbled and cooed over an infant. Many of the women were crying. I shook hands with each of Omar's five maternal uncles, who smiled wearily and touched my cheek. Uncle Sherif, the second-to-youngest, asked me if I ever had a chance to meet his father. I told him I wished I had.

"I am sorry," he said, choosing his words in careful English. "Very sorry you could not meet. He would like to meet the *khateeba* of his first grandson."

"I'm sorry, too," I said, without knowing what else to say. In the background, a radio had been tuned to a recita-tion of the Quran. A male voice chanted verses across static, in a tense, stripped, longing melody that is now as familiar to me as my bones. I saw a girl named Saraa coming toward me from across the room. We had met at the cousin's en-gagement party; with her wide dark eyes and expressive mouth, she was one of the most beautiful women I'd ever seen. She had been happy then. Now when she kissed my cheek, her face was wet. I took her hand. She led me to a room where five or six other young women were sitting to-gether. In hushed voices we introduced ourselves, giggling at the inadequate words to which we were limited.

Marwa, Uncle Ahmad's daughter, began reciting a prayer for her grandfather's soul. The other girls cupped their hands in front of their faces. I did the same. It's a strange feeling, praying to your hands, filling the air between them with words. We think of divinity as something infinitely big, but it permeates the infinitely small—the condensation of your breath on your palms, the ridges in your fingertips, the warm space between your shoulder and the shoulder next to you. I spent hours there with these women and girls whose names I couldn't yet keep straight, but who were already my family. They told stories I didn't understand, laughing and weeping by turns. I went back and forth to the kitchen for tissues and glasses of water, or sat silently, hoping they somehow understood what I didn't know how to say.

After that day, whenever I went to a family gathering an arm would slip through mine and pull me away to be kissed and fussed over by the other girls. As I learned more of their language, their conversations would burst colorfully to life; they were articulate, funny, frank, opinionated about news and politics. Marwa likes to tell the story of my odd entrance into the family. "One day she danced at a wedding, the next she sat through a funeral, and on the third she was one of us," she says, usually with a laugh. And that is how I felt.

Writing *Muslim* on employment and visa forms was harder than I expected. Modest as it seemed, this was the first public affirmation of faith I'd ever made. Finding the courage to write those six little letters took a long time. After this small triumph, I was shocked when the forms were returned to me labeled *Christian*. Religion is not a private affair in Egypt; if you have a Christian name, the government will not acknowledge your conversion to Islam until you take the *shaheda* in front of a state-approved sheikh. I had to laugh. In a bizarre, autocratic way it reminded me not to take myself too seriously—as monumental as religion is to a believer, its public face is usually ridiculous. If I was going to survive as a Muslim in a Muslim country, I needed to develop a healthy appreciation for the absurd.

There was no avoiding it—I would have to go to Al-Azhar, one of Sunni Islam's most highly respected judicial institutions and the oldest continuously operative university on earth, for a state-sponsored conversion. I had a reason beyond bureaucratic necessity: tired of being questioned by police when we were out together, Omar and I had decided to "register the certificate," the first of several steps necessary to formalize an Egyptian marriage. Registering the certificate, or *katb el kiteb*, refers to the drawing up and signing of a marriage contract, in which the price of the dowry is fixed, the terms of divorce decided, and the legal status of any shared property set out. In some senses *katb el kiteb* more closely resembles a western prenuptial agreement than a marriage contract; while a couple is considered religiously married after they sign their *kiteb,* they are not considered socially married—and are expected to abstain —until their wedding.

The period between the registration and the wedding is confusing for young couples, who are married in the eyes of God yet prevented by their families from spending too much time alone. This waiting period has no basis in religion and in modern Egypt it has become an excuse to throw an ostentatious party between a couple's engagement and their wedding. Omar and I decided to register for a different reason: we wanted to travel together, which was legally impossible unless we could present a *kiteb* at military checkpoints and hotels. If I married Omar as a Christian, I would have fewer rights as his wife. If we wanted to travel together, we had to draw up a marriage contract; and before we could draw up a marriage contract, I had to "legally" convert. It was a numbingly complex set of requirements, as only an Islamic police state can demand or deliver. And it necessitated the discussion of my name.

"Call her Zeinab," was Uncle Sherif's suggestion, because he liked me. His mother, Omar's grandmother, was another Zeinab, and his daughter another. It was a somewhat old-fashioned name, after a magnetic and fearless granddaughter of the Prophet, and unusual in a generation of Laylas and Yasmines.

"When Zeinab was a baby, the Prophet Muhammad would carry her around during prayer," said Omar when the name was offered. "He would put her on the ground as he knelt and pick her up again as he stood." Standing nearby, Ibrahim cradled a newborn cousin, so the scene was not hard to imagine. Though Omar was trying to be helpful, the subject of my Muslim name made him uncomfortable.

"The name Willow is not anti-Islamic," he said, with a protective glance in my direction. "It's a kind of tree. She cannot leave her name, too . . ." The *kamen* (*too*) gave him away; that sentence was supposed to end, *because she left so much to be here, she should not be asked to do this as well.* Since I was not Egyptian, it wouldn't quite be as bad as all that—I wasn't legally required to change my name, as an Egyptian convert would be. And like the other discreetly Muslim expatriates I knew, the world would go on calling me by my English name. *Zeinab* would become my name only to those who found *Willow* too difficult to pronounce.

"Zeinab is a tree as well!" Uncle Sherif pointed out. "A small tree, fragrant—"

"A tree in Heaven," said Omar.

Though I was touched by my future in-laws' eagerness to help, I was not enthusiastic about the idea of formal conversion. It felt insulting, as though the *shaheda* I recited with God as my witness was not good enough for the dry old men in turbans who oversaw the intersection of religion and state. Whether one's Muslim name is made legal or not, formal conversion requires the convert to choose one. While the idea of taking a new name was symbolically satisfying, it also made me feel divided. I already had a second name. *Willow* was an adolescent derivative of Gwendolyn, my legal name, which was too long a word to attach to a child in conversation. Willow stuck. Adding another name seemed redundant.

"I have too many names," I said to Omar.

"God has ninety-nine," he said, smiling and squeezing my hand. "You'll have three. That's not so bad."

The next morning Omar and I tried to make our way through the extensive campus of Al-Azhar. We shuttled between buildings in which we could and could not wear shoes, looking for one *Ish'har al Islam* labeled el Aganeb, "foreigners declaring Islam." We were both on edge. I was irritated by the whole process; it was more Egyptian bureaucracy. Had I taken a step back, I might have felt privileged to formally declare my faith in such a historic place. Instead I felt vulnerable. By the time we found the right building, I was close to panic. Conversion is a personal process, and to bureaucratize it is, I still think, a little cruel. The hours between my arrival at Al-Azhar and when I slept that night are hours I still find hard to explain.

I was ushered into a room with a sheikh in it. He seemed inanimate, smiling on a couch, a creature with the spiritual gravity of a small sun. I had never met a sheikh before. He was talking with an American woman in a head scarf who seemed to be organizing some kind of event. They finished their conversation as I filled out the requisite paperwork. (Why do you wish to convert to Islam? The question seemed unanswerable. I scribbled something complimentary and generic.) Then the sheikh turned to me.

"Hello, Gwendolyn," he said, in perfect English.

I wish I could remember more of our conversation. He asked me a series of questions and made a few encouraging remarks. When I stood up again he was still smiling. This is what I took away from what he told me: you were put on this earth to do good, and you must remember that duty every day.

"You have chosen a name?"

"Zeinab."

"Sister Zeinab, when you repeat the *shaheda*, you will become like a little baby. Imagine!" He laughed. "You will start from nothing. What you do with that is between you and God."

Afterward, I was asked to sign a ledger thick with the signatures of other converts and the dates of their announcement. Seeing hundreds of names—British, German, Japanese, Spanish, Russian—I began to calm down. Until that moment, Islam had meant something very private to me—it defined my relationship with God and with Omar. I had never felt part of a world religion with over a billion adherents; during the silent inward process of conversion, I don't even think I realized that this is what Islam is. Yet here I was, looking at the names of men and women who were now *akh* and *ukht,* my theological brothers and sisters. The world seemed substantially smaller.

Now that I was an "official" Muslim, Omar and I could do our *katb el kiteb,* giving us the freedom to travel together. It should have been romantic, analogous to getting a marriage license at the courthouse, but since I was a foreigner, this, too, was tangled in bureaucracy. First, I had to get official permission from the U.S. Embassy. It was delivered with sour congratulations; they probably assumed I was a gullible woman being duped into a green-card marriage. Then Omar and I had to take this permission slip, along with my Azhar-approved record of conversion, and go to another warren of government offices. When it finally came time to sit down with a notary and draw up our marriage contract, I was hot and irritated.

"Name?" he asked briskly. He spoke in slow, formal Arabic so that I would understand.

"Gwendolyn Wilson."

"Where were you born?"

"New Jersey, *Al Willayet Al Mutaheda Al Amrikaya*."

"Yoo Ess Ayy." He abbreviated my sarcastic elongation and smiled, eyes twinkling. "Dowry?"

"One Egyptian pound." Enough to buy tamarind juice when this is all over, I thought.

He nodded, jotting away on a series of forms. "One Egyptian pound now, two in case, God forbid, of divorce."

Omar took a pound note out of his wallet and presented it to me with a grin. "*Itfaddali*," he said, *You are welcome to it*.

"How much cash do you have on you?" I said. "I should have asked for more."

The notary, revealing a decent grasp of spoken English, laughed.

Omar and I signed all four marriage contracts—one for him, one for me, one for the government, and one for Allah knew who—and with a few official stamps, we were husband and wife in the eyes of the Arab Republic of Egypt. The contract laid out the terms of our marriage: I was entitled to a slew of things if Omar took a second wife (Egyptian men can legally marry the Islamic four), my dowry reverted to him if we broke things off before the wedding, et cetera. As the almost-wife of an Egyptian, I could be fast-tracked for a long-term resident visa or citizenship, if I liked. I suddenly had rights in Egypt, not as a member of the foreign elite, but as a demi-Egyptian.

Omar and I left the Ministry of Paperwork and walked into the street. Dust hung in the air and settled in layers on the buildings, blunting their outlines. Omar took my hand and kissed it—he could do that publicly now.

"We did it, *ya meraati*," he said; *Oh, my wife*. I laughed. With that, Omar and I were technically married before we were publicly engaged. Today one of our running jokes is that we are *mitgowezeen awee—very* married. Adding together all the social and legal rituals, we have been married three or four separate times. This marked the first.

Meetings in the Desert

Eliza removed her husband as soon as possible for the interior, and some account must now be given of their adventures. Her pen is . . . curbed only by her fear of the Turkish Censor, and by her desire to conceal her forebodings from friends at home.

        —E. M. Forster, "Eliza in Egypt"

OMAR AND I LEFT THE CITY SHORTLY AFTERWARD ON OUR FIRST trip together. We took a public bus—taped Quran blaring over tinny speakers, dust, solemn men spitting sunflower-seed husks on the floor—six hours southwest into the Sahara, to a small oasis called Farafra. When we arrived it was two in the morning and the surrounding plains were a startling blue-white: there was a moon, and it had turned the sand the color of ice. Feral dogs watched us uneasily as we, alarmed by the utter silence after the constant noise of Cairo and the road, walked from the bus stop toward our hotel.

In the sunlight of the following morning, Farafra took on a more earthly character. It was a series of dirt roads lined with one- and two-story buildings, punctuated by cultivated groves of date palms fed by cold-water springs. After wandering around the town—most tourists stayed in locally-run hotels along its outskirts and didn't venture into the commercial and agricultural district, so we attracted some attention—Omar and I decided to take a jeep trip into the deep desert. This part of the Sahara, known as the White Desert, was crossable but not habitable, and had been left fairly pristine. We heard that there were limestone formations twenty or thirty kilometers toward the interior that were worth seeing. Saad, a famous local guide, was making a trip out to one of his camps in the area, and we hitched a ride with him. One of his sons, a boy of five or six, napped in my lap on the way out, oblivious to the spine-wracking jolts of off-roading over sand. Half an hour later, feeling limber, we arrived.

Away from the oasis, the landscape had changed—the sand was the color of cream, streaked here and there with drifts of darker matter. It rolled away in small dunes, dotted with arches and hills of white limestone that crumbled when touched. As I walked around, dazed, and stumbled on a darker drift, I discovered that what looked like patches of black sand were really the broken remnants of fossilized shells, left over from a time when the Sahara was a shallow sea, millions of years ago. This is what the limestone was made of. After that, every time I looked upward I had visions of long-extinct fish and huge Paleolithic sharks swarming in the air above my head.

We spent the afternoon scrambling over dunes and falling down, laughing as though drunk, and in the evening we joined Saad at his camp. There was a bonfire going and clustered around it were ten or twelve American tourists, half a dozen Cairo literati, and a few men from Saad's tribe, all passing cans of beer back and forth. A hand drum and a reed flute were produced, and the Bedouin and a couple of the more politically-minded Cairenes began to sing Palestinian liberation songs. The tourists, blithely unaware of the content of the lyrics, clapped along. Omar and I looked at each other and smiled, our expressions ironic but without bitterness. We had already learned that as often as not, these oblivious collisions between westerners and nonwesterners were as comical as they were tragic. They must be comical; they betray a mutual impotence that is devastating if it cannot be comical. Omar took my hand.

We left the fireside and climbed up one of the limestone embankments to look at the stars. The bright earth below us threw blue half-light on our faces.

"When I was a child," said Omar, "I used to imagine that I could travel through space in whatever room I was in. I imagined I could see stars like this out my window."

I looked at him without remembering to be American, and for the first time did not see an Egyptian. I saw my partner. He had been a little boy, he had grown up, he had dappled the air with stars; he would one day be an old man —if I was lucky, and everything held together, I would grow old with him. To be trusted with the history of another person seemed like the best—the only—privilege there was. I understood the words God was said to have spoken to Amir Abdul Qadir, the Algerian scholar, while he was in exile in the nineteenth century: "Today, I lower your lineage and raise up Mine." There was a divinity insensible of ethnic heritage, a truth hidden but not erased by geography. It demanded to be recognized and protected.

"I'm going to start wearing a scarf," I said.

Omar was silent for a moment. We had never talked about the *hijab,* or head scarf; he had never expected or encouraged me to wear it. My comment must have startled him considerably. He leaned over and kissed my forehead, twice. "What made you decide this?" he asked.

"I want to do something to make this separate from everything else," I said. "I want to give you something bigger than anything I've given anyone else." It was an impulse more spiritual than religious; *hijab* lent itself to my purposes, rather than I to its. Having read the relevant verses of Quran and hadith, as well as the arguments of major scholars, I remain unconvinced that *hijab* is *fard,* or obligatory, as opposed to *sunnah,* preferred. My decision, made as it was in that particular moment, was almost defensive; it was a way to say that anyone who could not see Omar as he was would not see me as I was.

Over the past several years my relationship with the veil has shifted, yet persisted; it has become a way to define intimacy in a wider sense, and in the circle of men who have seen my hair I have included some of Omar's and my close friends. When I am in the United States, I still go bareheaded in some circumstances. In other words, I have never been a model *muhajeba,* but in a sense this has allowed me to maintain an appreciation for the veil that might otherwise have faded after the inconvenience that comes with wearing it settled in.

After I'd spoken, Omar was silent again. "Where did you come from?" he asked finally. "How did I find you?"

"I don't know, I don't know," I said, laughing.

He called me *aziza,* the feminine of "precious," a word that has none of the ironic implications of its English counterpart. A word used to describe an anxiously awaited infant, a beloved friend, a well in the desert.

I got an e-mail from Ben not long after this. He announced that he was leaving the States, and would be back in Cairo the following week. He intended to study Arabic to try to get a job in government intelligence when he went home. Omar and I were nervous about Ben's arrival. He was a mutual friend—it was through him that we knew one another—but though he was respectful of cultural differences he found Arab restrictions on personal freedom absurd, and had said as much to me. Omar and I worried that Ben wouldn't understand what we were doing—really, what I was doing. We decided to tell Ben we were dating. He wouldn't believe for long, since Omar didn't date, but it would give him time to get used to seeing us together. I also decided to postpone covering my head for a couple of weeks.

We met him at the airport. He was easy to find, wearing his signature newsie hat and black-rimmed glasses, like a latter-day Ernest Hemingway in the Cuban bush. There was a bit of old-school expatriate in him, I thought; the sort that had rejected the ruling race mentality but still carried the safari aura around with them wherever they went. He greeted us in heavily accented Arabic.

"It's good to see you," said Omar, reaching out to hug him.

Ben gave a long sigh and shook his head. "I can't believe I'm back in Cairo," he grinned. "What happened?"

"Are you glad to be back?" I asked.

"I'll tell you after I've had some *shisha*," he said. "These are for you." He handed me a stack of comic books. I suppressed squeals of delight and Omar gave me a funny look; he had yet to learn about my comics habit.

"Here such things are only for children," he said.

"Not where we come from," responded Ben. In a semiprescient second, I knew how things would progress from there, and I was afraid.

Omar looked uncomfortable. By the standards of the Middle East, rules had already been stretched; Ben's gift to me in public made our relationship ambiguous. Was he my brother? Or perhaps Ben was the fiancé, and Omar a guide or chauffeur? But Ben didn't realize his transgression; he was only aware that something had gone wrong, and looked concerned. None of us knew how to proceed.

"What?" asked Ben.

"Nothing!" I assured him, smiling maniacally.

"We should go," said Omar.

"What did I do?" said Ben.

"Nothing," Omar repeated.

Ben looked at me with an expression that said, *So it's started already.* I could see that Omar also felt apprehensive—it was not that the simple act of gift giving bothered him, it was only that such a situation (man gets off plane, hands unrelated woman stack of comic books) would never have reason to occur in the Arab world. There was no protocol for it. He didn't know how to react, and so he was nervous. Both of them needed reassurance, and needed it from me, but I could only stand there without speaking, sure that it was going to get worse.

The next day, I agreed to meet Ben for breakfast at an expat café in Maadi. I had to run an errand at Al-Azhar afterward—I didn't tell him I was going there to pick up the English translation of my "official" conversion documents.

"You've converted," he said as we sat down at a booth. The wood floors, the ads for hamburgers and fries, and Ben in his glasses, all made me feel as though he and America had conspired to stage this breakfast as an intervention.

"Yes," I said, surprised. "How did you guess?"

He sighed. "Why else would you need to go to Al-Azhar? There isn't much of a happening scene there aside from Islam."

There was a pause. "Well?" I asked finally.

"I guess it's not shocking," he responded, in the same tone he had once used to tell me I was drinking too much. "I mean, you did get that tattoo."

"Ben," I said, "half of the religious texts I own come from you. When you came home for Christmas the first year you lived here, you brought me, like, six Qurans."

"Yeah, but I was under the impression that you were basically an atheist," said Ben. "I didn't think—anyway. So you're a Muslim. Why?"

"I have a different answer for this every week."

"Pick the best one then."

"I like Islam."

He smiled and seemed more like himself. "That's good. That's reassuring. I might not have believed you if you said anything else."

My tea arrived and I took a long swallow; it was hot and hurt my throat.

"So no more drinking and lechery? Aren't you going to miss it?" asked Ben, looking melancholic.

I felt a twinge of sympathy. It was through Ben that I had gained a detailed appreciation for whiskey and Tom Waits, the combination of which had seen me through many mishaps. "Of course I'll miss them. The drinking, anyway."

"Fair enough." He paused. "What are you going to say to everyone back home?" Though he meant our college friends, the word *everyone* unsettled me: in my mind it expanded beyond the question, taking in people I knew from old internships and sublet apartments. Everyone. I let my head loll back against the booth. "I don't know. It's terrifying."

"Do you think it'll be that bad?" he asked in a way that suggested he was no more optimistic than I was.

"I'll be lucky if it isn't worse. You've lived in a Muslim country and you haven't been jumping up and down with enthusiasm, so I can only imagine what the rest will be like."

He looked hurt. "I just worry about you," he said.

"I know. Believe me, I wouldn't tolerate this kind of cross-examination from people who didn't have a right to worry about me."

"What do you think they'll say?" he asked.

"They'll say I'm a hypocrite," I said flatly. "Because Islam is about stoning gays and chopping off body parts, as we know. They'll say I'm a hypocrite, and there won't be a damn thing I can do to change their minds." It was as if I could protect myself with cynicism; as if by being sarcastic and diffident and pretending to expect the worst, the fear and embarrassment that were coming would hurt less. It wouldn't occur to me until later that my friends—perhaps even my family—would think my conversion was an unfavorable judgment on their own values and lives.

A few years later I would meet a girl in Cairo whom I had known for a single weekend in New York, a friend of a friend with whom I'd gotten heroically intoxicated and wandered into the atrium of the World Financial Center at midnight. After September 11, pictures would circulate of the atrium's pale ruins, the palm trees broken and white with ash. "It seems like another lifetime that we were there," the girl would tell me in Cairo, dark-eyed and a little shy. She saw only clashing lifestyles: then I had had short pink hair and held my liquor, now I was a practicing Muslim. She couldn't see—and I could not have shown her—that for me there was a larger story in which those two ways of living were vitally connected, one that embraced not only that evening and this, but the atrium, the ash covered palm trees, the emerging imperative that certain things be understood. Though she dressed and spoke the same way she had that night in New York, she had left the atrium, but I, in some sense, was still there. Every day my life was affected by what had happened on 9/11; every day I had to get up and negotiate the boundaries between that tragedy and my religion. Every day.

Ben was silent for a minute, considering something. "Maybe," he said, "I don't know. You might be surprised. I can help—I can play backup. People will be less worried if I'm there to tell them you're still sane."

"Thanks," I said, too tired to bristle. "So, do you want to come to happening Al-Azhar?"

"Sure," said Ben.

We paid the check and caught a cab outside, and I rehearsed the things I now knew I would have to say to the people I had left behind.

Arrivals and Confessions

Behold, We have created you all out of a
male and a female, and have made you into
nations and tribes, so that you might come
to know one another.

—Quran 49:13

I DIDN'T EXPECT ANYTHING MORE SUPPORTIVE OR ENTHUSI-
astic than Ben's reaction to my conversion. Keeping it a secret clearly was not a practical long-term solution. Living
in a Muslim country, I felt even guiltier about my secrecy;
Omar's family knew, but I hadn't told my colleagues at
school, and wasn't even sure that revealing my religion
wouldn't put my job in jeopardy. This was the main reason
I had put off my decision to wear a head scarf.

I was as afraid of the reaction of Muslim friends to my
conversion as of non-Muslim ones. I didn't want to be special and symbolic any more than I wanted to be feared; I
wanted to be a regular Muslim, for whom Islam was a matter of course, independent of either censure or reward. I was
too exhausted by what Omar and I had undertaken to even
handle praise; I wanted only normalcy.

There would be no avoiding the crisis when it came, so
I decided to force it. I ran up the flag, so to speak, by putting on *hijab*. The first scarf I ever bought and wore was

apple red, a color that ensured my ultraconservative colleagues would be as shocked as my non-Muslim ones. The
first day I walked into school "swathed," as Jo put it, the
principal stopped in her tracks, wide-eyed, and without a
pause asked "Is this a veil I see before me?"

For a second I couldn't get words to come out of my
mouth. "It's a permanent religious bad hair day," I said finally. She laughed. The moment of tension passed. I kept
up this attitude throughout the day; when people were surprised, I was cheerful and neutral, which left some puzzled,
some amused, some alarmed, and some delighted. I had
achieved what I set out to do, which was to avoid philosophical conversations with those who were not Muslim,
and clichéd spiritual raptures with those who were.

Looking back, the way I chose to "come out" taught me
something vital: anything undertaken with honest intentions
can be justly defended. I never by word or action claimed
to possess a higher or a universal truth, only a very personal
one; I think this was one of the main reasons I was able to
slip quietly into "ordinary" Islam, without the fanfare that
accompanies conversion. I never tried to become a mascot;
I was just a person, with the usual quirks and faults, who
was now Muslim.

My moderate Muslim colleagues and friends—moderate
is a terrible word, since many of them are very passionate
about their religion—accepted me without a batted eye. No
one went into ecstasies about the God-given blessings of
conversion, no one cross-examined me about my theology.
They simply began to greet me with *as-salaamu alaykum* instead of "hi," and included me in the silent wry glances that

would go around the room when secular or western coworkers launched into critiques of religion. The men began to treat me with the same protective chivalry they extended to other Muslim women; the women, typically put off by the androgyny of western girls, stopped treating me like a man. The transition was silent but complete.

Ultraconservative teachers, of which there were a few, became guarded and uneasy when I began to wear a head scarf. Converts are a favorite prey of fundamentalists; they are often isolated, confused, and in need of reassurance, which radical Muslims are only too happy to give. In my case, they were confused. The way I wore my scarf, and the colors I chose, made it clear I was not crying out for help or seeking support. Mainstream Islam is too abstract and ordinary a thing to offer much comfort to the average initiate; it demands belief quietly and without celebration, offers few indisputable answers, and requires one to draw on inner spiritual resources far more often than communal ones. It must have been disturbing to radicals that a convert could find mere Islam more appealing than their tight-knit community. This is the death knell of radicalism: Muslims who have achieved a personal understanding of the religion can inspire doubt in extremists simply by standing in front of them. It's a simple fact, but one with the potential to change the world.

To my friends and immediate family in the United States, I wrote a letter. With them there was no space I could occupy besides that of a convert; Islam for the average American was never ordinary, could never be ordinary. The day I wrote and sent this letter via e-mail is cast in sharp relief in my memory, all the more painful because it is something I would rather forget. Later, I would pick the letter apart, grafting its contents into these pages, a line here, a paragraph there. It was the first and most honest explanation I made for my faith, painful as it was. A Muslim writer friend once asked me why this kind of apologetic writing is so awful to us.

"I think it's because it shouldn't be necessary," I said. We were trying to decide why our best work, rather than giving us confidence, brought on bouts of depression. "It shouldn't be necessary, and the fact that it is means something is terribly wrong."

It seems an obvious thing to say; of course there is something wrong. One need only watch the news to see it. But I was not talking about the obvious wrong, the cycle of war and jihad, but about the emotional reality created by it: the fact that we now demand proof of common humanity. To provide that proof is to give away your dignity as rent to the ideal of peace. Using your own history to explain some trivial difference between East and West, or getting a reader to empathize with someone he believes to be his enemy, does not bring happiness—only a degraded sense of having been useful.

I could not have put this idea into words when I wrote the letter announcing my conversion to the people I loved back home. The ability to articulate the kind of pain it caused would come later. But I felt it, acutely, overwhelmingly, like vertigo. I could almost see the distance I was putting between myself and my past and the people who inhabited it. How could I explain to them that I had not deviated, but was walking in a straight line, as true—truer—to myself and my principles as ever? I did the best I could, but the letter could only have been bizarre to those who read it; I have not read it in full since the day I sent it.

Replies were slow to come, leaving me to invent worst-case scenarios in my mind. I was crippled by my own stubborn refusal to talk to Omar about my fears. *Someone* had to remain unhurt by my inconvenient life. It was a deluded way of thinking, but I clung to it, and waited.

Everything around me seemed muffled, colorless. I was slow to respond to questions and to go about tasks. My life unrolled in front of me, blank: I am not the sort of person who can walk away from the people she loves, or even the people she has loved. I could not imagine moving forward without them.

But I didn't have to.

Timidly, as though I might break, my family and friends began to speak up. My parents were supportive in a weary and slightly self-recriminating way, as if my decision to do something this terrible resulted from a defect in their parenting. They didn't say so, but guilt flowed between the lines. Guilt and acceptance were better than fear and denial, however, so I began the months-long process of reassuring them that I had not been brainwashed, and that Islam was a fourteen-hundred-year-old spiritual tradition, not a result of bad parenting.

A few of my friends recognized that my conversion was the result of a process that had begun years earlier: that my steady accumulation of Islamic texts, my extracurricular interest in Arabic, and the infamous tattoo were not coincidences. One, a guy I had known at BU, even said, "Anyone who didn't see this coming wasn't looking." Most responses fell somewhere in between. In subsequent years, the conversations that my letter provoked have been revealed to me bit by bit, often by accident; people did react with the mingled fear and disgust I had anticipated, but undercutting this was a current of tenderness I did not expect. They didn't want me to sense the nega-tivity, and made an effort—sometimes collaboratively—to be kind. The reaction was, given the state of the post-9/11 world, extraordinary.

I wrote using a more intimate vocabulary than ones employed to describe political affiliations and absolutist theologies and strategy, one that put our relationships at the center of the dialogue rather than our ideologies. I did not ask them to understand Islam, but to understand me. It was a plea that put too much trust in what had already been established—mutual affection and mutual vulnerability—to be ridiculed. When I deviated from this attitude a few months later, sick from the onslaught of misinformation and emotional sterility I saw in the media, and began to lecture them about my religion, I was pulled up short. "Who salted this earth?" a friend asked me in an e-mail, "*We are fine. We love you.* You can stop playing information nanny."

I was over the first hurdle. The weight of the secret I had been keeping was gone, and I felt physically lighter; I would not be irrevocably cut off from my home and I could keep the people

I loved. There remained, however, the issue of my marriage, and as December crept closer a nagging tension returned to the back of my skull. My parents and younger sister, Meredith, were coming for Christmas. Omar and I planned to announce our engagement to them when they arrived.

"What if they don't like me?" was Omar's constant question.

"Perhaps you shouldn't veil when they're here," suggested Sohair. In the days before my family's arrival, she and I were trying to arrange things to be as nonthreatening to them as possible. They should be isolated from the shrieking fundamentalist imams on Fridays, protected from harassment in the streets, kept in as clean and orderly an environment as possible. It struck me that both she and Omar were very aware of how frightening their city was to westerners—the noise, the pollution, the women without faces, the soldiers with semiautomatic rifles. They were resigned to it; had been brought up with the knowledge that they were seen as exotic at best and at worst, barbaric. If they had been hurt or sad, I could have reassured them, but resignation is unassailable.

"What should we avoid talking about?" Sohair asked at one point.

"Israel," I said immediately; here at least was a tangible issue. "Anything having to do with World War Two, actually. Better to avoid the whole era." Omar had strong opinions about Churchill.

"Do you really think World War Two will come up in conversation?" Sohair asked doubtfully.

"If it shouldn't, we can assume it will."

★ ★ ★

At last my parents and sister arrived, along with Jo's father. We distributed them between spare beds. Ben, who was out of town for the holidays, lent my family his apartment. Postponing our news as long as possible, we made plans to fly to Luxor for a few days to visit the old pharaonic temples after Christmas, and in the meantime wandered the alleys of Cairo, taking routes I had learned by trailing in Omar's wake.

"I'm amazed by how safe it is here," said my father a few days into their visit. "There doesn't seem to be any petty violence or theft."

I realized it was true; I had never felt physically unsafe in Cairo. The twin pressures of Islamic moral code and the government's strict policy toward criminal behavior meant that there was almost no street violence and comparatively little theft. As Egypt moves deeper into the twenty-first century, there has been a dramatic downshift in the fortunes of the average citizen, so this is becoming less and less true; the elite get richer while the rest of the country slips further into poverty. The frustration and anger caused by this imbalance has bred violence. But in 2003, it was still possible to walk from one end of Cairo to the other without fear of mugging or physical assault. At the time, it was the safest place I had ever lived.

Sohair invited all of us to dinner a couple of days before we were due to leave for Luxor. Omar and I would have to break our news there—otherwise my family would find out when we arrived in Upper Egypt and the two of us had to present our *katb el kiteb* papers at the hotel. I began to feel ill. I was less afraid of hysterics than I was of grudging tolerance. If there was trouble, if he was hurt or hurt my family, I wasn't sure what I would do.

On the night of the dinner party, Jo and I led our small troupe of relatives to Sohair's flat. When we came through the door I was overwhelmed: there was a five-course meal sitting on the table, Ibrahim was wearing a tie and had recently gotten a haircut, and Omar, clean-shaven, hovered in the doorway clutching his oud. These were not unconfident people; they knew their own worth, and at some point it must have occurred to them that the situation into which they had been thrown by taking an American girl into their family was somewhat unfair. They were articulate, kind, and intelligent; they should not have been compelled to such efforts to prove they were civilized. The fact that they did so anyway, without complaint, put me at a loss for words. I wondered what I could give them that would equal what they had given me. I shook my head, recovering, and began the introductions.

The dinner exceeded all of my expectations. Mutual goodwill was so apparent that people immediately began to respond to one another as individuals instead of ambassadors. I didn't say much; I watched my mother talk to Omar's mother about work and travel, observed Ibrahim's enthusiastic monologue about his electric guitar —to which my father listened smiling—and took in the encouraging looks that Jo gave Omar when he spoke. I started to hope that kindness might be enough to get us where we needed to go.

After dinner, Omar and I walked my parents and my sister back to Ben's apartment.

"Are you all right?" Omar asked me in Arabic as we climbed the stairs to the apartment.

"We'll see," I said.

As we sat in the living room, Omar and I made small talk, but it sounded too much like nervous chatter to make me comfortable. I watched my parents in their strange surroundings and felt a stab of guilt. My father was smiling through his professorial beard, which was still more black than gray, unaware of what I was about to say. Despite applying sunblock every morning, the back of his neck had burned.

"So you liked Sohair and Ibrahim?" I ventured.

"Very much," said my mother, "they're really wonderful." She was sitting cross-legged on a chair. She sat this way at our long farmhouse table at the house in Colorado when she read the paper. The normalcy that had been missing from my life, the normalcy I craved, suddenly irritated me; I didn't want to have to explain good people to good people, protect good people from good people, yet again and again that is what I felt I was being asked to do. Adulthood came to me like that: a realization that no one else was going to fly this plane.

"How would you feel about having them for in-laws?" I asked.

There was a pause. I held my breath.

"I would be honored," said my mother cautiously.

"Okay," I said, with a little gasp. "Okay."

After that all of us hurried to reassure one another. My parents wanted to make sure Egyptian marriage law wouldn't limit my human rights; we promised them it wouldn't. Then they assured us that they thought Omar was wonderful, and so was Egypt, and so was Islam. It came out all at once, but it was obvious that they meant it. It came from a desire to trust and protect us. I felt the blood rush to my head and was only dimly aware that Omar had taken my hand and not let go.

We ran back to my apartment to relay the news to Jo and her father. I think I was a little incoherent, but Jo guessed from my demeanor that it must have gone well, and flung herself into my arms.

"We're going to have a *wedding!*" she squealed.

Jo's father clapped Omar on the back. "Welcome to the family," he said. Omar laughed, delighted. I had told him earlier that *family* in the American sense often refers to family and close friends.

"You see," I told him later, "we do have a culture in America."

"I never doubted it," he said.

After that, things happened quickly. When we returned from Luxor phone calls came from other members of Omar's family, eager to meet mine. We decided to have a small engagement party. Jo and my mother and I threw one together in a hurry, moving all the furniture in our living room into the stairwell to make enough space. My father showed up to the party in a galibayya he had bought in Luxor, his head wrapped, with surprising facility, in a turban. Amu Fakhry, who wore a suit, was delighted, and didn't stop laughing for five minutes.

"He is a *Saidi!*" he exclaimed, meaning an Upper Egyptian. "Your father is a *Saidi!*"

With that, the atmosphere was established; no one was quite an American or quite an Egyptian, and everyone spent at least part of the evening speaking in his second (or third) language. The date of the wedding was set for the following November.

Everything I did from this point onward was in homage to that December. What happened was something so fragile and brave that it is difficult to put into words; my family and Omar's family agreed to love one another for no other reason than that we had asked them to. Nothing else would ever be quite as important; it no longer deeply mattered to me whose rules I followed, Arab or American or eastern or western, and the words themselves faded in significance. I had caught hold, and seen others catch hold, of something that could not be touched by geography. Alan Moore calls it "the very last inch of us," that immutable integrity. To live beyond the threshold of identity, to do so in the name of a peace that has not yet occurred but that is infinitely possible—this is exhilarating, necessary, and within reach.

The Butterfly Mosque

The Furthest Mosque is not of earth hewn
nor of water nor stone, but of right intent
true knowledge and just sentiment
—Rumi

DURING THE WINTER AND SPRING THAT FOLLOWED, OMAR and his family shepherded me as little as possible so that I could have a degree of the American independence I was used to. I consider that year my Arab childhood, because I was allowed to make the same social, practical, and religious mistakes a child is allowed to make, and afterward, though I had an unusual degree of leeway and support, I was expected to shoulder the responsibilities of a married Arab woman. Omar's Uncle Ahmad, a successful businessman and head of the extended family, said after our engagement was announced that no one was to question my integrity— what is commonly called honor—and that anyone who did would fall under his displeasure, and that everyone was to be as patient and understanding as they knew how.

I wanted to deserve that confidence. So I corrected and overcorrected when I was accidentally rude, which happened often during the first several months: I would wander into gatherings of the family chiefs (where I would be doted on with amusement and offered coffee until someone came to collect me), forget to help aunts and cousins with chairs and plates and food, and get into the wrong kind of political discussion with elders to whom I was expected to defer on all points.

What I lacked in poise I tried to make up for in dedication. I would sit through a five-hour wake in near-silence, dance at a wedding until my feet ached, and listen to the stories my grandmother-in-law told with complete attention but without understanding more than one word in three. The joy that this brought my family-by-marriage made adjusting to middle-class Egyptian life seem like a light burden. To this day an auntie will occasionally grab me and gather me in her lap like an overgrown baby and tell me I am the beloved of her heart. In those moments I forget how exhausted I have been, and think there is nothing I would not be willing to do for the people—in Egypt and at home—who have loved and defended me.

I would need them in the months that followed. At first, it seemed as though the break through that December was the sum total of what needed to happen to make everybody comfortable. But goodwill is not enough. Between my culture and Omar's was a pit full of dangers: poverty, terrorism, wars of attrition, racism, colonialism, and malice. Egyptians were furious that their American "allies" preached democracy at gunpoint in Iraq, yet allowed democratic Egyptian reformers to rot in jail under the regime of President Mubarak. The sense of having been humiliated and deceived by the West was overpowering, and it had not very subtle effect on how Egyptians treated westerners. As a result, I have seen countless American expatriates come to the Middle East with what they thought were open minds and hearts, contracted to work in schools or NGOs and bright-eyed with the desire to heal the warring civilizations, only to be rejected and humiliated by the people they set out to help. They turn around and go home, adding first-hand experience to the ranks of anti-Arab cynics.

They fail to realize that people who have lost dignity and opportunities to the "clash of civilizations" cannot be expected to welcome peacemakers who have lost nothing. That anger has to go somewhere. Pampered expatriates are convenient targets for spite. Had I not had a pressing reason to stay, I, too, might have become cynical and left. Omar's family embraced me, and my colleagues accepted me, but the rest of Egypt would not be so charitable.

Shortly after our parents' Christmas visit, Jo and I moved out of our expensive apartment in Maadi and into a much smaller one in Tura. This way, Omar and I could live closer together, and Jo and I could save money. In describing Tura I have to remember that for many of its inhabitants, living there is an accomplishment. The real slums of Cairo are far worse. Omar's family spent part of his early childhood in one of them. He describes having to cross rivers of sewage on his way to school, and going days without running water or electricity as the badly maintained—and often pirated—utility infrastructure blinked on and off. His family did not own a telephone until he was ten years old.

Compared to this, Tura must have seemed like a breath of fresh air: planned, paved streets, regular and fairly solid buildings, reliable water and lights. Sohair worked with a diligence I can only envy and a courage I fear I will never have to buy the flat where she lived with her sons. Despite our differences, I admire the tenacity of the people who live in Tura; many of them have stories similar to Sohair's, and have spent the better part of their lives pulling themselves up from poverty through very hard work.

The area has improved a little since I lived there. Today there are small gardens around the military-owned apartment complex where we rented our flat, and in some buildings the stairs have been tiled and the elevators are maintained. When Jo and I moved there, though, the situation was more stark. On the outside, the neighborhood looked worse than the worst American slum I had ever seen. Garbage was strewn in heaps at the edge of potholed parking lots; the institutional apartment buildings were dark and filthy, and their crumbling cement stairs were dotted with cat excrement and bits of bone and gristle the animals had pulled from bags of refuse. The air was thick with industrial fumes and at times became almost unbreathable, causing lymph nodes under one's ears, chin, and arms to swell painfully. Tura is sandwiched between three landmarks: an infamous political prison, a cement factory, and the Nile. Until it was immortalized in Alaa Al Aswany's novel *The Yacoubian Building*, Tura was known only by its proximity to the factory, and is still commonly referred to as Tura El-Esment, *Tura of the Cement*.

I remember it as a harrowing, sunless place, and whenever I say the name aloud a perfectly formed memory surfaces: I am trudging through the filthy dust outside the prison with a bag of fruit in my arms, and when I look up at the dun-colored, wire-topped walls, I am acutely conscious of the journalists, reformists, and dissidents being held inside. Then I see the mosque, a little jewel-like thing that looks far older than the prison itself. Its corniced minaret stretches above the wall like a plea for help; the mosque, like the prisoners, was trapped there for no other reason than that it was in the way.

I never learned its name. In Cairo there is a mosque on almost every street corner, so only the largest and oldest are given memorable titles; the rest are most often called by their cross streets. Omar and his family had lived in the neighborhood for years and never learned the name of the mosque behind the prison wall. When I had been in Tura for several weeks, I began to call it the butterfly mosque, because it reminded me of a butterfly caught in a jar. I would fantasize about freeing it and imprisoning in its place the modern, ugly, loud mosque that was the focal point of Turan religious activity, and was visible (appropriately enough) from the bathroom window of the flat Jo and I shared.

This mosque we quickly came to hate. Its muezzin announced the five daily prayer times in gravelly shrieks, broadcast at full volume over a set of speakers that were comically expensive and well-maintained when compared to the degree of poverty in which so many of the mosque's attendees lived. To call this institution a fundamentalist mosque sounds almost tongue-in-cheek; it was rabidly conservative, and if it had been situated in a less neglected neighborhood, there's a chance its leaders would now reside in the prison just a half-kilometer away. As it was, Tura was a convenient location for extremism to fester, and so we awoke promptly at four a.m. every morning to the screams of the muezzin, who rattled windows and set dogs to howling for a considerable radius. Few people ever complained. Most were too afraid of the extremists to speak up; the rest were too worn down by the brutality of daily life in a poor neighborhood in a police state to be bothered. And daily life was brutal. There is no kinder word for it.

Tura was a neighborhood that required capitulation and assimilation. It was not enough to be good natured or attentive or even Muslim; to be accepted there we would have had to convert to the church of lower-middle-class Cairo, a badly educated, puritanical segment of society. The fundamentalists south of Tura at least had a measure of idealism; the conservatism of our neighbors arose from undiluted desperation. Theirs was a culture of suspicion, grasping and covetous, whose elaborate rules and limitations were the products of minds ever-conscious of the nearness of ruin, the very real possibility that one's family could slip back into poverty. No one was comfortable, no one was safe, and so Jo and I, with our strange clothing and papery skin and alarming habits, were considered threatening.

When Omar warned us that Tura was much more conservative than our old neighborhood, and said we should pay a little more attention, we readily agreed, but the fact of the matter is that we had no idea what to pay attention *to*. "More conservative" to us meant that we should both be home when male guests came over and avoid wearing T-shirts or tight pants. We didn't know "more conservative" meant that two single women had no business living alone, and if by circumstance they were forced to do so, they should have no contact of any kind with the opposite sex, make as little noise as possible, and not go out at night.

I don't think Omar realized this either. The Middle East is one place for men, and an entirely different place for women. He was almost as puzzled and alarmed as we were by the neighborhood's summary rejection of its two palest residents. It would take me months to understand why we inspired so much fear, and to guess at the questions my neighbors must have been asking themselves. Would we cheat someone, lead someone's son astray, or call down the wrath of our infamous embassy, and in doing so ruin a family? The place breathed panic, and we added to that panic, and so we were hated.

I clung to politeness on principle. One Friday afternoon I was buying fruit from a local vendor—dusty oranges, which, when peeled, gave off a delicious scent at odds with the general odor of factory fumes—when the latest prayer session let out at the fundamentalist mosque and a column of men trickled through its doors into the hazy light. I kept my eyes downcast and tried to avoid them, but found myself caught between a man and his small son, who had wandered a few feet away from his father.

"*As-salaamu alaykum,*" I said to the man, thinking it would be ruder to say nothing. He stared at me for a moment before wordlessly gathering his son in his arms. I flushed and looked around, hoping no one had overheard. Refusing to return this traditional greeting is one of the worst insults one can offer a fellow Muslim. I hurried home.

When I described what had happened to Omar, he didn't believe me.

"He was probably just confused," he said. "He doesn't expect *as-salaamu alaykum* from a foreign woman."

"But I was wearing a head scarf."

"Perhaps he thought you were wearing it to be culturally sensitive."

"Omar, he looked *right at me.*"

Omar reached over to play with the hem of my sleeve. "I get so worried about you," he said. "If I had known—it's not usual for people to behave this way. They don't behave this way to one another."

It was true. Sohair's immediate neighbors, who were familiar with my situation, were very kind to me. And I saw my own neighbors being kind to each other. But it was small comfort.

A few days after we moved in, I woke up to a ringing doorbell, so late at night that it was almost early. Unnerved, I stayed as I was, cocooned in the stained blue quilt that matched my stained blue mattress. After a pause, the ringing continued. Because she could sleep through anything, Jo had taken the room looking out to the busy road that ran along the Nile, so I wasn't surprised when her light stayed off. Fumbling in the dark, I pulled on a robe and went to the door. Through the peephole I saw a guard and one of the local *zabelleen,* the Cairene untouchables, whose lives and livelihood revolve around the collecting and sorting of the city's garbage. I hesitated in the doorway. By Egyptian rules, I was well within my rights not to answer; I was a woman, they were two men, it was the middle of the night. On the other hand, refusing to answer did not necessarily mean the men would leave. Since one of the men was a military guard, it could be important—I wouldn't have put it past the local authorities to announce a fire by sending long-winded delegations door-to-door. I opened mine a crack.

"*Aiwa?*" I asked coldly.

"*Mise' al'khayr hadritik,*" responded the guard, using the polite form of *you*. The *zabell* stood with his eyes politely downcast. The two men didn't look especially threatening, so I stayed to listen. The *zabell*, I gathered, after his request was simplified several times, wanted to buy an ancient, broken vacuum we had found in a closet and put outside to be salvaged. I stared at him.

"Just take it," I said, baffled.

"Really?" asked the guard.

"Yes, for God's sake, good-bye."

He apologized and I shut the door and went back to bed.

The next morning, I caught up with Omar in the staff room at school and told him the story.

"The weirdest thing happened last night," I said, trying to decide whether I should be casual or serious and settling on casual. "A guard came to our door at two in the morning with one of the *zabelleen,* trying to buy that old vacuum we found."

He leaned forward. "What?" There was carefully restrained anger in his voice. I tried to hide my uneasiness.

"Yeah, they showed up like it was the middle of the afternoon on market day—"

"He came to *your door* in the *middle of the night* with *another man?*"

I could sense something was very wrong.

"Yes."

Omar stood up abruptly. "I have to make a phone call," he said, taking out his mobile.

"Was that bad?" I asked, feeling ridiculous.

"That was a test," he said curtly, and headed for the door.

On the bus home I pressed him for details, but he was evasive. Eventually I gathered that the military guards who patrolled our complex liked to press their advantage with inhabitants they perceived to be weak. They were attempting nothing so overt as rape or theft, but something psychological—in international politics and on their own streets, westerners bullied them; now they had a chance to bully vulnerable western women. Better yet, one of these women was about to become a member of an Egyptian family, which presented its own unique possibilities.

Outside the luxurious world of expatriates and the westernized elite, a middle-class Egyptian family functions as a chain forged to protect intangible (and for a westerner, unthinkable) virtues like honor and status—which, in reality, represent that family's influence over whatever tiny corner of the Egyptian socioeconomy they've managed to carve out for themselves. The guards had identified me as my new family's weakest link. Now they were out to discover how far I could be pushed and, by extension, how far Omar could be pushed.

Omar, as it turned out, could not be pushed at all. He went to the local administrative office, and the result was the sentencing of the guard in question to eight days in prison. Omar came back to our apartment and told Jo and me this, as a reassurance.

"Prison?" Jo looked at me anxiously.

I bit my lip. I wanted to resolve the situation but I couldn't stand the thought of sending anyone behind that awful half-kilometer of dun walls and barbed wire.

"I'm not sure anyone needs to go to *prison* over this," I said. "I really feel like he was just being an idiot to see what he could get away with—I don't think he was out to hurt anyone."

"It will teach him a lesson," muttered Omar, but I could see he was beginning to waver. Later, he would argue with the guard's commanding officer on his behalf, and the sentence would be reduced to a pay suspension.

Despite Jo's and my fervent prayers, the guard was not transferred to another building. He continued to sit in our filthy concrete lobby like a two-legged Cerberus, chanting the Quran and glaring at us with open hostility as we passed. Relief only came in the early morning, when he slept on his stool with a blanket pulled over his head. We learned to tiptoe around him when we left for school in the chill of seven a.m.

After this falling-out with our guard, Jo and I began to rely heavily on the goodwill of the local grocers, who ran a *duken* on a side street near our building. Since there was no local coffeehouse, possibly due to the influence of the fundamentalists, the *duken* was the default center of local life. Everyone passed through its doors to buy their eggs, olives, cheese, and bread, as well as cooking oil and matches and other household necessities. For some reason—I don't know what, though I am thankful for it—the grocers took pity on us and it was because of them that our stay in Tura was not completely unbearable.

I was nervous around them at first; I had learned better than to be too open with any man to whom I had not been formally introduced. For the first few weeks I practically snuck around the store, collecting all the things I needed instead of asking the shop boy, and avoiding eye contact whenever possible. It was not always an easy maneuver. In college I took modern standard Arabic, the language of the press; the colloquial dialect of Egypt used a completely different vocabulary. In order to understand the label on a packet of beans, I had to stare at it for several minutes, which gave other people in the shop ample time to stop whatever they were doing and stare at me. One day, when I was scrutinizing the labels above a row of spice jars, I heard a voice over my shoulder.

"*Erfa*," it said, and a hand pointed to one of the jars. I looked up wildly. It was one of the grocers. He was about thirty, had a mustache, and was smiling mildly. "*Ismaha erfa*," he repeated.

"*Shokran*," I muttered.

"*Afwan*," said the grocer gently. "*W'da camoon. Camoon.*"

"*Camoon*," I repeated, *cumin. Erfa,* I was fairly certain, was cinnamon.

He nodded. "*Sah, hadritik.*"

It was the beginning of the pattern that would characterize our interdependence, for such a relationship can't really be called friendship in the sense that we mean it in the West. Jo and I shopped at Mohammad and Namir's *duken,* and they taught us street Arabic. We would come in, together or separately, and after wishing us good morning or good afternoon or good so-late-it-can-only-be-Cairo, Mohammad and Namir would quiz us.

"What's this?" Mohammad would ask, holding something up.

"That's an egg," I would say.

"Red or white?"

"Red."

"And this?"

"Cheese."

"What kind?"

"*Falamank*? I don't know for sure."

"It is *falamank,* and it's fresh, have a little."

They were always courtly and mild, and by treating us this way, in front of other customers, I think they helped chisel away at some of the suspicion that our neighbors had built up about us. Mohammad and Namir subtly defended our honor by insisting that within the confines of their shop we should be treated like Arab women; that is to say, with the proper degree of respect. I first noticed it when I was at the store one afternoon buying our daily bread, and a round-faced, middle-aged man approached me and asked, without preamble, "Excuse me, but are you American?"

Such a question, innocuous in the States, was hugely forward in Tura. In the split second it took me to decide whether I should answer according to my rules or the neighborhood's, I noticed that Namir and Mohammad had stopped stocking the shelves and stood very still, looking at the man with an expression that was not friendly. Without speaking, but very clearly, they were saying *Stop, go back, and approach her more suitably*. The man understood, and ducked his head so that he looked up at me instead of down, a symbolic gesture of submission.

"I'm sorry, Lady," he said in Arabic.

"It's nothing," I replied. Mohammad and Namir had relaxed, but were still listening.

"I ask only because my wife is also American," the man continued, switching back to English, "and I thought perhaps you might like to visit her. She is always eager for familiar faces. She is in the United States now but she will be back next month." He recited their address, and gave a short bow.

"I'd be happy to," I said, charmed and confused at once. "Thank you." It was inconceivable to me that any other American should exist in Tura.

"Not at all," said the man, bowing again, and left.

There was a near-audible sigh as the door closed behind him, and the owners of the *duken* went back to their sweeping and stocking.

"*Kulu tamem?*" asked Namir, *Everything's okay?*

"Yes," I said. "Everything's fine."

He looked as though he wanted to say something else but stopped himself, deciding instead to slip an extra loaf of *fino* bread into my bag on top of the sale, a gesture of sympathy I never fully understood. In the coming weeks I paid attention to the women I saw in the neighborhood, hoping to spot the mysterious American, but I never found her. Perhaps she was one of the women who veiled their faces, resisting identification, beyond the reach of race or provenance. Or perhaps, despite my own experience slipping in and out of Turan behavior, I, too, could be fooled.

I still bear the internal and external scars of that place. I incubated so many intestinal parasites that I learned to distinguish between bacterial and amoebic dysentery by the presence of a certain kind of pain. One kidney infection turned severe and nearly put me in the hospital. And the insects: the swarms of mosquitoes that raised welts on Jo's and my arms and feet, the maggots and full-grown caterpillars we found in our food, the spiders that left bites as delicately colored as stargazer lilies, which would go numb, bruise, and open into sores if left untreated. We developed a condition I jokingly termed "anorexia bacteriosa": a deep-seated disgust that arose from repeated exposure to vile things in our food, which caused us to eat smaller and smaller meals spaced further and further apart, until we would only eat when driven by faintness. For a long time I couldn't stand the feeling of a full stomach, and rarely ate more than it took to stem hunger. Anything more and I began to imagine I was full of carrion and rotting. Photographs of Jo and me from this time period reveal two women who are only vaguely recognizable: ashy-skinned and solemn, with dark rings around their eyes.

All this could have been avoided: an Egyptian woman would have learned very early how to distinguish between a good tomato and one infested with maggots. Through a network of neighborhood women she would have identified cheap, good butchers (having no such network, Jo and I simply didn't eat meat); through her mother she would have learned to hang her carpets in the sun once a week to kill germs and insect eggs. She would have put *feneek* and kerosene under the door to keep away roaches and ants, and put her bread in the refrigerator to keep it from growing mold overnight.

I, too, learned to do these things, but much later than my situation required me to know them. Omar was sympathetic but confused. To him, Tura was the natural state of the world; he couldn't imagine why anyone would be unable to function in it. Jo and I were too proud to ask Sohair for help, and she was too sensitive to our need for independence to interfere. Years later, when I told her about the way we had been forced to live, she felt so dismayed and guilty that she became visibly upset. I tried not to bring it up again—understanding, by then, why my confession had caught her off guard. To her, a buffalo carcass hanging in a butcher's window looked like cuts of meat for stew and kebab; to me, it barely looked like food. There is almost nothing to say when instincts are so mismatched. She could not have known how helpless we were.

In the meantime, I learned a lesson that was as crucial as it was debilitating: all the formal education in the world, at the best universities and under the best authorities, cannot teach you to understand an environment you've never seen for yourself. I have come to see the concept of *expertise* as something of a myth; there can be no Middle East expert who has never lived unaided in the Middle East. Using academic theory to explain and predict the behavior of real human beings under stress is at best shortsighted. Living in that concrete box of an apartment in Tura, what I knew intellectually became less and less useful to me, and what an ordinary Egyptian knew practically became more and more so. A tolerable understanding of Safavid art, an appreciation for Arabic grammar? I would have traded my entire education for an insect-free house and three square meals a day of clean food.

The proximity of the fundamentalists, who hated us, and of ordinary Egyptians, who feared us, did have one upshot: it helped me understand the difference between the kind of antiwesternism that gives rise to terrorism and the kind that doesn't. In the years since 9/11, theories have been proposed linking Islamic terrorism to the poverty of many Muslim countries—despite the fact that the 9/11 bombers came from upper-class backgrounds, the terrorists in the July 7, 2005, London subway attacks came from middle-class backgrounds, and the activity of *poor* terrorists has been limited to Muslim-on-Muslim (or on Jew) nationalist campaigns in Israel-Palestine, Pakistan, and postwar Afghanistan and Iraq. One might argue that it simply takes more money to fly a 747 into a skyscraper than it does to load a homemade bomb into a produce truck, which means only wealthy extremists can engage in international acts of terror and that poor ones would if the opportunity arose. But the fact remains that violent extremists have been culled from every imaginable economic background.

Clearly, the catalyst is something more complicated than income. Jo's and my neighbors in Tura did not hate us for religious reasons; they hated us because they saw us as a danger to their security. Their antiwesternism did arise from economics, but it had no jihadist element whatsoever. In fact, I think that if we had been physically threatened, our neighbors would have rushed to our defense. Trouble with a western government was something they wanted very much to avoid.

I think this holds true on a larger scale: of the Middle Easterners I have met who resent the West (and specifically the United States), the vast majority resent it because they perceive it to be a military and economic juggernaut bombing whole countries into rubble, putting local industries out of business (though this title is slowly passing to China), and succeeding and succeeding where the Middle East fails. Religion never enters the discussion.

On the other hand, the fundamentalists we could see from our bathroom window hated us for very religious reasons. It became clear to me, living in the shadow of that brainless minaret, how little the anger of our local extremists had to do with military America. While the situation in Iraq gave them political legitimacy and direction, and a dangerous amount of emotional leverage with average Muslims, it was not the *reason* they were angry. They hated the America that exports culture. They were aghast at the suggestion that enlightenment could be bought on tape, and that right and wrong were fluid and could change from situation to situation. They hated being made to sympathize with adulterous couples in American movies. They hated the materialism that was spreading through Egypt and the Gulf like a parasite, turning whole cities—Dubai, Jeddah—into virtual shopping malls, and blamed this materialism on western influence.

I would struggle to explain to Egyptian friends (for this alarm was not limited to extremists) that consumer culture functioned in a surprisingly complex and sophisticated—arguably unhealthy, but still sophisticated—way in the West, playing on subculture and social memes and giving rise to an entirely new system of symbols. Because materialism, in the sense that we mean the word today, arose in the West, it is at home there; a retrovirus sitting quietly in the genetic makeup of the civilization without doing monumental harm. But the Middle East is peopled by cultures that struggled for centuries to rid themselves of anything iconic or graphic or unnecessary; there, materialism acts as a kind of cultural smallpox, leaving mindless ostentation and artistic sterility in its wake.

What seemed to threaten the fundamentalists most, reading between the lines of their rhetoric and behavior, was the sheer *accessibility* of western culture: the fact that everything a person could want, from consumer goods to emotional highs to sex to spirituality, was public and available to anyone. Nothing was hidden, nothing required serious effort to attain. In the West, anything that must be hidden is suspect; availability and honesty are interlinked. This clashes irreconcilably with Islam as it is practiced in the Middle East, where the things that are most precious, most perfect, and most holy are always hidden: the Kaaba, the faces of prophets and angels, a woman's body, Heaven. The fundamentalists, in their own way, were mourning the loss of legitimately beautiful ideas. They knew they could not make the ritualized, morally appraising culture of traditional Arab Islam—in which one must be worthy of truth, love, and God to attain them—more attractive than the lifestyle endorsed in the West. So they demonized attraction itself.

I thought a lot about extremism on Fridays, when I listened to our neighborhood imam give sermons. I would stand in the doorway of our bathroom and look out at the minaret that rose beyond it like a bony finger, and beyond that, at a graceful bend in the Nile fronted by green rushes. I could only follow small portions of the *khutba* or sermon; Omar and Ibrahim often filled me in on the rest. A typical *khutba* by the Hammer of the Infidel, as my mother would christen the imam, was limited to quotidian things: the correct way to behave in communal prayer, the length of one's garments, even the foot with which one should enter and leave the bathroom. But every few weeks, angry, it seemed, at the religious fatigue of the men who were required by Shari'a law to attend Friday services (women could go or not as they chose), the imam would let loose: heaping gory and imaginative curses on the American soldiers in Iraq, condemning the immorality of Muslims who did not abide

137

by stringent Wahhabi codes of conduct, orating self-contained monologues about the dangers and sins of the material world. He was careful never to say anything critical of the Mubarak regime or to explicitly endorse violence, and managed, somewhat miraculously, to avoid unpleasantness with government security forces.

In self-appraising moments, I think about whether or not I would have stayed in Egypt without Omar to keep me there. I spent so much of that year exhausted, isolated, and sick; even though Omar's family did everything in their power to make me happy, having grown up in this environment they could not understand why it remained so persistently alien to me and frightened me so much. Even in love, bolstered by the support of Omar's family, and half married, I consciously kept myself from visiting home until I had been in Egypt a full year. I knew, though I didn't breathe a word of it to anyone but Jo, that if I left there was a chance I would not have the strength to come back. Despite my best efforts to hide it, there were some in Omar's family who sensed this. Uncle Sherif, who had given me my Muslim name, had a way of looking at me with worried sympathy and silent assessment. It was as if I was a wilting flower and he was trying to decide whether I needed more sun or less, more water or more heat, to survive in this foreign climate. I did not want to tell him or any of my family-by-marriage what I did need, because they could not have given it to me, and this would have made them unhappy: I needed to be able to walk in the street without being harassed, to be able to sit in a café by myself, I needed protein, I needed books. I did not believe that the color of my passport entitled me to these things in a country whose own people could not have them, and so I could not in good conscience move among other expatriates. I was stuck between two kinds of silence: the silence that kept me from telling the people who loved me what I needed, and the silence that kept me from seeking the sympathy of westerners.

But what a silence. I had become a true believer: I had seen something larger than culture, and my faith in it was feverish, unchanged by anger and opposition. To me, faith in human potential is intertwined with faith in God and inseparable from it. Privately, Omar and I—and increasingly our families—could flourish in our third culture, which over the months and years developed its own truths, its own language almost: Arabic and English bent and cobbled together to express a broader set of ideas. Publicly, our worlds were still divided. But the existence of this private revolution fueled a new hope: I began to believe that similar things were possible in the public sphere. Once I had seen connectivity between the hemispheres, I could not unsee it, even when I was at my weakest and so desperate for familiarity that I felt I might not have the willpower to continue.

For the first time in my life I became more passionate about what I had to do than about what I wanted to do; whether this zeal for duty came from Islam, or from wanting to fight for Omar, or from having seen through to something more persistent than the cumbersome civilizations between which I moved, I don't know. There is infinite space within a human life. What I had to do was make my life work in Egypt and I stuck to this with a diligence I did not realize I had, and which manifested itself in ways I could not have anticipated.

One day I was riding in the women's car on the subway and as the doors closed I heard a girl scream: a high-pitched, frantic sound, the sort she might make if she was being threatened or attacked. "What's going on?" I asked a middle-aged woman standing nearby. She conferred with another passenger; in the meantime the girl stopped screaming and was surrounded by impromptu nurses who pressed her to take handkerchiefs and water and candy. "Her hand got shut in the door," the middle-aged woman reported back to me. "She got it out. She's fine now."

I realized that I had, unthinkingly, risen from my seat and taken two or three steps toward the girl when I heard her scream. Had there been a real problem—if it had been a thief or someone with a knife—I would have walked right into the conflict to intervene. For a moment I felt dizzy. I thought of a similar incident on the subway in Boston several years earlier, when a girl had screamed on a packed rush hour train. She had only been squeezed between two other passengers as people crowded into the car, but when she screamed I flinched, cowering instinctively in my seat. Something had changed in the intervening years. I realized that despite the bewildering number of behaviors I had had to alter to survive in the public sphere in Egypt, I was not less myself—in fact, I was becoming a better self. I didn't know I was capable of growing into the sort of person who stands up and walks toward a fight. As the metro clattered on, I felt, for the first time in months, like everything was going to be all right. I had gained so much more than I had lost.

I was reminded of the reverse situation: when Mohammad and Namir stood up for me without thinking, for no other reason than that they believed it was right. I realized what it meant: to do the right thing you must sometimes defend people who do not understand you, or who fear you, or who are angry at you. There are times when you have to operate purely on faith and continue to trust human decency even when it is no longer visible. It did not matter that there were Egyptians who were afraid of me because I was American, and that there would be Americans who were afraid of me because I was a Muslim; what mattered was that when I left the room, they loved their husbands or wives, they joked, they mourned their beloved dead, and they struggled to provide for their children. There was nothing so great that it could not be built on that commonality.

As unexpected as the events in my recent life had been, in my eyes they were connected by a straight line. It ran from the mountains of Colorado through the atrium in the World Financial Center, through the scent of soap on Omar's hands, through the butterfly mosque, through the moment on the subway. If these things could not be honored and defended together it spoke to a failure far greater than a clash of civilizations. The struggle for the Islam I loved and the struggle for the West I loved were the same struggle, and it was within that struggle that the clash of civilizations was eradicated.

Zawaj Figaro

I seek for a treasure
outside of myself;
I know not who holds it
nor what it is.
> —Cherubino, in *The Marriage of Figaro*

SHORTLY AFTER JO AND I MOVED TO TURA, I QUIT MY JOB at Language School to write full-time. A few of my articles had been published in the United States, and in Cairo a new English-language opposition paper, *Cairo Magazine,* had just been launched. I went to the first open meeting without expectation, bringing with me a few clippings of work I'd done for the *Weekly Dig* back in Boston. The magazine had rented offices in a building on the edge of a genteel but shabby district, near one of the palaces built for King Farouk in pre-revolution days. The World War II–era buildings felt vaguely European, with hexagonal facades of flaking plaster fronting the streets, which were bathed in dust. Climbing the stairs of the building at the address I'd written down, I came to a door hanging loose in its frame, beyond which I heard voices speaking a dozen varieties of English.

"I *told* you, I just don't like the glossy paper."

"It's just the sample stuff! The second issue will be in—"

"It's too *tabloid*."

"I know. Yes. I agree. The second issue will be matte. There's someone at the—"

The door opened, revealing a woman about my age who I immediately knew was American. We were wearing near-identical yoke-necked sweaters over button-down shirts. I'd made an effort to pull myself together and look like how I thought an American college graduate should look, and was glad I had succeeded.

"Are you here for the meeting? Come in." The woman smiled and opened the door wider: beyond her, half a dozen people were making their way through a haze of cigarette smoke with laptops and copy paper in their arms. The office was a series of rooms painted powdery colors, lit by bare fluorescent bulbs. Large old-fashioned windows looked out over a dim alley, the sort Mahfouz would have written about, home of a thousand dust-caked histories. In the main room was a large whiteboard already crowded with deadline reminders and story leads; around it in a semicircle were sitting eight or ten people, almost all under thirty-five, with their notebooks at the ready.

"We're just about to get started," said the woman who had let me in—her name was Faye, and she was the managing editor. "You can go ahead and take a seat."

"Thanks." I slipped into a chair at the outer edge of the circle as Faye called the meeting to order. We all introduced ourselves. The culture editor, a silver-haired cheerful-looking man, was Richard Woffenden, a longtime fixture of the expat community. The rest of the permanent staff was made up of young Egyptian and American reporters. There were two interns from the journalism school at Cairo University who were barely out of their teens. Even at that first meeting, I could sense that the people involved were unusually driven, that their goal was not only to tell the big stories, but to foster young Egyptian writers who, by virtue of their firsthand experience, could tell them better. That's a kind of altruism one doesn't often find among reporters scrambling to publish and be noticed.

My first assignment was relative fluff: *The Marriage of Figaro* was going to be performed in Arabic at the Cairo Opera House and the magazine needed someone who knew both enough Arabic and enough opera to write about it. That was how I found myself sitting along the wall of a rehearsal room one afternoon not much later, under dappled light, listening to a young soprano named Reem sing the part of Cherubino, and thinking about synchronicity. In college, shortly after I got sick, I had gone to see a student production of *Figaro* with some classmates. At that point, I wasn't used to waking up day after day after day *sick*, my partying truncated, my grades in constant danger, managing pain and sleeplessness. I had trouble sitting still for long periods and was only comfortable moving or lying down; during the second act I began to feel light-headed and achy. But when I forced myself to focus on the stage, I was surprised to find that comedic opera was actually *funny*.

"What do you think?" asked Reem in English, sliding into a chair. She was glowing and slightly out of breath. Beyond us, the Countess was lamenting her unfaithful husband; the Count sat in a corner with his understudy, arguing about Turkish coffee ("It's bad for your voice!" the Count claimed).

Through the starburst-patterned lattice over the windows, which gave the room the aura of a mosque, the sky was blue; the usual pale blanket of pollution and dust had cleared.

"I love it," I said to Reem. "It's funnier in Arabic than it is in Italian. Classical Arabic is so serious, you know? Anything sub-Quranic sounds hysterical in classical anyway, so when it's stuff like, 'Who's that at the door?' and, 'If you want to play, little Mr. Count,' you want to fall out of your chair."

"Sub-Quranic." Reem laughed. "I have never heard this word."

"I made it up." I flipped open my notebook. "Even though you're performing Figaro in Arabic, you've kept the original Italian setting and costumes. Do you think there is such a thing as universal art? Art that anyone can appreciate, no matter where he's from?"

"Do *you* think so?" Reem asked.

"No," I said, "I don't. I think there are universal ideas, but there is no universal art form to describe them."

"Maybe you are right," said Reem politely.

"You disagree?" I wondered if what I had said made sense to her.

She tilted her head. "I think every person knows what stories are," she said. "That is universal."

I turned this statement over in my mind, unsure, as with so many conversations across second languages and inherited perspectives, of whether we had achieved a profound understanding or none at all.

I often wondered the same thing about the situation in Tura. Jo and I were never integrated into the neighborhood, and I doubt we could have been if we lived there for decades. But as time went by our neighbors passed from open hostility to grudging tolerance. Occasionally they would even forget themselves and be kind, because it was far more usual for them to be kind; they were kind to one another, and the abrupt chilly way they treated (or avoided) Jo and me is a mark of how much we must have frightened them. When I describe our strange relationship with our neighbors to other Americans, I ask them to imagine two single, sari-clad, Bengali-speaking Indian women of obscure purpose setting up shop in small-town Oklahoma. It's the sort of situation that might never result in harmony, but one should not take that failure as a symbol of an imagined greater failure; it does not mean that there is no hope for understanding. All it means is that in close quarters, we overthink, second-guessing our own innate assumption of common humanness, which, I now think, boils down to a common need for kindness. We are cruelest to those who remind us of our capacity for cruelness. It was this that made Jo's and my relationship with our neighbors so bitter: it was clear that they did not like who they became around us.

I have seen the reverse as well: westerners from the most liberal backgrounds, whose beliefs are tolerant and broad-minded, find themselves unable to function in a society that requires them to live so conservatively and in such limited circumstances. They are forced to resort to the ruling-race social tactics they hate in order to get by, and then hate the Egyptians for making them hate themselves. This is the heart of the clash of civilizations: not the hatred of the Other, but the self-hatred produced by the Other. This is what makes hatred so easy to propagate, and so difficult to counter even for those who question its authenticity.

Though our relationship with our neighbors was improving, life in Tura remained somewhat arbitrary, as if the goal of the place was to cultivate ambivalence. One day the fruit seller would hand us the first tangerine of the season with a smile and refuse payment; the next day a *khamaseen* sand storm would send choking dust through the tiniest cracks in our walls, invading our mouths and nostrils, and we would cough up black slime for days. Or the Hammer, overcome by some merciful impulse, would prefix his dawn prayer-call with a few minutes of Quran recitation so lush and beautiful that I awoke holding my breath. Then, inevitably, he would start his angry howls and I would wonder what I was meant to feel.

I was reconciled to these persistent contradictions in an unexpected way. When I told Omar about the black kitten I raised when I was young, he bought me a Siamese cat as a present. She turned out to be pregnant. Jo and I watched her grow from a sleek feline into something shaped more like a football, and we spent time on our dial-up internet connection to learn about cat gestation and birth. On the day she went into labor she lay down at my feet and looked up at me helplessly: the first kitten was stuck.

"What do we do?" I asked Jo, whose horrified expression reflected my own.

"In the movies they always boil water and lay down a sheet," she said. We sat in silence on the couch for another minute. "I'm calling Sumaya," Jo said finally, referring to an acquaintance of ours. "Her cat had kittens a couple of months ago." She got up and hurried out of the room. I stroked the little brown-and-cream head pressed against my ankle.

"Sumaya says we have to help get the kitten out," Jo said, returning with the phone in one hand. "She says it will probably be dead. If we don't get it out, the other kittens will die, too."

I stared at Jo, feeling nauseated.

"Okay," I said. "I—okay. How do we do that?"

Jo looked down at the cat, which was making little pained noises. "I think—I think one person has to hold the cat and the other has to pull out the kitten. I'll hold the cat," she said, before I had a chance to interject. We washed our hands and lifted the cat onto a clean, faded pillowcase. With one eye closed—the way I watch horror movies—I tugged a tiny, half-birthed body free of its mother. Sumaya was right: it was dead, its nose and mouth an airless, bloodless white. Six other kittens followed. Four were black or gray and black, and two were spotted gray and brown, like little smoke-colored leopards. Their father must have been one of the feral Egyptian Mau said to be descended from the temple cats of the pharaohs. Nowadays they roamed the streets and garbage dumps, unwanted pests.

The kittens immediately started dying. Jo found the mangled remains of the two feeblest ones the next morning. The mother cat had eaten them. Another kitten was deformed and too weak to nurse; it only survived another few hours. When we found a fourth kitten dead two mornings later, Jo burst into tears.

"I'm tired of picking up bodies," she choked, pressing her palms over her eyes.

I put my arms around her, feeling sick. There was a sweet, fetid smell in the air: a death smell. The grotesqueness of our surroundings was suddenly too much for me. The layer of grime—dirt and grease and worse—that had been all over the apartment when we moved in had never quite gone away, no matter how much we scrubbed. A block away, the cement factory chugged out its awful fumes. Even the Nile, so deceptively serene, ran with sewage and the corpses of animals. No wonder the kittens were dropping off one by one. This was a place where nearly 3 percent of human babies died before their first birthday. How could anything born in this environment survive?

Only the two spotted kittens made it through the first week. I watched them in apprehension, looking for signs of weakness. They surprised me by thriving. Both were athletic feeders, and within a couple of weeks grew round and thick-furred. When they were barely bigger than teacups they began tottering around the apartment on unsteady legs. Jo and I would pick them up to keep from stepping on them, holding them to our faces to inhale their warm milky scent. My attitude toward the little drama began to change. If not for Jo and me, all the animals would have died. Instead, the cat and two kittens were alive and healthy. Another Turan experience defied categorization. What had occurred? Was it awful or wonderful? Should I give thanks or give up?

I had to let go of my need to compartmentalize. In Tura —and it is tempting to extend this generalization to the rest of the developing world—very few beautiful things are unmarked by arbitrary hardship. The reason Omar and his family and their neighbors could function in such an uncertain environment was because they did not expect life to be tidy or orderly, and their happiness did not depend on experiences that could be labeled. In colloquial Egyptian there is no term for *a good day*. Neither, I should add, is there a term for *a bad day*. There are beautiful days, black days, inky days, and blessed days; days can be described but not categorized. This was the secret of life in the gullet of the Nile. *Kun*; "Be." Good and evil, chaos and order, joy and tragedy—they were all brought into being with the same single word. *Kun, fa yakun*; "Be, so it is."

I had been a Muslim for six months, yet I'd never gone to a mosque for Friday prayers. After enduring months of sermons from the Hammer of the Infidel, I suspected that going to Friday prayers would be worse for my faith than staying home. In my mind, brick-and-mortar Islam was divided into a banal and aggressive present, represented by the Hammer; and an ethereal unreachable past, represented by the butterfly mosque. Between the two floated the Quran, which seemed at times to relate to neither; its words seemed to represent an accidental glimpse of universality, a momentary lifting of the curtain between lesser and greater truths. Something as cumbersome as organized religion couldn't do it justice.

I've had conversations with members of other faiths about this dilemma; about the peculiar music of holy books, so rarely reflected in the legalism of the faiths that spring up around them. A devout Christian friend from back home in Colorado once read me her favorite passage from the Book of Job: "And though worms destroy my body, yet in this flesh shall I see God." She paused afterward and then said, "We'll never get there." When I had been in Egypt for half a year, I knew what she meant. I had seen enough of bureaucratized conversion and unqualified sheikhs to wonder whether modern Muslims would ever "get there" either. The first time I went to Friday prayers in a mosque, I braced myself for disappointment.

I should have trusted Omar, who has a faith in the persistence of goodness that fate tends to reward; he can find poetry anywhere. He took me to pray at Sultan Hassan, an enormous medieval mosque in the Old City, just below the citadel built by Saladin in the twelfth century. During the week it is open to tourists before the sunset prayer, but on Fridays it is packed with the faithful and closed to casual observers. We parked the car a few blocks away and approached on foot, pressed along in a crowd of people—a thousand, maybe more—going to pray. At the threshold of the mosque, the entryway towered several stories above us and we took off our shoes. A wide corridor of stone led to the central courtyard. Like many mosques in arid parts of the Muslim world, the main prayer space of Sultan Hassan is open to the sky. The effect is of a cathedral without a roof: a square, tiled courtyard bordered on each side by a beautifully detailed half-dome, one for each of the four schools of

Sunni law. The half-dome directly opposite the imam is reserved for women; men pray in the open courtyard. Since the dome provides shade and the stone platform beneath it is raised, allowing a good view of the imam who leads the prayer, Sultan Hassan is one of the rare mosques in which the women's space is actually better than the men's. When Omar and I arrived, men and women were arranging themselves in neat lines, waiting for the prayer to begin. The noon sun baked the tiles of the courtyard; they were warm under my bare feet. Swallows dove and swirled in the half-domes, catching insects that had sought the shade. Omar let go of my hand.

"I'll be down here with the men," he said. "I'll meet you at the edge of the women's platform when the prayer is over."

I looked up at him, feeling anxious. "I'm afraid I'm going to do something wrong," I said.

Omar smiled. "If you do, they'll take care of you."

"Who are 'they'?"

"Your sisters." With that he turned and waved to Uncle Sherif, who was standing in the men's section dressed in white robes, and who, seeing me, grinned and pressed one hand to his heart. I smiled back before moving to stow my shoes at the base of the women's platform and climbing up to take my place there. I stood next to a woman who looked just a little younger than me, and who was wearing a gauzy pink head scarf that hung down her back. Another woman, whose dark lashes framed startling pale green eyes, came to stand on my left. The perfumes of the two women next to me met under my nose: lotus oil and something that seemed like Chanel but probably wasn't. The scents mixed with the coppery smell of dust became an integral part of my first memory of that place.

The call to prayer went up, vibrating across the courtyard. Without a word, the woman on my right pulled me closer, so that my shoulder touched hers. The woman on my left reached over to gently rearrange my scarf, veiling an exposed stretch of my collarbone. There was nothing condescending, irritated, or even fully conscious about their gestures; they were simply closing a gap in the line. They would expect me to do the same for them, if their scarves slipped or they absentmindedly stood too far from their neighbors. For me, the ritual of prayer was transformed by this physicality. As I bowed and knelt and stood, there were shoulders against my shoulders, knees against my knees, the back of another hand against the back of my hand. The line levels everyone. No Muslim is exempt from it; a saint must stand shoulder to shoulder with a murderer if a murderer is who he finds to his right.

On an ordinary day, the people around me refused to line up for anything—not bread, not bus tickets; if you wanted something you had to wade into a mob. Yet here in the mosque they fell in line with organic precision, taking great care that no one stand an inch ahead of his neighbor. The voice of the imam filled the courtyard, yet in the strange acoustic space of the half-dome, I could hear the women beside me breathing. Below us in the men's section, Azhar students from east and central Asia stood side by side with the ironing men and fruit vendors who usually grumbled that foreigners didn't tip well. European Sufi converts with red or blond beards and blue embroidered vests stood next to their natural adversaries, the short-robed conservatives, in a moment of fellowship. I began to see what filled that empty ideological space between the fundamentalist mosque and the butterfly mosque: a living tradition that could be dynamic, could evolve and be touched in brief but valuable moments—the words I loved. There were things in that line worth saving.

The sheikh who gave the sermon that day was someone I had met, sort of, at a family wedding several weeks earlier. That evening I had been feeling confident: I wore a red embroidered tunic and a head scarf draped in a style that was popular, and finally had a handle on everybody's name, all of which made me hope I looked less out of place than usual. I circulated between tables of guests under the supervision of three or four of Omar's youngest cousins, lively giggling girls who had appointed themselves my guardians. After the banquet was over and people began drifting to the dance floor, the girls' mood changed: they held an urgent whispered conference, and then started pulling on my sleeve. It took me a minute to decipher that someone important had arrived and we needed to get out of the way. Others were already clearing a path near the door. The girls tried to pull me along behind them but I stumbled on the edge of my skirt and limped a few steps before I could untangle myself. In the midst of this drama, I realized I was about to trample on the edge of someone's well-tailored galibayya. I looked up in alarm.

It was Ali Gomaa, the grand mufti of Egypt, looking as startled as I was.

He had been appointed to his position only a week or two earlier, promoted overnight from his professorship at Al-Azhar University to one of the most prominent positions in the Muslim world. Before his promotion he had instructed some of Omar's maternal uncles in religion, which explained his presence at the wedding. His appointment was a source of renewed hope for Sunni moderates, embattled for years by the advancing wave of fundamentalism coming out of the Gulf. As mufti of Egypt—the highest religious office of the most populous Arab nation attached to the oldest institution of Sunni law in the world—Dr. Ali, as he was affectionately called in Cairo, could and would wield a considerable amount of power.

I filed away my brief encounter with Dr. Ali as a good story and forgot about it. A week or so after that first Friday prayer, however, Omar announced that Uncle Ahmad had arranged something special for me. "You have an interview with the mufti next Sunday," he said.

I blinked. "What?"

"An interview. With the mufti." Omar grinned. "Does that make you happy?"

It took me all week to come up with the right questions. *I might never have an opportunity like this again,* I thought, so I wanted to make the most of it. I had been reading Irshad Manji, whose infamous complaint *The Trouble with Islam* had just been published. By and large, I hated it. I saw

155

Manji as the Janus face of the fundamentalist imam in Tura: both were self-appointed experts who disemboweled Islam in order to politicize it in a particular way. But Manji's book voiced real grievances, and I wanted to see what the traditional Sunni establishment would do with the ideas it put forward.

My first question was simple: In the West, where there is no entrenched hierarchy of trained clerics, do ordinary Muslims have the right to practice *ijtihad?*

The word *ijtihad* comes from the same root as jihad—the root itself means roughly "to strive." But whereas jihad refers to physical and psychological striving, *ijtihad* refers specifically to interpretation; striving to correctly interpret the will of God through the Quran, the Sunnah, and the hadith. For centuries the official power of *ijtihad* has rested in the hands of sheikhs versed in Islamic jurisprudence. Such sheikhs are called *mujtahids.* Typically, one has to go through something like a seminary school to become a *mujtahid.* This is where the newest Muslims—the Muslims of the Far West—take issue. Many activists in Europe and North America believe that all Muslims should have the right to practice *ijtihad.* Islam, they argue, has grown larger than the Fertile Crescent, and the opinions of a few old men in Medina have little relevance in Los Angeles. This idea was the crux of Manji's book. "Open the gates," was starting to become a rallying cry among those who believed that each Muslim should be free to interpret and apply Islamic law according to his own intellect.

My second question dealt with religion and culture. With the debate over Islamic dress boiling over in France and elsewhere, I wanted to know how much cultural leeway the mufti thought Islam permitted when it came to clothing and socializing. What should a Muslim do in a non-Muslim country to reconcile Islam with local cultural norms?

The third question was the most abstract and, in fact, more than a little insolent. It was prefaced like this: In Islam, the will of God is supposedly absolute. As stated in the Quran, "Nothing occurs which He does not will." This was a verse often used by gay and lesbian Muslims to defend their sexuality as natural and normal. Since conservatives often declared homosexuality "against the will of God," this created an interesting contradiction. How would the mufti respond to and resolve it?

On the day my interview was scheduled, Omar and I arrived at Al-Azhar mosque right before *maghrib*, the sunset prayer. We took off our shoes and padded barefoot across the marble courtyard to the oldest surviving section of the building, which had been constructed in the tenth century. We met Uncle Ahmad in a long hall containing a series of classrooms that had been added in the thirteenth and fourteenth centuries, one room for each dialect of Arabic, Turkish, and Persian spoken by Azhar University's medieval students. Today, the classrooms are used as offices.

"*Habibi!* I love you!" A robed sheikh crossed the hall from one of the offices and kissed Uncle Ahmad on both cheeks. After everyone was introduced, the sheikh ushered us into the office from which he had appeared.

"*Itfaddali*," he said to me, motioning to a chair. I looked around, tugging at the unfamiliar drape of my head scarf, which I had worn in a particularly conservative style for the occasion. The office was roomy and tall, whitewashed, with a small antechamber that served as a waiting room. A chart on one wall was covered by a list of names in calligraphy— a religious lineage, Omar told me later, linking the mufti with his sheikh, and with his sheikh, and so on, all the way back to the companion of the Prophet who is said to have initiated the mufti's Sufi order.

"Would you like something to drink?" the sheikh asked me in Arabic, rummaging in a small refrigerator.

"Yes, thank you." I sipped the Pepsi he handed me, feeling slightly out of place. I had no idea when the mufti would appear or what I was expected to do when that happened. The sunset prayer saved me for a short interim as everyone separated to perform it; afterward I found Omar and together we negotiated our way back to the office through the enormous crowd that had gathered. The cheerful sheikh we had met—who was, I now gathered, the mufti's public liaison— opened the door just wide enough for us to bypass the crowd and squeeze through. The mufti sat behind a desk at the far end of the room, rifling through a stack of papers. On the coffee table in front of him sat my Pepsi, looking a little idiotic. The sheikh offered seats to Omar and me and left.

Putting aside his papers, the mufti looked up. "*Salaam alaykum.*" He politely avoided meeting my eyes.

"I'll translate for you," Omar murmured. He turned to the mufti and began phrasing my first question. Even though I was skeptical of the idea that *ijtihad* was the silver bullet of Islamic reform—dependent as it was on individual perspective, it was just as likely to produce fringe cults as enlightened visionaries—I thought it would be pretty wonderful if I was the source of the "opening of the gates." I congratulated myself for being a revolutionary. But as Omar spoke, I realized my self-aggrandizing was premature. I had left the mufti a simple way out of the question.

"It's unnecessary for all western Muslims to practice *ijtihad*. There are some very good *mujtahids* in the West," said the mufti according to Omar. "In many of the United States, in fact." He began writing names down on a piece of paper. Among them, I noticed, was Hamza Yusuf, a young American sheikh who had gotten press for his thoughts about the reconciliation between Islam and the West. "Not everyone is qualified to make the decisions of a *mujtahid*," the mufti continued. "There's a lot to learn—history, language, the passages of the Quran, how to use the hadith—it's a study in itself. If everyone were to take this bit or that bit of the law and interpret it for himself—use it to justify his desires—there would be chaos."

"You have to understand," Omar would tell me later, "in the West, you see *ijtihad* as a way to make Islam more open, more diverse. Here we see it as how we got fundamentalism. *Ijtihad* is the excuse the fundies use to project their corruptness onto Islam."

Omar moved on to my second question—reconciling non-Islamic culture with Muslim social mores. He cited the veil and the fear it inspires in most westerners.

The mufti paused. It was clear from the expression on his face that he had thought about this a great deal. "In a non-Islamic culture, you are an ambassador of Islam," he said finally. "Our religion teaches that it is bad to isolate yourself from your community, from the people around you. To push them away. It is important to present Islam in a good way, in a way that those around you can understand. Islam is bigger than the veil. The veil is important, but Islam is bigger than the veil. If wearing the veil in a non-Muslim country will only bring hostility toward you, don't wear it."

I was stunned. This was not an idle statement; the mufti could no longer say anything idly. This was fatwa—a personal fatwa; a ruling meant for me alone, but policy nonetheless. Sitting across from me, Omar looked floored. In Egypt and most of the Arab world, the head scarf—a relatively minor point in Islamic law—had become a symbol for the entire religion. Its importance had become so inflated that many saw any compromise as akin to blasphemy. For someone in a position of religious power to make such a conciliatory gesture took great courage.

"Is there anything more?" asked the mufti. There was a line of people in the antechamber, growing impatient. Omar asked my third question. I could tell he was trying to make it sound less impertinent than it really was.

The mufti sighed, glancing wearily in my direction. "Of course the will of God is omnipotent. But there is a difference between what God wills and what God asks of us. Whether or not we obey and do what He asks is in our hands. When we do not, we are not straying outside of God's will—we are simply being disobedient."

Having affirmed the existence of both fate and free will, the mufti smiled at Omar and handed me my list of American *mujtahids* with a polite nod. We took this as our cue to leave. We thanked him—Omar much more eloquently than I—and made our way out of the office into the crowded hall.

In a cab on the way home, Omar asked me what I thought of the whole thing. I hesitated before answering. "Part of me wanted to find a leader with a really sweeping, visionary agenda. And the mufti isn't that—but I think I'm glad he isn't. He can do a lot more good from the center than he can from any extreme. In order to create any kind of change at all, he has to be a canny politician. And he's certainly canny."

"And he didn't remember you from the wedding."

"Thank God for that."

Arabic Lessons

Al qitu cat'u, al far rat'u, al nahr river'u.
—early-twentieth-century Arabic-English
teaching song

As my confidence increased, I began to ask for the things I needed and to find ways to make myself more independent. First among these was to get formal training in the colloquial Arabic I had been picking up haphazardly from sources like Mohammad and Namir. I began taking lessons with a tutor named Sameh twice a week at a language center in Maadi. It's ironic, or maybe appropriate, that one of the people who most helped me to thrive in Egypt was not only a man but a Christian.

Sameh would be my Arabic teacher for almost two years. Perhaps because he, too, was part of a minority in Egypt, he understood the mechanics of the place the way a minority or an outsider must. This didn't seem to dampen his enthusiasm for his country. Sameh, like Omar and the friends and family members I admired most, seemed to have his eyes trained permanently on the horizon, as if he could will it closer. It's a kind of idealism I have seen only in this part of the world, where there is urgency to all rebirth and reform, because everyone is aware that this very moment is the last and best chance to save a faltering civilization. Omar and Sameh, each in their own ways, were architects of a Middle East that does not quite exist yet, but in which determined people could already begin to live. No one willing to participate in it would be a foreigner, and so Sameh insisted that I learn not to speak like one. The first afternoon I came into his classroom, I think I wanted to show off; while chatting with the student who had the lesson before mine, I doodled a sentence in Arabic on the board. When Sameh came in he paused for a moment to read it.

"Did you write this?" he asked. I said that I had. Without speaking, he carefully erased my diacritical marks and drew in the correct ones, then smiled in a way that suggested he had forgiven me this time but in the future would find such precociousness annoying. The tone of our lessons was set.

One evening, he asked me a strange question.

"Why did you come to Egypt?"

I looked up, surprised. Sameh had one hand under his chin, and the delicate blue colored tattoo of a cross that distinguished him as a Copt was visible on the inside of his wrist. The space of the table was between us: we never sat or stood side by side, and never ever touched, not even to shake hands. The garden door was open, even in the dead of winter; these were the things that we did to make our lessons proper. For a man and a woman who are unmarried to be alone together in private is a violation of Shari'a law; that tension is increased by social stigma when the man is a Christian and the woman is a Muslim. By leaving the door open, we made the classroom into a public place, technically speaking—though the language center itself was a public place, half of the time there were no other classes in session. For good measure, we rarely spoke about anything personal, and this is why his question surprised me.

"I came because I wanted to see what it was like to live in a Muslim country," I said, remembering too late that this was his country, too, and he was not a Muslim.

He wasn't offended. "Try it in Arabic," he said.

"I went to Egypt because I want to live among the Surrendered," I replied obediently.

"Is it a good/nice/pleasant country?" He switched to Arabic as well, using an all-purpose adjective that made his question sound cautious. I was meant to understand that he was really asking if I was happy.

"Egyptians are the best people." I resorted to a polite idiom.

Sameh laughed. "*Beged*," he said, "Seriously."

I thought for a moment. "Egypt is a good/nice/pleasant country," I said. "There's too much pollution, of course, and it's very crowded, but the people have . . ." I ran out of words and put one hand to my chest, in a gesture that can mean thank you; no, thank you; or I am deeply touched.

"Grace/charity," said Sameh, "or kindness?"

"Yes," I said. And for the first time, I realized that it was true; that in spite of the terrible stresses of life in Egypt, despite the chaos and suspicion that characterized public life, the Egyptians had preserved pieces of a better time and could be tender to strangers. I'd seen it only a few days earlier when I was stuck in a nasty patch of foot traffic and breathing car exhaust, trapped behind a pair of extremely fat women. I had to catch a bus, and I found myself thinking, *Why would anyone ever want to live here?* It was too dirty, too difficult, too isolating. I began to run flat-out as the bus moved slowly away from the stop where it had been idling. Egyptian women, as a rule, never run; when necessary, they shuffle elegantly. I cared more about the bus than about propriety, and pelted through the rubbish that had blown against the sidewalk.

A car pulled up beside me—in it was a middle-aged couple. "Get in!" called the woman in the passenger's seat, opening the back door. I scrambled inside, *salaam alaykum*ing as the man in the driver's seat smiled at me, half-laughing. He sped to catch the bus, beeping furiously. The bus driver contained his annoyance and stopped when he realized what was going on. I pressed my hand to my heart and thanked the couple as I got out of their car. "Hurry, hurry!" said the woman. I had never seen the couple before, and I would never see them again.

There were no seats left on the bus, so I leaned against a pole in the aisle, blushing under the cool amusement of the other passengers. A woman sitting nearby reached over to tug at the hem of my shirt. It had inched upward while I ran, revealing a ribbon of bare skin. "Better to wear a coat next time," she said, and I thought, *Why would anyone want to live anywhere else?*

"That's true," said Sameh in English. "Sometimes I think about leaving, then I wonder whether I could be happy in another place, even if it was more organized and less of a pain."

"And cleaner," I said wistfully.

"Also cleaner. It's hard to make a good start in life here, but . . ." He trailed off and looked pensive.

"Someone has to stay," I said. It was a phrase I would hear over and over from educated Egyptian friends, the ones who could have found work abroad, outlets for their talents, but who decided to stay here. Christian or Muslim, they were deeply religious, romantic, well-read; they had asked the question, *What is Egypt?* and found that it came to them to answer. This was something I could now understand. There were questions being asked of all of us that had no easy answers. But there were too many good things and good people at stake not to fight for those answers.

"Yes," said Sameh. "Someone has to stay."

I knew that this was the way Omar felt as well. No matter how many checkpoints we had to endure, no matter how loudly the extremists howled at the dawn, he was committed to his culture. His mind was constantly occupied by it. Every errand we ran was an opportunity for a history lesson, an oral essay on Islamic thought, a digression about Arab contributions to mathematics and astronomy. Coming from anyone else it might have gotten annoying, but love, if not blind, is certainly deaf. He had the intellectual enthusiasm of the self-taught, and it was infectious. I learned more wandering around with Omar than I had in four years of college.

"There is a legend," he would say as we passed the yellowing walls of the Citadel, "that Murad Bey el Alfi once escaped assassination by—"

"Jumping out of that window on his horse."

"I've told you this story before."

"Yes, several times."

"I'm sorry!" He would laugh, and I would console him, leaning my forehead against his shoulder as passersby stared.

It didn't take long for me to absorb Omar's dedication to the landscape. Cairo is so cluttered with monuments that many—like the butterfly mosque—have fallen out of common memory, walled up with a shrug. On the eastern outskirts of the city, toward the Suez road, there was a nameless ruined watchtower that I came to love. A low concrete wall between it and the road declared that this was military ground and thus inaccessible; I guessed about its history from the car window each time we passed.

"Saladin," I said. "He must have built it to keep a lookout for crusaders."

"Or Napoleon," said Omar, "to keep a lookout for the British. Or the British, to keep a lookout for everybody else."

I shook my head. "There's almost no mortar left between the stones. That kind of erosion takes time."

"It could be Mamluk."

"It was Saladin," I repeated, raising my voice flirtatiously. Omar grinned. "Okay."

We would never know. A watchtower behind a wall, a mosque behind a wall; to most Cairenes taking an interest in these things was perverse. Walls are built for a reason, especially in a military dictatorship. Omar was one of the few people whose soul could stretch out in a city most found stifling. Through him, I was learning to be unbothered by walls—to accept them as part of the landscape instead of struggling against them or pretending they didn't exist. Omar had a remarkable ability to remain free in a country full of barriers. As much as I admired this, I was uneasy about what it meant for me. There was nothing America could offer Omar that he did not already have. In empty moments, I began to wonder whether I would live in my own country again.

Iran

Oh come to Shiraz when the north wind
blows!
There abideth the angel Gabriel's peace
With him who is lord of its treasures; the fame
of the sugar of Egypt shall fade and cease
—Hafez

AT THIS POINT, I REALIZED THAT IT WAS IN MY BEST INTER-
est TO start thinking about the Middle East as a home.
Whether it would be permanent or semipermanent remained
to be seen, but either way, my future was firmly tied up in
this place. I felt an urge to push further east, and see more.
Maybe I could find a country so unfamiliar that Egypt would
seem less so. Iran, being Persian and Shi'ite, seemed like a
good place to start if I wanted to visit a part of the Middle
East very different from the one in which I lived. I'd studied
the Iranian revolution—I knew names, dates, and facts from
which individual human experiences cannot be guessed.
Similarly, I knew how Shi'a Islam developed as a movement,
but when I looked at photographs of an Ashura procession
or a Shi'i passion play, there were things I didn't understand.

"Who *does* understand Shi'a?" Omar asked philosophi-
cally when I brought it up. We were sitting in a café with
his friend Mohammad, a blind musician.

169

"The Shi'i, we assume," said Mohammad. "Otherwise there is no point in us trying to understand." Mohammad had spent the first six months of our acquaintance speaking to me only in Arabic or French. He was won over by the fact that I had neither fled the country nor westernized his friend, and he had recently begun to use English—in which he was perfectly fluent—for my benefit when we spoke about complicated things.

"I think it's more like a political movement than a separate sect," said Omar. "When you think about what happened after Karbala—"

"No, no, no," said Mohammad. "They don't think of it this way. It's a completely different spiritual idea."

"But in basic religious things, they're the same as us," responded Omar. "They fast and pray."

"They don't pray *juma'a* on Fridays. They're waiting to pray behind the Mahdi, you see." (The Mahdi is the future savior in Islamic tradition.)

"What? No."

"Well, now it's a question: you must find out, Willow, whether the Iranians pray on Fridays."

It surprised me, as I was researching ways to get into Iran, how little contact the country had culturally with the bulk of the Arab world. Egyptians viewed Iran with almost as much fear and suspicion as Americans do, and were just as confused about the intricacies of its religious life. While there were hundreds of Arab satellite channels available all across the Middle East—including a dozen out of Iraq—Iran spoke only through the occasional televised passion play. Omar was dismayed by my desire to go there and resisted the idea at first. Eventually my stubbornness prevailed, and he contented himself by learning some rudimentary Farsi so he could threaten the appropriate people if I got into trouble.

I began the complex visa application process. Once a week for almost two months, I took the metro downtown and walked to the Iranian consulate, which occupied a dignified Victorian-era house in Doqqi. Its employees came to know me by name. We played a courteous game in which I lied about having any knowledge of Iranian politics and they pretended to believe me. We talked instead about Safavid art. They seemed reassured by my religion and my willingness to cooperate, and in the end I obtained my one-month tourist visa with what was—despite the amount of time involved—far less hassle than Americans usually face in the application process.

One afternoon during this diplomatic project, Sohair called me from work with an intriguing question.

"Beloved, I need your help with a phrase."

"Sure," I said, "what are you working on?"

I heard papers rustling. "I'm translating the latest message from Al-Qaeda," Sohair replied.

This took a moment to sink in. "The latest message from Al-Qaeda?"

"Yes, it was sent to some news agencies several days ago. It talks about Iraq, of course, and the bombings in Madrid. I have a phrase—'fie upon the hypocrites.' Does this make sense?"

I laughed. "Definitely. It's exactly the sort of thing people in the West expect Al-Qaeda to say. It sounds like a warped version of Shakespeare."

She laughed, too. "Good. They use a very flowery, classical kind of Arabic, so I wanted it to sound the same in English. There is one more word I'm having trouble with: *ghazwa*. Do you know it?"

"No, I've never heard it."

"It refers to the battles of the Prophet Muhammad against the pagans. It's used to describe an attempt of a Muslim force to overcome a non-Muslim one. I have *battle, siege, incursion, attack, foray* . . . what do you think?"

I chewed on my lip. We have very few words in English that convey multitiered meaning; usually we rely on adjectives to describe what a single noun can't.

"You might want to break it up into two words. *Holy battle* or *holy attack* or something." I knew these were awkward phrases at best.

"Hmm. It isn't quite like that."

"It's not as strong as *jihad*?"

"No no, not as strong as *jihad*. And *jihad* is more abstract; more about struggling than attacking. This is specific."

I thought of something and brightened. "What about *crusade*?"

Sohair seemed surprised. "*Crusade*? Really?"

"I'm serious. It's the only word we have that conveys 'attack' and 'holy' at the same time."

"I don't think it can be *crusade*, my dear, *crusade* has a very specific meaning for Muslims. Use of that word has caused all kinds of problems in the past. When George Bush used it in one of his speeches a couple of years ago, there was chaos in the Arab world."

"But that's exactly what it is," I said, more for my own benefit than Sohair's. "It's an attack for reasons that are specifically religious, whose end goal is to topple another faith from power. Al-Qaeda is on a crusade."

Sohair was saintly at putting up with my unfashionable opinions, from the nature of a crusade to the reason you can't blame Israeli children for being born in Israel. "That may be," she said, "but the word *crusade* will certainly be taken the wrong way. For an Arab reader, *crusade* could only mean an attack on the Muslim world from the West."

"Then there are two crusades," I said. "It's *crusade vs. crusade.* I wonder if we have a word for *that* in English?"

"I think you call it *war*," said Sohair.

Shortly before I was due to leave for Iran, the war came to me. Looking back I see that it was inevitable. Ben, having recently completed his Arabic courses, had just returned to the United States. Less than twenty-four hours after Jo and Omar and I had seen him off at the airport, the phone rang in our apartment, and he was on the other end.

"Willow?"

"Ben? Are you okay? What's going on?" I thought for a moment that he might have left something important behind.

"I was just interrogated for an hour and a half by the FBI."

My heart began to beat faster. "What? Why?" I heard a click; the call was being monitored. There is nothing subtle about a phone tap.

"They knew where I went to lunch last Saturday. In Cairo."

"*Here?*"

"They said they could take away my citizenship . . . because of the Patriot Act—"

"What?"

"Willow, they asked me about you. They asked me about you and about Mehdi." Mehdi was a mutual friend of ours from college, who had the misfortune to be Persian, and who was, as far as I knew, a simple computer geek.

"Me and . . . why? What did we do?" As soon as the question was out of my mouth I recognized how self-evident the answer was.

"They wanted to know why I was flying back and forth from Egypt so much. They wanted to know where I got the money from —I told them my parents pay for my tickets, but—they think we're terrorists, Willow. They think we're fucking terrorists."

"But we're the good guys," I said weakly. It was the most coherent thing I was able to contribute to the conversation.

"It's so messed up. They asked for Ireland's information, I think they're going to talk to her—" Ireland was Ben's ex-girlfriend, and a daughter of two conservative Washington lobbyists—"and God knows who else is going to get dragged in. I called you as soon as I got home."

"What should I do?" I asked.

"I don't know, I just thought I should tell you what was going on. I don't know."

"But I'm leaving for Iran in two weeks."

"Are you out of your damn mind?"

"I already have tickets," I said. I remembered a conversation I had with a friend of mine who worked with asylum seekers back home—he told me that one of the questions the authorities ask to determine whether or not someone qualifies for asylee status is "Are you afraid to return to your own country?" I was afraid; at that moment, and for a long time afterward, I was afraid to return to my own country. It was a feeling so alien that I found myself unable to cope with it emotionally. I had always been a member of a comfortable majority—I was middle-class, educated, white, of no unusual political bent. I had always felt, though I would never have admitted it, that the laws protected me before anyone else.

I was online a few days later when Ireland sent me an instant message with more bad news: the FBI had been to see her and she was deeply disturbed by what had taken place.

"Okay, first of all, they can't take away your citizenship. That's bullshit. The Patriot Act doesn't give them that power," she wrote. "They were just trying to scare Ben. Second of all, you can refuse to talk to them without a lawyer. Have one meet you at the airport when you go home this summer. Okay?"

"Okay," I wrote, bewildered. For the first time in my life, I was glad to have a Republican on my side. I would come to appreciate how much the true conservatives had done to combat some of the more unconstitutional aspects of the Patriot Act: as much or more than their liberal counterparts.

"Please don't go to Iran. Okay? Please."

"What would that prove?" I wrote. "I'm not doing anything wrong. I'm not out to hurt anybody. If I change my plans, it'll be like admitting I have something to hide. And I don't."

"Willow . . . why are they watching you so hard? Just don't go!"

"I'm theoretically the citizen of a free country," I wrote, with more cheerfulness than I actually felt, "and I'm going to act like it until they lock me up and tell me otherwise. Plus, the tickets are nonrefundable." Smiley face.

I messaged Mehdi as well, to see if he had heard what was going on. He was melancholic.

"What gets me," he said, "is that while they're on my ass watching my every move, that's one less real terrorist they're not watching. And that's depressing. And by the way, your e-mail is being monitored; I can tell because my encryption programs are bouncing off it."

I had taken America for granted. It had been a safe haven in the back of my mind; it was home, it was where I could always go if things got really bad. I had never felt truly unsafe in the Middle East, but I realized that this was because I knew I would be evacuated, rescued, spoken for, and defended if there was ever real trouble. Now that the privileges afforded me as an American were under threat, I saw that I liked them just fine, and furthermore, that I had been relying on them without knowing it.

I began to have nightmares. I dreamed of getting shot and bleeding to death, of being lost in airports and unable to fly home, and once, that Omar and I were stuck in an invented borderland between Egypt, the United States, and Israel without our passports. The entrance to each was blocked with the concrete barricades Egyptian police use at checkpoints. We couldn't remember which country we had come from or where we were going, and no one would let us in.

In an effort to be as transparent and cooperative as possible, I sent my complete Iranian itinerary to the American consulate in Cairo. Then, carrying $2,000 cash in my pocket and swathed from head to toe in a black polyester robe, I flew to Tehran, with a slight fever and the grim feeling that if I were the FBI, I would investigate me, too.

My first impression of Iran began in Dubai. I had a short layover there on the way to Tehran, and sitting at the gate waiting to board the plane, I began to wonder whether I had the right idea about the country I was headed toward. In my mind, I had envisioned Iran as like Egypt, but worse; I had cast it as an Arab Sunni country, and was expecting the specific militancy of Arab Sunni extremism. I didn't even need to be there to realize I was wrong. None of the women on my flight wore head scarves. I saw a slew of stylishly tailored jeans, highlighted hair, and lipstick, and felt extremely underdressed. The travel agency I was using suggested I wear a black manteau, the housecoatlike outer garment that the Council of Guardians made mandatory during the Islamic Revolution in 1979. There was no such thing in Egypt, so instead I wore an abaya, a long traditional robe that was roughly similar.

Based on the appearance of the other women on my flight, I began to wonder whether I should have bothered with the unfamiliar garment. When we landed in Tehran the scarves came out and were draped over heads with obvious distaste. There was an edge of defiance among the younger women, who wore tiny scarves halfway back on their heads, ponytails peeking out the back. In Egypt, few of the women on the plane would be considered properly veiled. Compared to most of them, I was dressed like a fundamentalist. This was a strange turn of events. Having nothing but the press to rely on for an impression of Iran, I expected harrowing brutality: a regime bent on total domination, a people struggling against fanaticism. But the Axis of Evil was nowhere to be found in the cynical nonchalance of "mandatory Islamic dress," and the catty girls from the plane looked less than revolutionary.

My guide met me at the airport. He was a kind-looking man of sixty or so, and was so courteous and mild as we started chatting about our schedule that I breathed a sigh of relief. I'd been dreading the situation that would inevitably have occurred in Egypt—getting stuck for a week with a desperate guy in his thirties who would make it his mission to get me into bed, despite the engagement ring on my finger and the scarf on my head. But Ahmad was married, with a daughter my age and a son slightly older, and seemed amused at the prospect of shepherding around someone so much younger than himself.

"Most tourists who come to Iran are middle-aged or older couples," he said. "Not many young people come here because there are no bars, no discos. There are no healthy ways to get into trouble as young people like to do. It's sad, really."

This was a phrase I was to hear many times from many people over the course of my time in Iran. What's happened to our country —it's sad, really.

Tehran was gray and overcast during my time there. The city bore few scars from the eight-year-long war with Iraq; I only saw one building with visible traces of shelling. A string of parks ran through the center of town and the streets were remarkably clean, the Elburz Mountains were beautiful in the background, and yet the air itself seemed low and listless as I wandered around with Ahmad. It took me several hours to realize that it was because I heard absolutely no laughter. In fact, the only raised voice I heard the entire day was in a restaurant, when a waiter called out food orders to the kitchen. The human stillness was so complete it was almost surreal. People were unfailingly kind as we visited museums and tea houses, and delighted to learn I was an American (Iranians don't hate Americans, they were all anxious to assure me), but the atmosphere was always solemn. "Ten years ago a woman could be thrown in jail for laughing too loudly," Ahmad explained, "and unmarried men and women are still sometimes harassed when they go out together. Maybe this is the origin of what you are sensing."

I shook my head, stunned. Maybe.

We passed by the old American Embassy on the way back to my hotel. "They left it exactly as they found it," Ahmad said. "After the revolution they just locked the gate. And painted the slogans on the wall."

The outer wall—institutional brick like the buildings inside —was covered in murals showing the Statue of Liberty with a skull for a face and an assortment of anti-American slogans. All the windows inside the compound were tiny and barred; a subtle and ominous suggestion that the United States knew the revolution was coming long before the storm broke.

"This is where they took the hostages?"

"Yes." Ahmad followed my gaze toward the death's-head Statue of Liberty. "I have nothing to say." He smiled helplessly.

That night I met Hussain at the hotel. As the director of the travel agency I was using, he wanted to welcome me to Iran and make sure everything was running smoothly; I also had to pay him. We had tea in the hotel lobby and he obliged me by talking politics.

"These places are always very crowded," he observed, looking around at the arrangement of armchairs and coffee tables; the lobby was quite full. His English was flawless, only slightly clipped, with a vague untraceable accent. "Only about half of these people are actually staying in the hotel."

"Really?" Hotels didn't strike me as entertaining places to hang out.

"Really. In the international hotels, you're less likely to run into the morality police. Boys and girls can come here to be together."

"I guess that makes sense." I paused, trying to find the words for what I wanted to say next. "When I was walking around Tehran today it seemed like most people were a little bit . . . unhappy. Is this just the way Tehranis are? Like New Yorkers?"

Hussain pulled out a pipe and some tobacco, which smelled faintly of vanilla. "Are you familiar with the Russian novelist Gorky?"

"I kind of avoid Russian literature. It's depressing."

"Gorky once said that a people who do not dance will die. We cannot dance, and look around." He gestured with his pipe. "We are a dead people. No dancing, no big parties —women can't even sing. None of the things that help people to live, we have. Of course we're unhappy."

I was mortified to have steered the conversation in such a depressing direction. I hadn't yet learned that despite the emphasis on privacy and discretion, Iranians are, unlike Americans, totally unembarrassed by sadness. "But it seems like the younger generation is able to get away with a lot," I said. "I see girls who are barely in hijab hanging out with boys all over the place. They don't seem very worried."

"That's because the government knows that if the young people wanted to stage a counterrevolution, all of this would be over in five minutes. Young people put this government in power, and young people could take that power away. Seventy percent of this country is under thirty."

I lowered my voice so my next question would not be overheard. "So why don't they stage a counterrevolution?"

Hussain sighed. "Because Iranians are sick of war. In the last hundred years, we've fought two bloody wars, and had two revolutions, a coup, and a countercoup. No one wants to go through all that, not again. People want reform, not revolution."

"I can understand that. I would, too." I rolled a sugar cube around in my mouth—I wasn't used to the way Iranians drink tea, sucking it over a lump of sugar kept tucked inside one cheek. "But a lot of Persian expats I've spoken to seem to think a counterrevolution is about to happen."

"Really?" Hussain smiled bitterly. "Well, you live in the Middle East. Something is always about to happen. Often the same thing is about to happen for years and years."

I laughed and then blushed as several people turned to stare in my direction.

Tehran, the Unfunny City, capital of an Islamist hyperreality, never quite became real to me. It seemed like a living novel; a story that was constantly inventing itself, often at the expense of the very real people who lived in it. The diffident way that fashionable Tehrani women wore their scarves; the rose-embellished murals of martyrs, two and three stories high, that were painted on the walls of buildings; the moralizing slogans; everything suggested to me that Iranian Islamism was less about religion than it was about a method of control. It functioned the way bureaucracy did in Egypt: a way to create hassles and delays so endless that people were too tired to fight back against the local tyrants. From what I could see, it was just as effective. I have never been less sorry to leave a place than I was to leave Tehran.

My next stop was Shiraz, a city about six hundred kilometers to the south. Beset by insomnia in Tehran, I was only half awake when I boarded the plane; I had my headphones on and was listening to Delerium to cope with my dark mood, and when a prayer for safe travel came on over the plane's intercom I simply turned up the volume of my music. The woman in the next seat looked at me in alarm. Only later did it occur to me that I might have been doing something illegal. In Shiraz I was met by Azin, a cheerful, witty woman of thirty or so whose scarf slid around alarmingly on her head. Constructed in a horseshoe shape around a bend in a dry river, Shiraz was blooming improbably with rose gardens and cypress groves, and was dotted with blue-domed summer palaces and shrines. This is a common sight all over Iran; most of the country is mountainous and dry, but even the smallest villages I saw were lush with carefully tended plant life. Where the water and arable soil came from remained a complete mystery to me. Shiraz was no exception: a city of cultivated beauty in a feral, sweeping landscape.

Azin took me to the tomb of Hafiz, one of the most celebrated poets and mystics in Islamic history, who is revered in Iran as a saint. The tomb—a graceful domed mausoleum surrounded by a garden—was adjoined by a *chai khaneh* or teahouse, a small stone courtyard with a fountain set in the middle and niches with large pillows to sit on cut into the walls. When we entered, a group of chador-clad women looked at me over their shoulders, curious.

"Your husband is Egyptian?" asked Azin, deftly maneuvering tea and sugar cubes on a brass tray, when we were seated.

"Yeah, Palestinian-Egyptian."

"And he let you travel by yourself?"

"Yes he did," I said cheerfully.

Azin shook her head, incredulous. "We have a stereo-type that Arab husbands are very conservative compared to Persian husbands."

"I think most Egyptian men are more domineering than Omar, to be fair. When I finally convinced him to let me he was almost excited—he gave me a list of things to look for and asked me to find out whether there are any Sufis in Iran."

"Sufis?" Azin looked doubtful. "Maybe before the revolution. But not now." She adjusted her scarf absently, the way women in other countries might play with their hair. "Do you like living in Egypt?" she asked.

"I do." It was true. And I was right; Tehran had normalized Tura.

"Why?"

"I guess it's because everything interesting or important, eastern or western, eventually passes through Cairo. It feels like the center of the world. It's been the center of my world, anyway, for a while." It was the first time I had been able to articulate the reason I could no longer see myself severing my connection to the city. Even if my marriage failed, Cairo was the reason I could never again pretend that America was somehow separate from the rest of the world. In *The Prophet,* Khalil Gibran says we cannot leave the places in which we have suffered without regret, that these places become our second skins. Cairo was mine. It made me sick and dirty and endlessly hassled, and it had given me Omar, and gotten me in trouble, and gotten me out of trouble. It was now an indelible part of my history, and since we love anything that is familiar, I could only think of it with affection.

Azin smiled. "The center of the world," she repeated. "It sounds like a poem." We sat in silence for a while, sipping tea through sugar lumps. Eventually the women in the corner rose, pulling their veils over their mouths, and left.

Later that day we visited a shrine erected for a brother-in-law of one of the imams. It was small and had a nondescript dome—I had a feeling I was going to have to feign the awe my Persian guides seemed to expect of me in everything. Egypt did everything on such a large scale—starting with the Pyramids and ending with the constant chaos of the streets —that it was hard for me to feel shocked anymore.

Azin and I had to wear chador inside the shrine; they were conveniently provided in a large box by the door. I pulled the garment over my head, swept the trailing end over one hand, and wished it wasn't strange for a foreigner to wear one in the street. Chador, a symbol of oppression to most non-Muslims, afford the wearer a kind of dignity totally lacking in the dumpy manteaux, which are, in the end, the mullahs' halfhearted compromise with western dress.

When we went inside my awe became unfeigned. The entire interior was covered in a mosaic of mirrors. I had never seen anything like it in my life. Each step was more disorienting than the last as my scattered image shifted around the interior. I stood in the center and swayed on my feet. A dozen people were seated on the floor, praying or reading.

"You can take a picture if you want," whispered Azin.
I shook my head. "Not while people are praying."

"It's okay, you're a foreigner. They understand."

"No, I don't want to be rude. I wouldn't want somebody to do that to me."

Azin nodded, pleased. "That's good. Really, that's excellent. It makes a big difference." She reached out and squeezed my hand. I smiled at her. We left quietly, the mirror-shrine preserved only in memory.

The Shrine of Fatima

We try men through one another.

—*Quran 6:53*

THAT EVENING, AHMAD FLEW DOWN FROM TEHRAN TO MEET me. IN the morning he and I made the long drive north through the Zagros Mountains to the city of Isfahan. The mood I had caught in Tehran hadn't lifted in Shiraz, but the Zagros, all dusty high plains and craggy, mineral-streaked mountainsides, were eye-catching enough to distract anyone from culture shock.

"If I may ask," Ahmad said at one point, "what made you want to come to Iran?"

I chewed my lip. "A couple of reasons. I'm interested in Persian history. I've been in Egypt for a while and wanted to see something else. I wanted to get a sense of another country."

"A sense?"

"A feeling about how things work here, the way people think about things."

"But you're very quiet." He said this in a way that implied *very bored.*

"Oh no," I said, alarmed. "No, Iran is beautiful. It might be the most beautiful country I've ever seen. And the people are very nice." I fumbled for the right words. "It's just that

I haven't had a break from new things in almost a year, so most of my awe has been used up."

We were silent for a few minutes.

"You are becoming a little bit Arab, I think," he said at last, gently.

The suddenness of the observation startled me. "What makes you say so?" I asked.

"The way you walk and speak to people. It's different from the way other Americans I have met behave."

"Oh. God. I guess it's a habit now."

"To please your new family?"

"To keep from sticking out. To keep from creating a scene wherever I go."

Ahmad nodded, considering this. We drove for a while without speaking, feeling awkward at having been so frank with each other. There was pain in my lower back and I felt a bit feverish, so I let the scenery blur in front of me, hoping for a nap. It was not to be.

"Look to your right."

Obediently I looked out the window and saw a cluster of domed black tents.

"Nomads?"

"Yes, tribespeople. Shahsevan, maybe."

I came fully awake. "Really?"

Ahmad smiled. "Really. Shall we go say hello?"

We drove down a dirt path into the gulley in which the tribespeople were camped and stopped ten meters short of the first tent. A large dog sounded the alarm, circling the car as we got out. I saw a veiled head peek out of one tent, dart back in, and then emerge as a girl of sixteen or eighteen. She was wearing a heavily embroidered red dress, cut like a *salwar kameez*. A long scarf was draped over her forehead and hung down her back. She smiled as Ahmad approached and introduced us.

"She's invited us for tea," he said.

We ducked into the first tent, which was pungent with the smell of unbleached wool. Inside, a circle of girls sat giggling into scarves. I smiled and sat where the girl in the red dress pointed, pressing my hand over my heart for *thank you*. She smiled back and busied herself with a small kerosene stove. I looked around at the other girls. Most were dressed like the first, in robes of bright green, red, or blue with gold embroidery. Their scarves were clearly meant to ornament, not hide, their hair, which they wore in thick braids across their foreheads. They fussed as they arranged themselves around us. Ahmad asked them a question that sent several of the girls into fresh fits of giggling.

"I asked if any of them are married," he said.

Terribly forward in Egypt, this was a standard opener in Iran. It turned out that one of them was, and had an eight-month-old son. I looked at her closely. Exposure to sun and wind had carved premature lines in her face, making her age difficult to guess. Her body looked like it had, at one point, been emaciated by disease or malnutrition. I had a hard time picturing her carrying a child. But her expression was so sharp and open that I wasn't surprised, either.

"What tribe are they from?" I asked Ahmad.

He repeated my question in Farsi. One of the girls answered with a name that seemed to surprise him, and there followed a short conversation.

"They say they are Abd'el Khaneh, which I have never heard of, and they claim they are Arabs," he said finally.

"They are?" It was a strange claim for a tribe in central Iran. *Abd* is an Arabic word for *servant,* and *khaneh* is Farsi for *house* (as in *chai'khaneh, teahouse*), so Abd'el Khaneh meant roughly *Servant of the House.* I wondered if the enigmatic "House" might refer to the family of the Prophet, which is known as "Ahl ul'Beyt," *family of the House,* in Arabic.

"Yes," said Ahmad, clearly bemused. "They say Arabic is their tribal language."

In modern standard Arabic, I asked the girl in the red dress whether she could understand me. She gave me a sideways glance and said something that sounded like Arabic and Farsi played over a radio with lots of static. I understood none of it.

"It might have been Arabic once," I said to Ahmad, "but now it sounds like some kind of mixed dialect."

"She doesn't understand you, either," Ahmad said, and then chuckled. "It's because of what we were speaking about. We've found Arab nomads in the middle of Shiraz province."

We had tea with the girls, whose brothers, back from their shepherding duties, slowly trickled in. Several of the boys had startling pale blue eyes. Most of them looked like they were between thirteen and eighteen, and crouched instead of sitting to drink tea, as though a sudden move might send them bolting out the door. One wore an old U.S. Army jacket. It must have been prerevolutionary, a surreal remnant of a time when Iran was a valued U.S. ally.

We thanked the girls for the tea and Ahmad promised to pass this way again with the pictures I'd taken of them. We got back on the road and drove to a mountain pass south of Isfahan, where I stood on a rock and looked west toward Iraq, and beyond it, to the Mediterranean, the Atlantic, and home. Though so many things had changed, the mountains, so like the landscape I'd left behind in Colorado, were too familiar for me to feel afraid.

There's an old Persian rhyme that goes like this: "*Isfahan nisf-e jahan,*" Isfahan is half the world. Even today it might as well be true; though the trade routes have mostly been given up and the poets and royal courts have mostly left, the energy and the architecture remain. Built on the Silk Road, Isfahan at its height might as well have been synonymous with Persia. It had everything—the favorite palace of a string of shahs, two universities and several small colleges, an enormous bazaar, and artists from across the globe courtesy of the polished Safavid empire. It also supported, and still supports, one of the most developed teahouse cultures I have ever encountered. A string of ancient stone bridges is home to a series of waterside *chai'khaneh,* many of which are built right into the bottom of the bridges themselves, so that sitting in one feels like being in a boat.

But the heart of the city is the Maidan Imam Khomeini, a circle of Safavid-era palace and mosque structures fronting a large bazaar. It was there that Ahmad and I went to hunt down a *sehtar,* a traditional Persian instrument Omar had begged me to look for. After interrogating a couple of bazaari

191

cloth merchants, we got directions to an instrument shop near the *maidan*. When we found it, I was surprised to find it was run by a pair of guys close to my own age who, with their band T-shirts, corduroy jackets, and cargo pants, would not have been out of place at a Pixies concert. They both smiled in a certain way as Ahmad and I walked in, and it all came together. The stick-it-to-the-mullahs fashion, the music shop —they could only be Sufis. Azin had led me to believe that Sufism had been driven underground by the revolution. Yet here we all were.

Our conversation was stifled by an almost complete language barrier; they spoke very little English and no Arabic, and my Farsi was limited to the polite expressions Ahmad had been teaching me. So Ahmad translated for us.

"Their names are Isma'il and Javad," he said. "They say they are members of the Ni'matullahi order."

It was a Sufi path I'd never heard of before, but after Ahmad explained I had been hoping to run into Persian Sufis, they filled in the gaps with enthusiasm. Music, they said, was central to their *dhikr*—a type of prayer like a cross between a hymn and a mantra —which was why they ran a music shop. Both were curious about the way Egyptian Sufis performed *dhikr,* and how many paths there were, and what they were named. I answered their questions as best I could, wishing Omar were there to do the subject better justice.

When I told them I was looking for a *sehtar* for my husband, Isma'il ran out of the shop, saying that none of the *sehtars* they stocked were good enough. He came back about ten minutes later with another one, picking out a melody that we heard floating down the street in front of him. He and Javad packed it in a case with great tenderness, tucking in picks and extra strings and bridges, giving Ahmad instructions about tuning. As we left, so did the uneasiness that had been plaguing me since Tehran. The fact that I could travel halfway across the world and meet people like Javad and Isma'il made me feel, in a strange way, safe; they reminded me that it was possible to encounter home in many different places.

Though I was free of my bad mood, there was still something deeply sad about Iran. Ahmad told me story after story about tourists he had chaperoned who were brought to tears over something. Sometimes it was simply the dome of a mosque that did it, but more often it was a strange feeling of loss or regret. One wealthy American man in his sixties found himself suddenly devastated by the fact that he had never found lasting love. A British diplomat, who spent thirty years in Iran as an ambassador before the revolution, wept openly about everything that had been lost in the last thirty years. It was uncanny. One evening in Isfahan, as Ahmad and I were sitting in a rose garden drinking tea, he himself began to look downcast. I asked him what was wrong.

"Nothing really," he said. "I was just remembering the past." He shook his head and smiled, then launched into a story about a British woman who, upon seeing the golden dome of the Hazrat-e Masumeh, was so undone by the current aggression against the Muslim world that she cried in front of thousands of pilgrims—in the end, nothing to be embarrassed about, as many of them were weeping, too.

"For God's sake," I said, "what is it about Iran that makes everyone *cry?*"

It was the first and only time I saw Ahmad laugh. "I don't know," he said when he recovered, "but now I wonder myself."

We went to an Indian restaurant for dinner that night. I ate with greater appetite than I had in several days, glad for a change from Persian cuisine, which rarely varied from meat cooked on a stick. At one point, Ahmad asked me how I had come to like Indian food.

"I'm not sure," I said. "I wasn't that into it before a friend and I found this amazing Indian restaurant in Boston, during college. It was expensive, but we ended up having these huge feasts there at least once a month—" Like magic, my throat closed up. I was bewildered. Surely this wasn't a dangerous topic. Yet I was on the brink of sobbing into my lamb masala. It was as if I saw, by virtue of the vast physical distance between Boston and Isfahan, how *over* my former life really was. I was momentarily overwhelmed by the magnitude of the break I had made with my own history. The world was too big, I was too small; I couldn't contain so many contradictions. I suffered through the rest of the meal and went back to my hotel, where I drew a bath and cried for half an hour.

The next day coincided with the anniversary of the martyrdom of one of the imams. Black flags flew all over the city, no cheerful music was permitted to play, and everyone looked even more downcast than usual. I felt exhausted but strangely peaceful. Something had clicked. I finally had a sense of what separated Shi'a from Sunnah on an emotional level. There had been a lot about Shi'a and its effect on Iranian culture that I found vaguely unsettling—the focus on sacrifice, the intense ritual mourning—but there was something ecstatic about this cultivation of sadness. After my own minibreakdown, it made more sense. Like Buddhism, Islam encourages spiritual detachment from material things. In Sunni Islam, this is accomplished through intense personal discipline and strict iconoclasm. But in Iran, Shi'a seemed to accomplish the same thing in a different way. Somehow, by making sadness an ecstatic, transformative experience, the fear of loss was annihilated. It reminded one that the only permanence is through God; everything else begins to fade as soon as it is created. I felt like I could finally understand the air of melancholy that surrounded Iran's beautiful gardens and palaces and mosques, making them seem humble—as if they said, in the same breath that they glorified art and nature, it doesn't matter, it is lost, it has already passed away.

We left Isfahan that day, driving out along the city's empty black-shrouded boulevards. Before arriving back in Tehran, we stopped in Qom, a holy city that had grown up around the shrine of what I mistakenly referred to as "one of the Fatimas," somewhat to Ahmad's dismay. I had a Sunni's indifference toward members of the Prophet's family further removed than his grandchildren. Beyond Imam Husayn and Sayyida Zaynab, I didn't bother to keep the prophetic lineages straight; I did not, and still do not, know which Fatima is buried in Qom. The Shi'i did know, and built an immense blue and gold mosque complex in her honor during the sixteenth century, and made the city one of the centers of Shi'i learning. To enter the shrine of Fatima one has to be both Muslim and, in the case of women, wearing a chador. In most parts of Iran any all-encompassing garment passes muster; the Arab galibayya and head scarf I had worn during my stay were accepted without a batted eye, and were, in fact, far more conservative than what most women wore. But at the shrine of Fatima the traditional Persian chador was enforced. Of the hundreds of women who pressed around me at its gates, a large number were not Persian—many looked southeast Asian, some were pale and blue-eyed—but all wore the black or blue-and-white-printed sarilike garment. I would have had no problem wearing a chador myself, but as I was swept along in the human river of pilgrims, I realized that the only way out was forward, into the shrine. I would have to enter it as I was. At the entrance, Ahmad caught up with me, just as I was stopped by a tall grim-looking man of thirty-five or forty: a member of the religious police. Ahmad gestured toward me and spoke to him. The policeman observed me closely, trying to decide, it seemed, whether to believe what Ahmad was saying. I dropped my eyes and looked politely at his shoes.

"You're American?" the policeman asked in English. There was no malice in the question, only a deep unease.

"Yes."

"And Muslim?"

"Yes."

He said something to Ahmad, who repeated emphatically what he had said before.

"Are you really a Muslim?" he asked me again.

I looked up at him. "I can say the *shaheda* right now, if you'd like," I said. I meant to be accommodating, but as soon as I said it I realized it sounded like a challenge. And maybe it was.

The policeman frowned, his unease increasing. For a long minute we stood like a tableau. I looked down again, waiting for his permission to enter; he thought silently. Ahmad, who I saw from the knee down, shifted from one foot to the other. I wondered how much trouble we were actually in—I wasn't sure how much power the religious police had in Iran. It occurred to me what this was and what it meant: an American Sunni Muslim, dressed like an Arab, waiting at the door of the very Shi'ite, very Persian Hazrat-e Masumeh; in the city that had been the birthplace of the Iranian Revolution. *Can I come in?* became, in this context, an extremely provocative question. It was a question of which agenda would swallow which. If there was an Islam that was larger than sects and nationalities, an Islam that could accommodate contradictions, and if I could be judged as an individual and not as the representative of an idea, then I would see the inside of the shrine. I was different, but I had done nothing wrong. Sometimes following the rules is a more radical act than breaking them.

"Go ahead."

I looked up, surprised. On the policeman's face was the barest hint of a smile. "Go ahead," he said again, and then, "You are welcome."

I stepped over the threshold into the stone-flagged court-yard. Ahmad trailed after me, smiling and shaking his head. I looked over my shoulder at the policeman, who was watching me with a thoughtful expression; forgetting myself for a moment, I caught his eye and grinned.

El Khawagayya

It's a rather nasty word even by the standards of Arabic, starting with a throat-clearing *kh* and continuing with *wAAga!*, like spitting phlegm.

—gn0sis, on everything2.com

"SO WHAT WAS THE MOST UNUSUAL THING YOU SAW IN Iran? Tell me about something you weren't expecting."

"Carrot jam."

Jo laughed. "Seriously."

"I *am* serious. Who makes jam from a vegetable? It explains everything. The revolution, the hostage crisis— everything." We were sitting in the living room of our flat, near the window, watching a flushed sun disappear into the dust on the horizon. The Pyramids jutted up like teeth at the edge of the Giza Plateau, throwing shadows east toward the Nile. The room was a mess. Jo was packing, preparing to leave for the States. Gifts I had bought in Tehran and Isfahan littered the table in pools of brown paper: enamel pencil cases, tiny painted boxes, printed cloth. I was on a strong course of antibiotics to combat the infection in my kidneys, but the accompanying back pain would linger for a year. On arrival in Cairo I found an e-mail in my inbox from Hussain, the director of the travel agency, thanking me for being one of his "good" clients—which I assumed meant one who didn't cause trouble with the testy Iranian authorities—and inviting me to come back soon with Omar.

"Don't go," I said to Jo as she bundled books into a suitcase. "If you go, who's going to play Punch Fundie with me?" Omar found Punch Fundie undignified.

"I don't know, muffin," she said. "I guess you'll have to find some other game." She held a kitten at bay with her foot as he sniffed around one of her bags, wondering if it might be a good place to pee. Though born in captivity, the kittens were never what I would call tame—they tolerated our affection grudgingly, proved difficult to house train, and looked at people with serious, predatory little stares. They were only sociable when they were sleepy, when they would curl up into spotted pools on the nearest lap. Jo clucked her tongue at the one that was now chewing on her toe. Withdrawing her foot, she flopped onto the couch with a sigh.

"I thought this was going to be a fun one-year-adventure-type thing," she said, "but I really feel different. This place has had a much bigger impact on me than I thought it would."

"Good or bad?"

"All experience is ultimately good." She saw my grimace and smiled. "No, no, I'm not just being polite. I will actually miss this city. I've learned a lot, being knocked around here."

The larger of the two kittens scooted out from under a chair and pounced on the smaller.

"I'm afraid that if I'm knocked around too much more I'll become a completely different person," I said. "Especially if you're not here to remind me who I was."

"This is your story now," Jo said gently. "You'll know what to do. You'll have Omar and Sohair and Ibrahim and your father-in-law and Sameh and lots of other people. Plus, we'll come and see you, and you'll come and see us—"

What she was saying was sensible but I couldn't help feeling a stab of anxiety. Jo's departure would mark a new season of my life in Egypt, one in which I would go for months at a time without seeing another westerner. As Omar and I saw her off to the airport, I was conscious of the bright sun on my shoulders and the wind coming down from the Mediterranean. They seemed like heralds of good news. I hoped I was ready for whatever they brought.

With Jo gone, Omar and I began to think about finding an apartment together. We had several terse conversations about whether this was a good idea—the wedding was still several months away because the American guests didn't have a long holiday before Thanksgiving weekend. From a religious point of view we were already married, so legally we could do whatever we wanted—the Egyptian side of the family, however, would be baffled by the idea that we were moving in together before throwing a wedding. I thought about going back to the United States for the intervening months but Omar couldn't bear to be away from me for that long. As so often happened, we were forced into a compromise that suited no one.

Aware of our culturally precarious situation, everybody did what they could to help us. Omar's uncles and cousins brushed off the awkward explanation of our plans and told us to go ahead with what we thought was most practical. His female relatives inundated me with advice about how to be a wife, and hints on the psychology of Arab husbands.

"My husband is very helpful around the house," said a paternal cousin, a jolly mother of one. "I'm lucky—when I cook, he does the dishes. He also cleans up after himself. He's not a traditional man." She paused.

"That's good," I said, uncomprehending.

She examined my face with a quick glance, looking for a particular reaction. Egyptian women can read a conversation like a doctor reads a body. Realizing I couldn't understand what she had left unspoken, she smiled kindly. "I think Omar is more of a traditional man," she said. "He will probably expect you to do everything around the house."

I stared at her in dismay. "Like what?"

"The cooking."

"Okay."

"The laundry. The cleaning." She hesitated. "Do you know how to cook?"

"No," I said. I was beginning to feel a little sick.

"That's all right." She patted my hand. "We can teach you. But you should be prepared—for a woman, there is a lot of work after marriage. Many responsibilities."

The feeling of sickness increased. I often felt feverish now—it was one of the strange adaptations my body made to cope with the extreme heat. And though I felt hot, my mouth was always cold, as if I had been drinking ice water. When I took my temperature it was inevitably an even 98.6 degrees. The result of all this was that I'd stopped sweating. The body is clever and honest. In heat so relentless sweat does little to cool you down; instead it robs you of the salts and minerals you need to keep your blood pressure stable. Egyptians do not sweat, not like westerners. Until now I had been pleased and a little awed by my body's ability to adapt, but suddenly it felt like a betrayal—yet another part of me rearranged for an alien way of life.

"Are you all right?" My cousin-in-law frowned.

"Fine." I stood up, forcing myself to smile. "Thank you."

I had not been raised to think of myself as a future housekeeper. The idea that housework was demeaning and oppressive had been drilled into me from such a young age and from so many sources that I could not remember where I first came across it. I believed it, and took the maxim to the next logical step: if housework was demeaning and oppressive, it must also be unnecessary. I was confused when the kitchenette in my college apartment got dirty. When dust bunnies accumulated under the bed, I had an uneasy feeling that the world was not functioning as it should. If people were not meant to clean, cleanliness should not require people. I still believed this, however unconsciously, and the idea that Omar might expect me to do nothing but cook and scrub floors filled me with terrifying images of domestic slavery.

He came over to my half-packed apartment that afternoon, where I was sorting through some of the books and utensils Jo had left me. As soon as he was through the door I burst into tears and asked him if he wanted me to spend my days hunched over dripping buckets of laundry.

"Of course not!" He gathered me in his arms. Standing, my head fit neatly under his chin. "Where did you get this idea? I'm not marrying you to have a servant, I'm marrying you because I love you."

I looked up at him. "Really?" It was a ridiculous question but I wanted to be comforted.

"Who do you think I am? Listen." He backed up a step and took my hands. "You have this idea of a stereotypical Arab man in your head, and you keep confusing him with me. You've done it before. You're afraid I'm secretly this man, and that you'll only discover the truth when it's too late. But I'm *not*."

He was right. Conditioning is very hard to escape, even with effort. I was still haunted by nightmare scenarios. There were moments at night, on the edge of sleep, when I was gripped by intense anxiety about my marriage. In fits like these I would invent paranoid contingencies, ways of fleeing secretly to the airport or the embassy if Omar became a fanatical tyrant.

"Sometimes I'm afraid of you," I told him, surprising even myself.

He looked hurt. "No," he said, "No, no. Be angry at me, be frustrated with me, but never be afraid of me."

He would never give me a reason to be afraid—never lift his hand in anger, or call me a demeaning name, or even raise his voice. Though Omar was mild and reserved by nature, this was also a matter of principle for him. The Prophet, his role model, never beat or belittled his wives, a fact observed with surprise by his followers and contempt by his enemies. Omar took that tradition very seriously. To him, the old Islamic saying that marriage is half of religion was absolute: his duty to love and protect me was part of his duty to God.

We began looking for apartments in Maadi, a short distance downriver from Tura. We settled on one in a dignified little building owned by a Coptic woman and her daughter. It overlooked a garden, home to a lone mango tree and a straggling English rosebush. The souk and the language center where I took lessons with Sameh were both a short walk away.

On my last day in the Tura apartment, Omar came over humming a little song he'd made up about "*sha'itina*," my grammatically garbled word for *our apartment*. He insisted my grammar mistakes were adorable and went several years without correcting them; it was left to Sameh to prevent bad speaking habits from setting in. Omar carried bags of clothes to the car while I coaxed the cats into a large birdcage, the best we could do in the way of pet carriers.

"Will you miss having your own room?" I asked him as I put the offended animals in the back seat.

"My own room?" Omar laughed. "Have you forgotten? I've never had my own room."

I blushed, remembering belatedly that Omar and Ibrahim shared a room, like most Egyptian siblings. In a city as crowded as Cairo, having your own space was a luxury very few people—even wealthy people—could afford.

"Will *you* miss having your own room?" Omar prompted.

"No," I said, taking his hand. "Being with you is ten times better."

In a day, I became mistress of a household, part of a network of households that made up Omar's extended family. By my American reckoning, it felt like I'd skipped forward a decade. In my early twenties I was supposed to be independent, living on my own and being spontaneous. That independence would prepare me for life as a wife and mother in a nuclear family, hundreds of miles from my nearest relatives. Instead I had become part of a vast tribe, linked to its communal reputation and destiny, and a participant in its welfare. Independence was replaced by interdependence. I would have to learn how to function in this unfamiliar role, and learn quickly.

The first day we spent in our new apartment was a Friday, the beginning of the Egyptian weekend. I woke up before Omar to survey my little kingdom: a small bedroom with shuttered French doors leading to the balcony, a living room, a bathroom, and a tiny kitchen. The collective space was so small that we had to put our dining table right next to the front door.

Still, it was clean and newly renovated—compared to the old flat in Tura it seemed luxurious. The walls were painted pale yellow and the tiled floor was cool in the dense summer heat. There was a gap under the front door that I hadn't yet noticed—when it admitted a procession of fat striped spiders and the geckos who hunted them, I would. The atmosphere of the place was gentle and expectant, as if the walls were waiting to see how I would cope in the private realm so closely associated with Egyptian womanhood.

Small as it was, this apartment represented one of the biggest challenges I would ever face.

Although Omar was sincere when he said he did not expect me to become a submissive homemaker, he was a man, and had very little idea what it takes to run a functioning Cairene household. There is a reason the *sitt el beyt* —the lady of the house—holds such a revered position in Egyptian society. She is the one who builds relationships with the vendors of the best meat and the freshest fruit, and argues for the lowest price; she knows herbal remedies for dysentery; it is she who cooks for ten people out of three pots when relatives drop by unexpectedly. In Egypt, women create the civilization the men merely live in.

I appreciated the fact that Omar respected me as an equal, but I knew his support was largely intellectual. "If it isn't a man's job or a woman's job to run domestic life, whose is it?" I asked him once, teasing. He tilted his head with an ironic smile. "A maid's," he said. I clucked my tongue in exasperation. In a world where there is no such thing as bagged salad or microfiber mops, keeping insects at bay and a family fed is a constant occupation. Since people are cheaper than goods in Egypt—the country produces few consumer products, but plenty of labor—maids are employed by housewives starting in the lower-middle class, where the gap between housewife and housemaid may be no more than a few hundred pounds per month. Even when Omar's family was struggling, there had been a maid to tidy the bedrooms and wash the cement floor with kerosene to repel fleas and roaches.

The idea of having a maid made me uncomfortable. I decided to do as much as I could myself, even though this meant I would spend nearly half of each day in the kitchen and the marketplace. On our first morning in the apartment, I went barefoot into the living room and looked out the window toward the mango tree, organizing my thoughts. I would have to go to the souk and determine which vendors sold the best produce at the best prices. There was the small matter of learning to cook without all the prepackaged conveniences of the first world. If I wanted chicken broth, I had to go to the market, pick out a live chicken, have it butchered, bring it home, and boil it. Laundry would have to become a routine, too. Because few people either owned or had ever heard of mechanized dryers, laundry was a process: after a load came out of the machine, you had to heap it all into a tub, haul it to the window where your clothesline hung, dust the clothesline, hang the clothes, then cover the whole mess with plastic sheeting to protect it from dirt and bird droppings.

This was going to be an adventure.

I dressed and left the apartment, closing the door quietly to avoid waking Omar. I loved being up early in the morning, when you could still hear the birds, and the air wasn't choked with smog. When I remember the route between this first apartment and the souk, something tightens in my chest—I miss the dark little gardened streets dripping dust from every surface. If you tapped a banana leaf you were rewarded with a shower of the stuff, which hit the ground in plumes, dispersing back into the air like drops of ink in water. What I struggled so long to understand about this city would be the thing I came to love most: beauty and ugliness are so crowded together that the line between the two is faint and you begin to mistake one for the other.

On the first street of the souk there was a particular *fararghi,* or poultry seller, whom I would come to patronize because his birds were reliably healthy. His name was Am Mahmoud. I would go and ask him to pick out a nice-sized chicken, which he would scoop up by the wings from a cage full of squawking inmates and present to me for inspection. If I liked it, he swiftly slit its throat, whispering a *bismillah,* and put it in a barrel to bleed out. Afterward, he dipped it in boiling vinegar and tossed it into a jerry-rigged device that looked like a small cotton gin (and functioned in much the same way) for defeathering. Then he gutted it, calling to the stray cats that inhabited the alley; familiar with the sound of his voice, they would come running for scraps. The bird I would cook for lunch was finally handed to me in a plastic bag, rinsed clean and still warm.

As often as I saw Am Mahmoud, he still looked at me as an outsider, a *khawagga.* One day I arrived to find the yellow-painted metal cages empty—his supplier hadn't yet arrived from the farm outside Cairo where the chickens, ducks, and doves he sold were raised.

"No chicken today?" I asked him in Arabic.

"Not yet," he said apologetically, spreading his hands.

"Okay, no problem." I swept my skirt aside with one hand to keep it from trailing in the dust, and turned away.

"Wait!" Am Mahmoud motioned to me. "You have other shopping to do?"

"Yes—"

"Come back in half an hour. I'll have a chicken for you."

"All right. Thanks." I smiled, bemused, and went to buy a kilo of zucchini from a stall in the next street. When I returned, Am Mahmoud gave me a bag containing the largest chicken I'd ever seen; it looked pale and naked in the half-inch of pinkish broth that had accumulated underneath it. I looked up at him. "Where did you get this?" I asked.

"A friend." He grinned.

It was only when I got the thing home and examined it that I realized he had sold me a turkey.

The next time I walked in the souk, I passed by Am Mahmoud's stall without looking at him.

"Madame . . . madame!" I heard him call after me.

"You sold me a turkey," I snapped.

"Yes," he said. "Not a good joke? Turkeys are only for New Year."

"Good-bye." I shook my head and kept walking, hiding a smile—it was too funny not to laugh a little. Egyptians find it hilarious that westerners are so divorced from their food that they can't tell poultry apart; I had lived up to the stereotype with admirable ignorance. I stayed away from Am Mahmoud for several weeks, pointedly buying my chicken from another *fararghi*. The marketplace is a test of social intelligence—if you have been cheated or tricked, the very worst thing you can do is pretend nothing has happened. It sets a precedent: you are an idiot, and every good merchant knows that idiots are easily parted from their money. After a suitable amount of time had passed, I went back to Am

Mahmoud, who greeted me with new respect. He never sold me another turkey.

One morning, a group of about five American or Canadian tourists were walking through the souk as I was doing my morning shopping. They passed me as I stood in front of Am Mahmoud's stall with a bag of greens balanced on one hip, talking to his mother or aunt (I never discovered which) while my rooster was cleaned. When I looked up, I saw that the tourists were staring—not at the bloody progress of the rooster, but at me. It was clear they couldn't place me. That I was a westerner must have been obvious; there is nothing ambiguous about the color of my skin and the shape of my features. But I was dressed in a scarf and a long skirt and speaking Arabic, and shopping for my dinner while it was still alive. I blushed and stared back, unsure of what to do.

Am Mahmoud's relative reached out and took my hand in hers, pulling me back into the shadow of the corrugated metal overhang that protected the stall. At the same moment, Am Mahmoud himself, cleaning his hands with a cloth, stepped between me and the street, screening me from the view of the tourists. Since his back was to me I couldn't read the expression on his face—he said nothing. The tourists moved on.

The incident passed without comment. Am Mahmoud finished cleaning the rooster and his mother or aunt fussed with a plate of feed for the doves that sat in a wicker cage at her feet. As I walked home and mulled the scene over in my mind, I realized that my status in Egypt had changed. I was still a foreigner, but I was no longer *simply* a foreigner. The word *khawagga,* the term most often used to describe a westerner in Egypt, is dismissive, even a little derogatory. It isn't as neutral as *agnabi,* the classical word for *foreigner.* But its original use was far more complex. Until about fifty years ago, a *khawagga* was a naturalized Egyptian; an émigré, typically a member of Egypt's vanished Greek, Armenian, or Turkish minorities. A love song from the forties speaks wistfully of a "*khawagga* brought up in Cairo," whose long braids have captivated the heart of the singer. *Khawagga* in its intended sense was not an epithet but an origin, and I had passed from one kind of *khawagga* to another. Am Mahmoud had protected me from exposure and embarrassment as he would an Egyptian girl.

In the years to come, many an auntie or uncle or family friend would proudly call me "the old kind of *khawagga*" when impressed by my diligence in learning the language or correctly observing some very Egyptian custom of mourning or celebration. Coming back one day from an errand in the souk, Omar laughingly told me that a fruit vendor had asked him, "Is Sir the husband of *el khawagayya?*" Baffled, Omar gathered he could be speaking about no other foreigner—I was the only white woman he knew who shopped at the souk with any regularity—and said that he was. The market had passed a favorable judgment. I had become *el khawagayya,* the rough, nonspecific masculine of *khawagga* feminized and made particular.

Divisions and Lines

And God is on your side
dividing soldiers from the fishermen;
Watching all the time
dividing warships from the ferryboats.
—Wolfsheim, "The Sparrows and the
Nightingales"

DESPITE MY PROGRESS, I WAS ALWAYS CONSCIOUS OF BEING
an outsider. I assimilated Egyptian habits without ever feeling Egyptian. I dried mint and coriander in bundles at the kitchen window, and began to wear a long cotton galibayya around the house; I began, also, to understand the psychological difference between living in a foreign country temporarily and living in one indefinitely. Jhumpa Lahiri calls living in a foreign country "an eternal pregnancy"; an uncomfortable wait for something impossible to define. As the months passed, I realized how astute that observation was. My days fell into a pattern—I would get up, shop for the day's meal in the souk, then work on articles or research until midafternoon, when I prepared lunch and ate with Omar after he arrived from school. In the evenings I took Arabic lessons with Sameh or visited friends and relatives. Despite the routine, I had a constant feeling of anticipation—for what, I couldn't say; it vanished if I thought about

213

it too long. Looking back I think it was the expectation of normalcy. It remained just out of my reach, inevitably scuttled by a bewildering social situation, a mistake, an unexpected event or responsibility. While bartering for a taxi ride, a bargaining tactic I had been using for weeks would suddenly backfire and cause unintended offense to the driver; in company I would say something people found shocking or hilarious, and their kind reassurance only made me feel worse—more idiotic and clumsier, so maddeningly *foreign*.

Yet most of my friends and family were surprised when I admitted my frustration, and told me I was better integrated than they would have expected after such a short period of time. I thought, cynically, that I seemed well-integrated because most western expats and tourists in Egypt weren't integrated at all. Many lived in wealthy enclaves, spoke little or no Arabic, and sported shorts of a length no Egyptian would consider wearing in any kind of weather. In other words, they were guilty of the same failure to make basic cultural adjustments that immigrants in much more difficult circumstances were censured for in the West. It was not the hypocrisy that bothered me as much as the absence of reflection: the inability or refusal to compare their behavior to their standards. More and more, I avoided what few Americans, Canadians, and Britons I knew.

In doing so, I ran the risk of falling into a particular category of white converts: those who are ashamed of the lives they led before Islam, and who try to erase their pasts by flinging themselves headfirst into Arab or Pakistani culture. Because Al-Azhar University is headquartered in Cairo, the city plays host to a large cadre of converts with this sensibility. I sometimes saw them in line at the *duken* or coming out of the mosque: the women were veiled up to their eyelashes and the men sported unkempt, vaguely pubic beards. In lieu of Arabic, they adopted fake foreign accents in their English. Though they were all undoubtedly serious and dedicated Muslims, from the outside it seemed like they were playing an elaborate game of dress up, aping Arab ways without understanding or self-awareness. My anxiety about meeting other westerners stemmed from something very different from these converts' cultural amnesia. Sometimes I missed my own culture and my own country. There were moments when the wind shifted and smelled almost green, replacing the metallic desert air for a few hours, and when that happened I would almost collapse with homesickness. I wanted the company of other westerners, but what they inevitably became in Egypt was too alarming and embarrassing for me to watch.

People almost always arrived with the best intentions. They want to learn, to see behind the stereotypes they were presented with on television. They are willing, they think, to follow unfamiliar rules, though they can't really agree to a contract they've never seen. They come here and find that many of the stereotypes they don't want to believe are perfectly true: there is an uneasy segregation between men and women, and it does lead to animosity and dysfunction between the sexes. Women are stifled in the mosques and harassed in the streets by men reduced to the behavior of idiots by poverty and despair. Though Pew polls have determined Egyptians are the most religious people on earth, piety has not stopped endemic dishonesty in business dealings large and small. Egypt is an ugly, dirty, hungry place. It is easy to stop at this conclusion and decide there is nothing more.

The doors to the country's quieter and more human beauty are locked: Egyptian life revolves around the family, and if you don't have one, it's difficult to participate. Shut out and bewildered, cheated in the marketplace, alternately flattered and sneered at in the streets, too many of the westerners I knew turned to a variety of casual racism. No amount of education could withstand it. It manifested first in language: a refusal to speak Arabic. Simple enough, and easy to attribute to laziness, but there was something malicious and contradictory about it—the American or Brit or Canadian would order a shopkeeper around in English, assuming he understood, then insult him or joke about him, assuming he didn't. It was a pattern I saw repeated over and over again until I came to expect it; each time I was so shocked that I assumed there had to be some excuse, some mitigating reason.

One incident that stands out in my mind occurred in a taxi: I was headed to a café with a group of American students who were doing a year abroad at the American University of Cairo. The group was all girls, and after telling the taxi driver where to go (and observing that he would probably take the long way and ask for more money), they started talking about their sex lives, half-shouting to be heard over the deafening traffic. One complained that her Egyptian boyfriend, culled from one of the self-consciously westernized upper classes, wouldn't go down on her. With an arch sneer, another girl said that Egyptian boys were so sheltered and segregated that they had no idea what to do with a vagina. I leaned my forehead against the window, watching the passing cars shimmer in the heat, and said nothing. The driver, a bearded man in his forties or fifties, probably didn't understand the conversation in full, but in this age of the internet *vagina* is universally understood. He shook his head, muttering, "God forgive us all," over and over again. I couldn't look him in the eye. I faked my way through the chatter at the café and went home. I never saw the girls again.

After it conquered language, the racial ugliness sometimes degenerated into something much more frightening. For western men, this commonly meant abusing local women. At one of the few expat parties I ever attended, I heard a German engineer brag that he was solving the Darfur crisis by patronizing Sudanese prostitutes. Cairo was home to a large community of Sudanese refugees and many of the women were war widows and orphans without any source of income but their bodies. A couple of Americans who were listening—intelligent, sensitive, educated people—laughed, and turned around to repeat the joke to those who hadn't heard. At home, these were the sorts of 'liberals' who would rather drink ipecac than utter a racial slur. A few mosquito bites, a couple of unpleasant tour guides, and their principles had evaporated.

Most of my Egyptian friends and all of my Egyptian family lived lives far removed from the breaking point between locals and expats—I was the only westerner most of them were close to, and for a few of my younger and more sheltered cousins-in-law, the only westerner they had ever met. But occasionally someone I knew and cared about would bruise under the pressure of that bitterness, and when it occurred there was almost nothing I could do.

It happened to Sameh. Two Brits I knew, both converts, needed an Arabic tutor, so I gave them his number and a glowing recommendation. A week or so later, at one of our lessons, I asked him whether they had called.

"Yes." He paused, tapping the tabletop with the end of his pen.

"Are they going to start taking lessons? Did you work something out?"

"Yes," he said again. He didn't quite look at me. "They bargained with me," he went on, keeping his voice neutral. "They said I was asking for too much money."

My face felt hot. "God, I'm sorry," I said. "I didn't think they'd—I'm sorry." One of the trickiest things to learn in Egypt is when and when not to bargain, but one rule is clear: you don't bargain with friends. Bargaining implies dishonesty. In the marketplace, dishonesty is expected; there, bargaining is a test of both the seller's and the buyer's abilities as storytellers. The seller claims his scarves are pure silk and imported from India, and the buyer claims he has seen the same scarves in Attaba for half the price. By bargaining with Sameh, my British friends had snubbed him, implying he was from a lower social category than theirs, that he was a menial to inspect and suspect as they would a driver or a cleaning lady.

I was suddenly exhausted by all the things I couldn't say: I hadn't told them that Sameh had become a friend, that his unspoken sympathy and determination to see me succeed had helped propel me through hard times. But because I said nothing, they heard only "Arabic tutor," and treated him as they thought an Arabic tutor—an Arab tutor—must be treated in order to be kept honest.

"What did you say?" I asked Sameh. My distress must have been evident on my face, because he smiled.

"I let them. I gave them a ten percent discount."

"Why? You'll teach them bad habits! They shouldn't—"

"It's all right," he said. "Don't worry about it. Did you do your homework?"

We worked for forty-five minutes then broke for tea and biscuits, as was our custom. The heavy twilight air poured in through the garden door. In an apartment on one of the floors above, a parrot complained to itself.

"*Ana roht lilkaraoke night fi club fi wust el balad imberah,*" said Sameh. "*Wahid sahbi kan beyishrab, w'ana kunt zalen minu.*" ("I went to karaoke night at a club downtown last night. One of my friends was drinking, and I was upset with him.")

"Why?" I asked. "I thought you could drink."

"Who do you mean by *you?*"

"Copts."

"Oh, no. You can't talk to God when you're drunk. But some people drink anyway."

There was a knock at the outer door of the center, and a loud voice called for Ustez Sameh, Ustez being an honorific for teachers and superiors. Sameh caught my eye, telegraphing the need for silence. He left the room, closing the door behind him. I strained to listen but heard only murmurs; a few minutes later, I saw, out the garden door, a line of men's shoes retreating along the sidewalk, screened by the outer hedge of the garden. Sameh returned.

"I apologize," he said. "They are students of mine from the Delta—they come to Cairo on weekends for tutoring. They aren't used to being around young women. I didn't think they were ready to see you."

It was a mark of affectionate respect; something a brother would do to shield his sister from undignified staring or impolite advances. The more cherished a woman is, the more inaccessible she is made. I felt mingled appreciation and restlessness; I was so loved, so protected, and so cut off, bundled into the vacuum between East and West. It did not seem fair that this should be necessary, or that I should have to tell two educated Europeans to treat an educated Arab with respect. So much of life seemed to be about separating the people who would hurt each other.

Land of the Free

All mankind is divided into three classes:
those that are immoveable, those that are
moveable, and those that move.
                              —Benjamin Franklin

THAT SUMMER, I PREPARED TO FLY BACK TO THE UNITED
States to see my family. I had kept my promise to myself:
it was July, a full year since I had arrived in Egypt. If I could
stay put for one year, I could stay put for two, three, indefinitely. I could get on a plane confident that I would come
back. Assuming, of course, that my government let me.

I planned my trip around the premise that I would be
detained. FBI agents had been waiting for Ben at his port
of entry into the United States, so I made sure mine was
Denver. If I was going to be arrested, I wanted it to be within
sight of my mountains. The alternative—being rounded up
with the usual suspects at JFK International Airport in New
York—depressed me. I carefully organized all the documen-
tation of my trip to Iran: boarding passes, receipts, itineraries,
phone numbers. And I made up a call list. Every journalist
and public intellectual working in the Middle East has one:
a list of people for a trusted family member or friend to call
in the event he or she disappears. The people on this list
are usually the journalist's friends in the media or politics,

people who could focus enough attention on the disappeared to keep anything truly terrible from happening. People who could buy time.

I was barely enough of a journalist to deserve the name, and I was not going to some desolate backwater. It was depressing to have to make such a list before traveling to the U.S.A. *The U.S.A.* In fighting the Middle East we had become the Middle East, a place where people could be detained for writing letters, for speaking forbidden languages, for thought crimes. Omar and Ibrahim and Sohair were so used to living in a restrictive political environment that they weren't even fazed when I told them I was under investigation. They were surprised that I was so shaken. Surely I expected it? I was a convert and a liberal. Several of Sohair's siblings, my aunts- and uncles-in-law, had spent time under surveillance or even in jail for subscribing to forbidden ideas such as secular feminism or democratic change, or to antisecular religious beliefs. To them, the refuge and freedom I had taken for granted was a luxury. It was something they had never had, and never aspired to; in Egypt hoping for these things can shatter a person.

The day I left, Omar and I drove to the airport before dawn. Smog had not yet settled on the city for the day, and the horizon was pale, promising the lemon-colored sunlight for which Egypt is famous. When we got to the international terminal and unloaded my bags, Omar kissed me on the forehead.

"Call me when you get there?" he asked.

"Of course." I smiled at him.

"Call me every day after that?" He smiled, too, though his eyes belied how tense he was. He didn't mention the FBI, thinking it would be bad luck, but I knew he would go home and perform extra prayers for the safe arrival of his wife in her country.

Landing in Denver, I felt a surge of euphoria. It was partially fear, and the strange high that comes from arriving changed in a familiar landscape. I reminded myself I had nothing to hide, but even with that knowledge I couldn't shake the political instinct I had learned living in a dictatorship: sometimes that doesn't matter. Sometimes the people in power are less interested in catching the bad guys than they are in making examples of convenient targets, thereby frightening the bad guys into line. It's a strategy far more efficient than real justice. As I walked down the gangway, dusty and exhausted, lugging my laptop and a carry-on, I had a sense of déjà vu: I remembered standing at the threshold of the shrine of Fatima in Qom, looking suspicious for almost identical reasons, and asking to be let in. I was walking that same fine line between an ideal and trouble of an unbelievably serious kind.

I still don't quite understand what happened next. I stood in line at passport control with the rest of the passengers from my flight, lamenting the fact that I wasn't wearing any makeup; I didn't want to be hauled off looking sloppy and pale. As I stood there, a man in a camel-colored trench coat walked by, like some noir archetype, and without pausing took a picture of me with his cell phone. For a split second our eyes met and I wondered if I should say something.

But he turned away and continued briskly down the corridor. It was so bizarre I wondered if I had imagined it. I was still feeling dazed when my turn came at passport control. I handed my documents over to the man working at the booth in front of me. He ran my passport, looked at the computer screen, frowned, looked up at me, looked back at the computer screen, and said, "Whoa." I felt a stab of nausea: this was it. But the man simply asked me a series of questions about my residency in Egypt, stamped my passport, and let me through.

I was free.

I have never undergone such a sudden reversal of my politics: for that moment, and for many moments afterward, I didn't give a damn about my right to privacy. What I assume happened is this: some intelligence agency or other dug through my e-mail, sifted through my records, interrogated some of my friends (Ben, Ireland, and eventually Mehdi were all questioned by the FBI), listened to a few phone conversations, and decided I was not a threat. They did all this while I was still in the comfort of my own home and going about my daily life. I far, far preferred this arrangement to sitting at Gitmo, waiting for them to get a warrant for information I would gladly hand over myself. This is not to say that the Bush regime's invasive approach to security in America was right—it wasn't right, it wasn't ethical, and it wasn't worthy of a free nation—but it was preferable to something far worse, and staring that thing in the face, I didn't even think of quibbling about my privacy.

However, the incident that began with an overambitious snitch in Cairo would have a lasting, hurtful impact on the other innocent people it involved. Though he was never formally indicted on any charges, Mehdi would be put on an automatic search list, subjecting him to embarrassing extra security procedures every time he tried to fly—possibly for the rest of his life. Ben would have ongoing visa and tax problems. I was the only one who escaped unscathed. I would never know why. Ben raised red flags because he traveled back and forth from the Middle East on a teacher's salary, and Mehdi raised red flags because he was Muslim; I was both Muslim and traveled back and forth from the Middle East. Was it because I was so openly antiextremist? Because my husband was a Sufi, a Muslim minority known to be persecuted by extremists? It would remain a mystery. Ben occasionally talked about requesting the official records of our investigation but always hesitated—best to let sleeping dogs lie, he said. Maybe in a few years, when all this has calmed down. When the country is more like the one we grew up in again.

Maybe then.

Boulder had not changed—I love Boulder because it never changes. Its residents are absurdly proud of the city, though people who move there or visit from the coasts never understand why: it's small and insulated, uptown and downtown run into each other after just ten minutes of walking, and strangers greet each other in the street in a way that seems to make city dwellers claustrophobic. There are no buildings over five stories high. Almost everyone owns a dog. Small as it is, for the American interior Boulder is a triumph of urbanization: it's neither a boxy bleak suburb nor a farming community nor a tiny mining outpost—the three forms of settled life that dominate the rest of the Great Plains and the West. It's a real *town*, the kind that grew up as a frontier whistle-stop and settled into prosperous middle age. Lying in a cupped palm between the mountains and the high prairie, it felt enfolding and safe—it was home.

I spent three weeks regressing into adolescence—meeting old friends and going to old coffee shops, with no earthy potatoes to scrub and no fruit to sort through looking for the tiny holes that belied maggots. I told no one how exhausted I was, or how much it exhausted me to answer questions. I found it particularly hard to talk about Omar.

"What's he like?"

I was sitting in a café called the Trident, where I had practically lived during high school, talking to a couple I knew who had been dating on and off for several years. With a white ceramic mug of tea in front of me—one of the unnamable and indistinguishable teas in which Boulder specializes, made from herbs that turn bright yellow in hot water—and the same jazz CD that had been playing for ten years wafting from speakers in the corner, it felt almost as though I had never left.

"He's tall. Quiet. Quietly funny. Very smart, but not in a condescending way."

When I didn't go on, the male component of the couple, whose name was Josh, changed track. "What about Cairo? Do you go out? Are there things to do?"

"Sometimes. There are things to do, but they're a little bit different than the things to do here. There's less . . .

subculture, I guess. People are kind of expected to do and think and wear similar things. You mostly visit people's houses—sometimes you go to movies or concerts. But there's no going out as in bar crawling or clubbing or partying, unless you're from a very westernized social class. And even then, your responsibilities to other people are much greater than they are here, so there's way less room to fuck up."

"It sounds a little stifling."

"It is a little stifling."

"Are you happy?" He pursed his lips.

"Hmm. Yes, but it's a different kind of happiness than the kind we're taught to expect here."

"In what way?"

I had never articulated it before. "I think . . . there's a kind of sanity that comes from making most of your life about other people. You have less time to spend with your own neuroses. Even though there's an awful lot of bullshit to deal with, in some ways people in Egypt seem mentally healthier than people here. There's a greater willingness to—" I fought for the right words. "People are so comfortable with the word *love*. It's okay to tell your friends that you love them—friends of your own gender anyway—really passionately love them. It's not considered weird."

They took a moment to digest this. Josh's girlfriend, Katie, pursed her lips: it was an attitude I would encounter often, an earnest effort to comprehend a way of living that really had to be experienced to be understood.

"But I'm having trouble with—I don't know how to put this," she said. "You can't go out with guys?"

"No. Not without Omar or someone from his family."

"Can you go out by yourself?"

"You mean to a café or something? Yes, and I do sometimes—but it's unusual to see a woman sitting in a café by herself."

"But you can't be alone with a guy."

"God, no."

"And you can't, like, go out dancing."

"Nope."

"Or to parties on your own."

"It depends."

"I'm sorry, that's misogynist."

She was surprised when I laughed.

"Come on," I said, "you don't see what's wrong with that equation? There are only two genders here. Creating a rule for one necessarily creates the same rule for the other. You could just as easily have asked whether Omar could go out with another woman or be alone with her, and I would have given you the same answer: no. When he wants to see his female friends, he has to bring me. What? You thought there was some mysterious pool of women who are somehow exempt from the rules, and who appear out of nowhere to run around with guys for the sole purpose of creating a double standard? If girls can't go out alone with guys, who's left for the guys to break the rules with?"

"So guys can't have serious girlfriends and stuff?"

"Not openly, not in the middle classes. It would make the whole family look bad—like they'd raised an irresponsible, irreligious son who isn't a good candidate for marriage. The families of girls can be really, really picky about the social history of any guy their daughter might marry."

"So there isn't a double standard." Josh leaned forward, interested.

"Oh, no, there is a double standard, but only because girls have hymens. If there was a way to check for male virginity, trust me, religious people would do it. Guys are expected to follow the same rules—it's just anatomically easier for them to get away with breaking them."

"But who are they breaking them with, if girls can't be alone with guys?" Katie had followed my logic with admirable precision.

"Who do you think?" I asked. "The kind of girls who charge by the hour."

"Is there a lot of that?"

"As I understand it, there's less now that the fundies are on the rise. A couple can't get a hotel room together unless they can prove they're married. If I had to guess, I'd say most guys have only had a few—experiences—before they get married, and a lot are probably honest-to-God virgins."

"Do you and Omar talk about—" Katie flushed, looking for my reaction to the question she was about to ask. "What—went on—before you were married?"

"No." I did not elaborate or invite elaboration.

It would be years before I could have what I would call a normal conversation—that is, one that wasn't half composed of dancing on cultural razor blades—with most of my friends from home. Most of the time, I was forced to adopt either an analytical attitude or a cavalier one about my new life. There seemed no other way to communicate; the molds for westerners who go abroad were cast long ago. If I was anthropological about my life in Egypt, I could break things down into easily digestible bites, none of which were ever the whole truth. If I was not the anthropologist, I could be the wayfarer in search of a spiritual homeland in the East— which was how many people cast my conversion. This seemed yet more dishonest. I didn't believe in spiritual homelands, and found God as readily in a strip mall as in a mosque. My faith did not require beauty or belonging—the deeper I went into my practice, the less it required at all.

The reason I had stayed in Egypt and invested myself in it so thoroughly was simple: this was the place I found myself in and the people I found myself among, and I wanted to do right by them. I had gone to Egypt to see what Islam was like as a practice and to find out whether the Arab world resembled the one portrayed in the media; I had stayed not to see, but to participate. I had discovered that both Islam and the Arab world were far from ideal—that the religion I loved was becoming steadily warped and was the source of many excuses for violence and ignorance and misanthropy. Yet I was not disappointed. This was what was so impossible to explain to the satisfaction of the people back home: I was not disappointed.

I doubt I could have explained why, at that point. The events of my recent life were too crowded together for me to digest them. My concern was not what had happened to me, but what would: what I needed to do next and who I needed to win over next in order to keep my fragile bicontinental existence viable. I didn't stop to wonder why the howling and snarling of the fundamentalists, who woke me at five a.m. every morning, and who were forcing us all to live in smaller and smaller boxes, had not turned me off Islam. I was familiar with the apostasy industry: the Ayaan Hirsi Alis and Wafaa Sultans who had made their fortunes by rejecting Islam. In her book *The Trouble with Islam*, Irshad Manji smugly announces that after similar run-ins with extremists, it "was Islam's job" to keep her from leaving the faith. I never thought it was Islam's job to keep me. My faith was not a contract, not a deal; there were no clauses I expected God to abide by and which, if violated, would give me an excuse to back out. Irving Karchmar, a Sufi convert and friend, and the author of the novel *Master of the Jinn*, said it best: at some point, the devoted pass from belief into certainty. I passed into certainty very early. Though I couldn't articulate it then, it was certainty that animated me; it was certainty that allowed me to watch the progress of the extremists and feel anger and disgust, but never disappointment. It was not my place to be approving or disappointed: I had submitted too completely for either. Through the bile and ignorance of the radical imams and self-righteous apostates, through the spin of the news networks and the pomposity of academics, I saw a straight, unwavering line. How could I be disappointed? I did not believe in Islam; I opened my eyes every morning and *saw* it.

I had a hard time communicating this to my friends, and I hesitated to even open the subject with my family. Eventually I would meet other Muslims, as well as Christians and Jews, who had gone through something similar and knew what it was to be astonished by faith. It's a word that makes many people uneasy and embarrassed; like sex, we talk about it as if it performs some efficient, necessary but un-mentionable function, and is somehow self-contained, af-fecting only a small part of daily life. But faith is in reality none of those things. I couldn't explain what it was to kneel to the inexplicable and feel not debased but elevated, in more complete possession of myself than I had ever been. I reminded myself that a few years ago these were not things I would have wanted to hear from a friend, that hearing them would have frightened me. When questioned as to why—why on *Earth*—I was not disappointed by the faith I had chosen, I only shook my head, barely understanding the answer myself.

I spent a lot of time with Jo, around whom I felt I made sense. It had been less than two months since she left Cairo. I modeled for her as she patterned and pinned my wedding dress. In the evenings I sat over long dinners with my par-ents. On some days I could almost pretend nothing had happened—that lurking in the shadows was some other life, lived happily and unremarkably in some American city, in an apartment rented with a couple of friends. Part of me wanted that life, whatever it was. The familiarity of Ameri-can soil was like a physical tonic.

The day of my flight back to Egypt came more quickly than I was prepared for. As I got into the car to go to the airport, I had to press my teeth together to keep from cry-ing. I realized I had never really thought about love. Some unspoken part of me always assumed the Disney version of love was the truth, that falling in love removed all obstacles and patched up all broken things. Leaving my family be-hind, all of whom wore brave, anxious faces, I knew I was wrong. Love is not a benign thing. No corner of my life remained unaltered by the consequences of what I loved. The most wonderful thing that had ever happened to me brought me neither peace nor comfort. But it did bring me Omar. And that was more than enough.

Nile Wedding

And the void weighs on us; and then we
  wake,
And hear the fruitful stream lapsing along
Twixt villages, and think how we shall take
Our own calm journey on for human sake.
—James Henry Leigh Hunt, "A Thought
of the Nile"

"WILLOW? GOD HELP US, IT'S *RAINING*—"

I sat up in bed, still half-dreaming, and tried to gather my thoughts.

"It can't be raining," I said.

"Look outside!" The voice on the other end of the telephone belonged to Nevine, our wedding planner. She was right: a chill was in the air and the sky beyond our salmon-colored shutters was a dark brooding color. The rose bush in the garden below danced under a stream of fat raindrops. It was my wedding day, and in one of the driest cities on earth, it was raining.

"Listen, I've ordered a bigger tent," said Nevine. "A third again as big as the old one."

"So everything is okay?" But Nevine had turned away from the phone to speak hurriedly to someone whose voice I couldn't hear. I lifted my free hand to my face and breathed the herbal scent of henna and eucalyptus: my palms and feet were covered in flowers, stars, and peacocks, all meticulously drawn in heavy red-brown dye. Though Sohair had arranged a traditional Sudanese henna artist for the rest of the bridal party, it was Jo who had painted my hands and feet, in what might have been the most ambitious henna design project ever undertaken by a westerner.

There was a muffled scrape as Nevine returned to the phone. "God willing, everything will be fine," she said.

"It's raining." Omar, half-shaven, stuck his head in the door, looking worried. I rubbed my forehead.

"Okay," I said. "Okay."

It was my idea to have an outdoor ceremony. I wanted something airy and colorful. *Ceremony* is perhaps the wrong word; Islamic marriage is a social contract rather than a sacrament, so a Muslim wedding is really a party, the purpose of which is to announce a couple's marriage to the public. There are no specific rituals as such, but over the years Egyptians have adopted many western customs, including elaborate wedding cakes, white wedding dresses, and even wedding singers. Rather than catering to two sets of traditions, Omar and I decided to ignore them both. Instead of white tulle, my wedding dress was blue-gray silk; Jo and my mother had hand stitched the entire garment, working from a design Jo created using a medieval Persian court dress as a template. A Japanese neighbor of my parents who had experience packing kimonos had undertaken the delicate task of folding and wrapping the dress to prepare it for its transcontinental flight from Denver to Cairo. The life of that dress, like my own, was the work of many hands.

For a venue, Omar and I chose the sloping, palm-lined garden of Villa Androws, a dignified old mansion on the west bank of the Nile, a mile or two upstream from Maadi. The garden ended in mossy stone steps leading straight into the river and could be approached by boat. It was an enchanting place, one of the last remnants of a very different Egypt, a country that was prosperous and secure enough to cultivate imagination. "My lost world," Omar said with a smile when we first visited the garden. It had been sunset, the only time of day when Cairo seems forgiving, and gives her inhabitants short glimpses of another destiny. Nevine had watched us anxiously for our reaction, playing with the Coptic cross that hung around her neck.

"*Wallahi gamila,*" Omar told her. *Really, it's beautiful.* She smiled, relieved.

"Yes," she said. "I save this place for couples who want something different, something special."

Together with Nevine, Sohair and I planned flowers, tables, and lights for an open-air celebration, assuming with total confidence that the weather would be good. In a wet year, Cairo gets half a dozen days of rain, always in late winter and spring. Outside of Alexandria, I have never met an Egyptian who owns an umbrella. After coordinating guests and clothing across nine time zones and three continents, all we wanted was an uneventful wedding day. The City Victorious had other plans.

The phone rang again as Omar and I rushed back and forth across our tiny apartment getting dressed. This time it was Ben, who sounded even more frantic than Nevine.

"They won't let us leave," he said, "so you guys stay put for now. We have to convince—"

"What do you mean *they won't let us leave?* Who's *they?*" A feeling like pins and needles ran up my neck and across my scalp. Nineteen Americans—plus one Frenchman, the fiancé of one of my college friends—were due to travel to the Villa Androws together in a minibus we reserved for the occasion. The driver was scheduled to pick them up at the hotel where most of our international guests were staying.

"The military police," said Ben. "They're saying we can't leave without a police escort."

My mouth went dry. It was a common scenario: Egypt is a police state, and over the course of recent decades its henchmen have decided that the greatest obstacle to their power is the very people they are meant to govern and protect. When a large group of tourists decides to mix freely with ordinary Egyptians the state panics. Escorts are ordered, cordons are put in place, everything possible is done to shield the foreign money from a population hated by its own government. I had slipped the net. There were no other foreigners in the circles I moved within, and since I spoke Arabic (not well, at that point, but passably), I had remained remarkably unmolested by what one journalist termed Big Nanny. So unmolested, in fact, that I had forgotten about it, and failed to plan for state intervention in my wedding.

"What is it?" Omar looked at me, the muscles tense in his jaw.

"They're not going to let the Americans leave," I said, and realized with horror that I was going to cry. "They want to send soldiers."

Omar began to curse in Arabic.

"We're working on it," Ben said on the phone. "I'll call you back."

The scene that followed is confused in my memory. Omar and I paced back and forth across the room, then sat silently, absurdly, as if we were actors dressed for some glittering play. I said several nasty things about Egypt; Omar, rather than arguing with me, listened with a kind of grim despair. No matter how hard we tried to patch over the gulf between us, it kept opening up, in ways and at times we couldn't predict. It was never going to get easier. That was the fatal truth. But when Omar got up without speaking and pulled me into his arms, I knew I had found something that meant more to me than security, and so had he.

The phone rang again. "Good news," said Ben, "we're leaving now. Your dad threatened to call the embassy, and your mom yelled, but it was your friend Saraa who finally cracked them. I don't know what she said, but it worked. She saved the day."

Saraa is a poet, quiet and lovely and sad. It was only by chance that she happened to be at the hotel with the international guests; she didn't have a ride to the wedding and had asked to take an extra seat on the minibus. Always prudent and graceful, she never told me what she said to the security officials that made them back down. I never prodded her about it. By then, having gotten into dozens of conversations that shocked and frustrated me, I'd learned not to ask for information that was not volunteered. In the moment, I was simply thankful.

"Okay," I said to Ben, "better run before they change their minds."

"Totally. Hey," his voice changed, "smile, okay? It's your wedding. Everything is going to be fine. Look outside."

The rain had stopped. The sky was still gray, but the clouds were high and thin, and I held out hope that we would at least stay dry.

"That's the driver," said Omar on his cell phone. He looked, if possible, more relieved than I felt. "Are you ready? Let's go."

The image of my wedding that stands out in my mind is this: Omar and I are crossing the Nile by sailboat toward a garden, in which stands a billowing white tent. Looking out, the water is the color of slate; looking down, it's the color of tea. All along the edge of the garden stand people I know: my family and my friends, wearing party dresses and suits and galibayyas and veils, pale-skinned and olive-skinned, copper-skinned and dark. My mother stands between Ben and Ibrahim looking anxiously at the water; she holds Ben's arm, and though I can't tell from far away, I later learn that she was worried the rocking of the boat would pitch us into the river. Ben reassures her and leans over to say something to Ibrahim, who laughs. When we reach the stone steps that lead out of the water, Ibrahim will take one of my favorite photographs: in it, I am stepping out of a peeling turquoise boat, framed by an embroidered veil, and a disembodied hand—Omar's—helps me to shore. It captures the energy of that final moment between uncertainty and solid ground.

The rest of the wedding was a pleasant blur. Everyone danced. I remember smiling at the sight of my grandmother's henna-painted ankles. My sister looked radiant in a lavender silk dress, borrowed for the occasion from a Syrian-Dutch friend. Over the course of the next few weeks I would get several offers for her hand in marriage, all of which she turned down with polite good humor. At one point I spotted Sameh in the crowd, smiling in an impeccable dark suit. I waved and he made his way toward me.

"You came," I said.

"I had to come." He paused. "You are not just my student. You are my friend."

I bit my lip. Then, on impulse, I reached out with my right hand: he grinned and shook it. It was the first and only time we would ever touch.

I heard cheering and turned: a group of Omar's cousins was gathered together with interlocking arms, collectively tossing Omar up into the air. He laughed, boots and vest askew, as he came back down, was caught, was hurled into the air again.

When the invitations to my wedding were sent out, I only expected a small handful of American friends and family to make the long and unpredictable trip to Cairo. Twenty showed up. Ben came with his family; Jo with her father; my parents, sister, and maternal grandparents came; and six or seven friends from high school and college, one of whom was a fire spinner and put on a show when the sun set. The regional director of the Red Cross, a famous Cairo University linguist, and several luminaries of the Egyptian left came at Sohair's invitation, along with a hundred aunts and uncles and cousins and second cousins from both sides of Omar's family. Omar's musician friends—Mohammad and his brother Mostafa, the blind virtuosos; and several others —brought their instruments and played for us. The result was that our wedding, originally intended to be a small private gathering, was a society event, and kept our wedding planner in business for a long time. For a party that almost didn't happen, it was a triumph: one of the rare moments when things that should logically go wrong go right instead, and better worlds become possible.

An Appointment

Follow those who ask of you no fee.

—Quran 36:21

AFTER MY INTERVIEW WITH THE MUFTI I HAD WRITTEN AN essay that I wanted to try to publish abroad. Egyptian media was saturated with his often controversial rulings, but outside the Muslim world he was virtually unknown. I sent a copy of the essay to the mufti's office first, as a courtesy, so he could verify that I'd quoted him correctly. I was told his daughter translated the essay, and was impressed enough to tell her father it was a good read. A few weeks later, at a family gathering in Doqqi, Uncle Ahmad pulled Omar and me aside.

"The mufti liked the essay you wrote," he said. "He has more time this Saturday to answer your questions."

I blinked. "I'm flattered he liked the essay," I said, "but I don't have any other questions prepared. Please thank him for the offer—"

Uncle Ahmad looked at Omar, who looked at me.

"You don't understand," said Uncle Ahmad with a firm but patient smile, "the mufti would like to see you. This Saturday. At eleven a.m."

In the Middle East, opportunity sometimes comes as a command. "Of course," I said. "I would be honored."

242

At that point, none of the high-ranking sheikhs at Al-Azhar, nor any of the leaders of the various Sufi paths, nor even the more fashionable Muslim televangelists were really on the radar of the western media. There were several reasons for this: first, Azhari and Sufi sheikhs are very selective about which journalists they speak to, and about what. By and large, western journalists are seen by the Arab Sunni establishment as ignorant and exploitative, reporting only the most sensational stories and ignoring the difficult work the moderate opposition does to hold back the tide of Islamic extremism.

This view is not without merit: in the years since 9/11 there have been repeated calls by western pundits for the Muslim opposition to step forward; after total silence in the western press, these pundits smugly concluded there is no Muslim opposition to speak of. Though Sufis have taken up arms against extremists in Iran and Pakistan, though bumper stickers pasted on the walls of Cairene shrines refute militant Wahhabi doctrine, the western press has chosen to turn a blind eye. Determined Islamophobes often claim that no fatwas have been issued against terrorism in response to the fatwas that call for it—this is blatantly false. Dozens of fatwas against terrorism have been issued since 9/11, many by high-ranking clerics. The silence of the press with regard to positive gains made by moderate Muslims has enabled damaging misconceptions about the religion and its leaders. Because of this endemic misrepresentation, sheikhs from across the political and sectarian spectrum turned press shy, granting few personal interviews with western reporters.

The second reason has to do with access: it's difficult for all but the most dedicated western journalists to figure out ways to approach sheikhs and *sheikhas* in the first place. Non-Muslims can only enter certain mosques, and only at certain times. Outside of organized colleges like Azhar, most sheikhs don't have Web sites or hold office hours. In today's sectarian environment, Sufi sheikhs can be very reclusive, and their contact with the curious and the press is often screened by protective lieutenants and followers. It's easy for stories about the inner workings of the Muslim establishment to be stymied by suspicion on the part of the clerics and exasperation on the part of the reporters, resulting in more bad blood on both sides.

I prepared for my second interview with the mufti feeling more than a little nervous. I wasn't sure what I would do with the result, but I knew I must do something. Clerics of the mufti's importance and authority did not hand out personal interviews every day. I wrote and discarded question after question. I finally settled on a theme: dissecting the fatwa, that much-maligned Islamic legal tool, for a western audience. When the day of the interview came, I dressed conservatively and with care: a floor-length black skirt and a black tunic, with slim black sandals. As Omar and I were leaving I reached for a black silk veil, then hesitated, reached out, and took one that was deep red.

When we reached the mufti's office at Dar al Iftah, the section of Al-Azhar responsible for answering requests for fatwas, Omar and I were shown straight into Sheikh Ali's office. He sat behind a large wooden desk and smiled when we came in. After glancing at his face—the striking Turkish-

Mongolian features only a little hardened by six months in a demanding office—I dropped my eyes and murmured my *as-salaamu alaykum*, leaving Omar to make a more extensive greeting.

"Come sit here, my daughter," said the mufti. More at ease, I looked up and smiled. Omar and I took the chairs drawn up in front of his desk. Eyes twinkling in an otherwise serious expression, Sheikh Ali offered me a chocolate from a bowl sitting at his elbow.

"*Shofti el film* El Samurai il Akheer?" he asked, speaking slowly in colloquial Egyptian for my benefit. Have you seen the movie *The Last Samurai?*

Charmed, I laughed. "Yes," I said, "I liked it very much."

His smile held just a hint of bitterness. "I am the last sheikh," he said. Humorous though it was, there was some truth to the metaphor: Sheikh Ali was the champion of unpopular—some would say lost—causes. He preached reconciliation between Sunnis and Shi'ites, spoke against face veiling, and fought for room to admit the secular demands of modern life into orthodox Islam. In many ways, he was one of the few Sunni religious authorities who could fill this role—his credibility was unassailable, even among his enemies. Though he would come to be loathed by the fundamentalists, I would never hear an unflattering rumor or a hint of scandal about him. Yet despite his potential as a leader in the moderate bloc, I knew, even then, that he was too conservative to appeal to the West, every sheikh's looming second constituency.

"Now," said Sheikh Ali, folding his hands, "what would you like to talk about?"

The mufti was an eloquent speaker. His answers to my questions were never less than the questions deserved, and he seemed to intuitively understand the difference between addressing a Muslim audience, for whom legalism is a way of life, and a non-Muslim audience, to whom the modern Muslim obsession with rules must seem bizarre and counterintuitive.

"A fatwa is a statement clarifying the position of Shari'a law regarding a particular human act, whether that act has to do with ritual—something between a person and God—or social, political, or economic dealings between human beings," said Sheikh Ali. "It can include family, state, and international relations. Fatwa follows certain criteria taken from the Quran and Sunnah: no one should pay for someone else's deeds, because the theory of inherited sin is not present in Islam. Actions must be judged by their intentions and goals, so the intention of the action in question must be good, and must be for God. In addition, suspicion is not a substitute for certainty. This is one of the foundations of straight thinking."

As Omar translated, this in particular impressed me. Islamic law stipulates that in order for someone to be convicted of adultery, four people must have been witness to the act of adultery itself—a caveat meant to make it nearly impossible for the state to interfere in the private lives of its citizens. The mufti's statement was a reprimand to the moral policing that resulted in scandals and honor killings based on suspicion and rumor.

"Also, when crafting a fatwa one must remember that God forgives those who repent—He does not want them to live with eternal guilt," the mufti went on. "Shari'a aims to protect human dignity and human rights within the context of humanity's social rituals and its stewardship of the Earth. Islam forbids tyranny, prostitution, suicide, drug abuse— anything that treats a human being as an object. A fatwa is determined under all these rules and goals, so that human beings can live more happily, safely, and peacefully."

Women

If I cannot liberate myself, then no one
from outside can liberate me.
—Orzala Ashraf, board member
for Afghan Women's Network

THOUGH MY WORK FOR *CAIRO MAGAZINE* AND OTHER PUBLI-
cations was increasingly important to me, most of the time
I felt like an unusually intellectual housewife. The work
I loved most was being Omar's spouse, and by extension
a member of our family. As the months passed, I came
to understand the group mind that develops when a large
number of people are interdependent. When I ran out of
milk, Ibrahim would appear with a fresh half gallon before
I could even ask; on the birthday of an uncle I would spend
hours in the kitchen helping my cousins-in-law bake cakes.
Determined not to be a fragile foreigner, I learned to do
many more things than wives of my generation were expected to know—like their counterparts in the West, young
Arab women were becoming less preoccupied with setting
a good table and more focused on their careers. Nevertheless, family was still synonymous with civilization in Egypt.
People lived for feast days, weddings, and birth celebra-
tions. The poorest relative would scrape together money to
give a cousin a wedding gift, or buy a gold medallion for a

newborn niece. As difficult as life was, Egyptians were never too cynical to celebrate it.

Henna parties, open only to women, were the events I most looked forward to. The night before her wedding, the family and girlfriends of a bride-to-be gathered at her house to dance and eat sweets until dawn, donning clingy dresses they would never consider wearing in public. I would emerge from one of these parties half deaf, exhausted from dancing, and practically diabetic with sugar shock, hands and feet covered in henna designs. The bride, always flushed with triumph, was a symbol of fruition, poised on the brink of social and sexual independence. Unmarried girls looked up to her in adoration, while married women gave her frank advice. It was a celebration I had seen nowhere else: part rave, part fertility festival, part crash course in sex education.

"It's so nice to get rid of the men for one night!" said an aunt at a henna party for one of Omar's maternal cousins. "They're sleeping at the mosque, poor darlings. I told them they couldn't come back until after the dawn prayer."

I grinned. "They're the lucky ones," I said. "They'll have energy at the wedding tomorrow. We'll all be asleep in our chairs."

She laughed and patted my hand. "You miss Omar, of course," she said with a wicked smile. "And he misses you. You're still a bride and groom."

"It's only for one evening," I protested, blushing. "We'll survive."

"He dies in her!" said one of the other aunts, carrying a plate of food. "It's so romantic." In colloquial Egyptian, to die in someone is to love her so intensely that the feeling consumes you.

"Of course he does," said the first aunt, pinching my chin. "She's a moon."

I hid my face in my hands, squirming under so many extravagant compliments, and both aunts laughed.

"Go dance!" said the second. "Omar will think badly of us if we don't teach you how to dance."

I got up and let one of the littlest cousins tie a bell-covered scarf around my hips, feeling lucky to be alive at this moment among these people. It was such a tantalizing contradiction, being a woman in the Middle East—far less free than a woman in the West, but far more appreciated. When people wonder why Arab women defend their culture, they focus on the way women who don't follow the rules are punished, and fail to consider the way women who do follow the rules are rewarded. When I finished an article or essay, all I received was an e-mail from an editor saying, "Thanks, got it." When I cooked an *iftar* meal during Ramadan, a dozen tender voices blessed my hands.

"Why aren't women allowed to lead men in prayer?" I asked Omar one day as he sat on the couch reading Ibn Arabi. He closed the book over his index finger to keep his place and slid over to make room for me. I felt a surge of affection; he never dismissed or belittled my questions, and when I asked them, they took precedence over whatever else he was doing.

"Women are the manifestation of God's beauty, which on Earth is veiled from men's eyes," he said. "So to put women on display in front of men is unworthy."

"That's a Sufi answer," I said with a smile.

"I am a Sufi," he said, smiling back at me. "But it's the truth."

In recent weeks, I had gone looking for other Islams. By now I was comfortable enough in my own faith to be curious about different interpretations. Though I was a westerner and a Muslim, I wasn't quite a western Muslim; my religious ideas and practices were products of North Africa. Using the internet, I started to read about Islamic movements in the West, hoping for a clearer picture of Muslim life in my own culture. That was how I discovered the Progressives. They were a group of American Muslims dedicated to reform, bringing the practice of Islam into line with its original humanitarian vision. One of their main goals was gender equality in the mosque, the linchpin of which was a campaign to allow female imams to lead mixed-gender prayers.

As precedent, the Progressives cited the story of Umm Waraqah, a matriarch from the time of the Prophet Muhammad who was given permission to lead both men and women in prayer. However, with this exception, all four schools of Sunni jurisprudence held that women should only lead congregations of other women, not of women and men. The reasons why were a contradictory mishmash of man's earthly superiority and his sexual weakness; he was more fit to lead, yet he could be undone by the sight of a woman

bending over in front of him. Having no desire to lead con-
gregational prayer myself, the issue had never bothered me,
but the opposition to the Progressives' argument was so
pathetic that I had to say something.

"What about Umm Waraqah?" I asked Omar. "They're
saying she set a precedent for women leading men."

Omar sighed. "Umm Waraqah was a very old woman
when that decision was made," he said. "And the story
only says she led her *dar*—her own house. Younger men
and boys, who were all related to her. It was a specific
situation."

"If she was only leading men in her house," I said,
pulling out the linchpin of the Progressives' argument,
"why did the Prophet assign her a muezzin?" A muezzin
is the person who gives the call to prayer—something you
wouldn't need if the people gathering to pray lived in the
same house. Traditionally, one muezzin serves an entire
district.

Omar looked at me more closely. This kind of reason-
ing was somewhat alien to Islamic jurisprudence, which fa-
vored the inductive over the deductive.

"That," he said, "is an interesting question."

"Besides," I continued, "*dar* doesn't always mean *house*.
Dar es-salaam is Heaven, which is far more than a house.
And *dar el-harb* is realm of war, not house of war."

Omar drummed his fingers on the carved wooden arm
of the couch. "Your Arabic is getting better. Sameh is a
good teacher." He looked like he was considering his next
words. "I know there are things that are hard for you to
understand," he said, "but be a little careful about whose

authority you trust. Plenty of people talk without anything to say, and without understanding."

"I know." I squeezed his hand. "I'll be careful."

Early that March, when the weather in Cairo was yellow with sandstorms, the Progressives in New York held a Friday prayer led by a female scholar, Dr. Amina Wadud. There was a chorus of praise from western observers and a mixture of bemusement and alarm from the Muslim world. Savvy by now from years of fallout over the Salman Rushdie death fatwa, many conservative leaders instructed their followers to leave the Progressives alone. "We know that the enemies of Islam have many tactics they use in trying to get a misdirected and emotional response out of the Muslims," was the remark of Sheikh Abdullah bin Hamid Ali, a member of the Zaytuna Institute. "And perhaps they do that in order to produce a situation where they can justify taking action against those they label as extremists, radicals, terrorists, and fundamentalists. I think that if people want to make up their own religion, let them do as they like. We just ask them to give us a little respect." It was an opinion repeated in orthodox circles across the globe, along with the surprisingly canny pronouncement that the prayer was a publicity stunt and would not result in any real change. Conservatives were getting smarter about media.

"Except for the usual trickle of sociopaths, it looks like this is going to be a pretty civil scandal," I told Omar, reading over reactions as they came in, "I'm impressed."

"Actually," said Omar with a little smile, "I was going to tell you that the mufti was just on TV. He's supporting the prayer."

I stared at him.

"He is? Is he still on? What did he say?"

"He didn't say that it's necessarily a good thing for women to lead prayer," Omar explained, "because to let an unqualified woman lead prayer simply to make a statement about women leading prayer is wrong."

"Right. Tokenism."

"But he said it was a matter for debate—that there is no scholarly consensus that women should not lead prayer. He says it's for each congregation to decide for itself."

It was by far the highest level of support the Progressives would get for their agenda. I spent the day glued to Arab news channels and MuslimWakeup!, the flagship Progressive Muslim Web site, waiting to see if there would be any more discussion of Gomaa's endorsement. I was shocked at what I saw.

"Why do we need approval from some guy in a beard on the other side of the world?" someone commented on the MWU! article about Gomaa.

"Who cares what the mullahs think?"

"I'm surprised that this is even posted here—these people are not our friends."

"MWU! is publicizing the endorsement of a man who supports terrorism."

I couldn't believe what I was reading. If this was progress, Islam was in trouble. Gomaa had never supported terrorism; I could only assume the anonymous commenter thought all clerics in beards and turbans were violent. It was disturbing to see such suspicion and self-hatred. Gomaa had gone out on a limb—it was unlikely he would receive support for his ruling from the rest of the Sunni establishment, and if he didn't get it from the West, where he was undoubtedly expecting it, he might be forced into a retraction.

"They're out of their *minds*," I said to Omar that evening. "They've been offered an olive branch from the traditionalists and they don't give a damn."

"Why does it matter to you so much? You've never even met these people."

I struggled with an answer. For so long there had seemed to be no overlap between my history and my religion—when I was in Egypt I had to translate my past, make it digestible and comprehensible and safe to other Muslims, and when I was in the United States I had to do the same thing to my beliefs. Here were people refusing to translate. They were westerners and Muslims in one fluid identity, and they felt no need to apologize or explain themselves. I didn't want to admit how burdened I felt by my conciliatory instincts. The contempt I felt for converts who turned their backs on their own people arose in part out of jealousy; I wished I could simply shrug people off as soon as loving them made my life difficult, as they did. It would be easier if I could simply choose one camp or the other. The Progressives allowed me to hope I wouldn't have to. That was why it gave me so much pain to see this opportunity slip away.

Sure enough, by the next morning Al-Azhar had issued a statement opposing the mufti's endorsement of the Wadud prayer—a highly unusual move in an organization that usually took pains to present a unified front. Gomaa would spend the next year covering his right flank, catering to conservatives with a series of fatwas that baffled western observers. A great moment had passed by, mishandled on all sides.

The Fourth Estate

When the people cast their votes
we can all go home and cut our throats.
     —Irving Berlin, "The Honorable
     Profession of the Fourth Estate"

IN 2005, UNDER PRESSURE FROM THE UNITED STATES, PRESI-
dent Mubarak called for an election. For the first time since
he was thrust into power by the assassination of Anwar
El Sadat, Mubarak allowed serious candidates from parties other than his own to run against him—a move that
inspired the City Victorious to breathless political optimism and heavy rioting for many months. The Ikhwan al
Muslimeen—known in the West as the Muslim Brotherhood—were still barred from politics, but ran dozens of par-
liamentary candidates as independents. In the presidential
race, one serious contender emerged: Ayman Nour, a young
progressive who formed a party he named Al Ghad, or Tomorrow. Nour's platform appealed to a wide cross section
of Egyptians: he was religious enough to be popular with
the young, but had political savvy that appealed to their socialist parents. He stressed freedom of speech, assembly and
the press, and talked of new infrastructure; from the very beginning it was clear he was a doomed man. Nevertheless, his
dedicated supporters demonstrated over and over again in

downtown neighborhoods, clashing with hired National Democratic Party thugs and rival parties. Cairo stepped out from its behind-the-scenes role as the site of negotiations and summits to become, for a short while, the center of international attention.

"Here's one from the board," said Richard, the *Cairo Magazine* culture editor, at a meeting one evening in early April. "State media coverage of the political demonstrations that've been going on downtown." He tapped the spot on the crowded assignment board where it was scribbled in. "As you've probably all noticed, there hasn't been much to speak of. This would mean talking to some of the higher-ups in the Egyptian Radio and Television Union about their election coverage policies. I'm not touching it. Who wants it?"

"I'll do it," I said. "I wouldn't mind some excitement."

"Good. Here." Richard handed me a list of contacts. "Off you go."

Several days later I found myself at the beginnings of a demonstration in Tahrir Square. Over a hundred black-clad riot police lined the traffic-choked space between the Egyptian Museum and the American University, acting as a human perimeter to contain the mayhem. State media outlets were claiming the protest was organized by the Muslim Brotherhood, and refused to cover the event on the grounds that the Ikhwan were an illegal party. The protest was so chaotic that it was difficult to make heads or tails of its ideology. It was not uncommon for women to be groped and molested at these demonstrations, so I stayed along the outer edge, away from the oppressive mass at the center of the square. After half an hour I gave up: there was so much infighting that determining the original intent of the protest was impossible. I left and took the metro home, overheated and frustrated.

The Cairo metro is divided into two sections: mixed cars in which both men and women can travel, and the women's car, in which men are not allowed. In the women's car, which seemed to exist in a feminine vacuum untroubled by the turmoil in the streets above, I spotted a familiar heart-shaped face encircled by a head scarf: it was the daughter of my upstairs neighbor, a girl a year or two younger than I was. She waved and came over to give me a kiss.

"What are you doing here in the middle of the day?" she asked in Arabic.

I hesitated. It was rare that I covered something so controversial, and when I did I was discreet about sharing details with Omar's family and our friends. The prevalent opinion in the world we inhabited was that a woman did not, strictly speaking, have the right to put herself in potential social, political, or physical danger.

"Covering the protest," I said finally, deciding the truth was simplest. My neighbor seemed unfazed. "I couldn't tell what was going on," I continued, more confident now, "they're claiming it's an Ikhwan demonstration but it didn't look that way to me."

She didn't bat an eye. "That's because it's not," she said. And that was how I discovered my dutiful, conservative upstairs-neighbor was an Al Ghad party member. The demonstration had been organized in support of Nour, a man to whom the state-owned media had no intention of giving free publicity. Claiming it was an Ikhwan stunt was their excuse to stay away. This information was essential to the article I wrote, and I had learned it not on the streets, but in the women's car.

The women's car was a moveable, segregated hothouse —a determined peace prevailed there, and produced a miniature society. I began to write an essay in homage to the women's car, picking out narrative threads that I thought might help a western reader understand its subtler implications. I sent the essay to the *New York Times Magazine*. When it ran, I showed a cutting to Sohair.

"I enjoyed this," said Sohair after she'd read it. I watched her anxiously for signs that she was just being polite. "It was very human. You did a good job."

"Thanks," I said. "I'm just happy they printed it. Usually the things you read in magazines about women's society in the Muslim world are anthropological—scientific, I mean, like the writer is studying the behavior of monkeys instead of human beings."

When several furious responses were published a week later, full of blistering language about gender apartheid, I was totally unprepared.

"But you generated controversy," my mother told me over the phone in an attempt to cheer me up. "You got people talking. That counts for something. Just imagine the Manhattanite ladies who lunch who read this and were absolutely scandalized, so scandalized that they actually *wrote in* to the *New York Times* to complain about it. It's worth it just to piss them off."

"I don't *want* to generate controversy," I said, feeling desperate. "Controversy is what mediocre people start because they can't communicate anything meaningful. I want *consensus*. And I didn't do that. I did the opposite of that. I didn't say the right things. I wasn't trying to defend the women's car in and of itself—just to show that these little human connections can happen anywhere. You can't stamp them out. Culture doesn't blunt them, language doesn't blunt them. It doesn't matter whether these people agree about the veil or gender or anything—all I wanted to do was make them *see* that, see that when they talk about Islam they're talking about real people who can feel affection for a stranger on the subway and that it *means* something."

This argument sent everyone I used it on into a short meditative silence. Controversy is seen as the best thing for a writer's career short of actual success, and the fact that I was so upset by it must have been a little baffling. But I didn't want to be fashionable, I wanted to be accurate. I didn't understand the literary economy that had built up around Muslim and ex-Muslim writers in the West: there was a market for outrage and anyone who created it, whether by condemning Islam or apologizing for it, was considered in vogue. It was a formula in which truth and consistency were secondary. Staying complicated—refusing to tell incomplete stories with pat moral endings, and remaining a Muslim professional rather than a professional Muslim—was going to be a challenge.

Later that week, Sohair asked me why I was so upset. I had been trying to hide my frustration from her and

Omar—revealing its source would mean showing them how hated they were in the West, something I tried very hard to downplay.

"You look pale," was what she said to me, mixing something on the stove in her apartment as I hung in the doorway of the kitchen.

"I'm always pale," I said.

"You look paler than usual, and also unhappy." She fanned herself with one hand: this was the time of year when the kitchen became stiflingly hot.

"There were a bunch of letters in the *New York Times Magazine* attacking my essay."

"No." She seemed genuinely shocked. "How? What was wrong with it?"

"I don't know. It frightened people. I should have said things differently. They didn't understand what I was trying to say."

"What kind of attacks? What was in these letters?"

"They said—well, one said it was the saddest defense of a dysfunctional culture she'd ever seen."

I can't forget the look on my wonderful, secular, educated mother-in-law's face when I said this: it was dismay mingled with pain, a momentary loss of confidence. It was her women's car, too. She didn't agree with it; she thought men should be expected to behave themselves in the presence of women, making a women's car unnecessary, but it was part of her history. She'd argued theology in it, commiserated over the rising price of meat, helped mothers wrangle mischievous children—this was the point; there was not *nothing* going on in these spaces westerners did not understand or inhabit. There were universes in these spaces, whether their existence was just or not. But I hadn't communicated that properly, leaving the door open for an anonymous American woman to negate my mother-in-law's relationship with her own history.

A week later, Japanese officials announced that a women's car would be added to the Tokyo subway to protect female commuters from inappropriate male attention; precisely the reason the women's car had been implemented in Cairo. The Tokyo car was hailed as a step forward for women's rights. The discrepancy would stay with me for weeks—it was the final proof that I had underestimated the amount of fear and prejudice surrounding Arab culture in the West. In my mind the week of mercy that had come after 9/11—the week when one of my Muslim friends was approached in a grocery store by a tearful man who said he hoped no one blamed my friend for what those evil people had done—was eternal. People in my own life had made a titanic effort to accept me after I converted. Sometimes the effort failed, but I appreciated it nonetheless. I had no idea that things were getting worse around the greater United States, and did not understand why.

The *Sheikha*

The teacher gives not of his wisdom, but
rather of his faith and lovingness.
—Khalil Gibran

LAILA WAS ONE OF THE FEW CONVERTS WITH WHOM I FOUND
common history, and who I admired and loved; her wry,
serene pronouncements on the nature of religion and human nature made it into several of my essays. Though half
Egyptian, she looked European, and had been raised in
Stockholm by her Swedish mother. Because of her heritage, she had always been conscious of Islam—I, on the
other hand, could not have told you what Ramadan was
a bare four years before I converted—but was brought
up without religion. Like me, she had been a reasonably
happy, productive western subculturette, playing drums in
a goth-punk band called Dark Lords of the Womb and
reading Kant as a teenager, until one day, as she described
it, "I woke in the middle of the night, thinking I heard
someone call my name. Immediately, my heart began to
race—I was having a panic attack." She paused.

"What happened then?" I prompted.

Laila wore a sybil-like expression. She first told me this story while we sat in a café near Tahrir Square, having ditched a mind numbingly bad performance of *Madama Butterfly* at the Opera House and walked through the evening filth across Qasr el Nil Bridge to have coffee. Wrapped in formal, jewel-toned silk veils—neither of us had much opportunity to dress up so we had taken advantage of the occasion—we were the object of many semibenevolent stares. They bothered her less than they bothered me.

"The panic attack stayed for months and months," said Laila. "It didn't go away until I converted."

"Wow."

"Yes. And then the panic attack went away, but I was a mess—you know how it is, at first after you convert you cry every five minutes."

I laughed. "It's so true! You get so *sensitive*—"

"See something sad, cry. See something happy, cry."

"There's this Donna Tartt novel," I said, referring to *The Secret History*, "that calls becoming religious 'turning up the volume of the inner monologue.' She's talking about the Greeks, but the principle is the same."

"Turning up the volume . . . yes, that's what it was like. A very strange experience." She smiled. "And here we are."

A few weeks after my Ali Gomaa profile ran in the *Atlantic*, Laila called to tell me some women from her Sufi order were planning a day trip to the north coast to visit a reclusive and admired Sufi *sheikha* named Sanaa Dewidar. Sheikha Sanaa and her family lived most of the year in Syria but summered in Egypt. If I was interested, the *sheikha* had consented to an interview. I didn't need to be asked twice: I packed a notebook and a tape recorder, and on a morning thick with smog took the subway downtown to meet Laila and her friends. They picked me up in a blessedly air-conditioned Hyundai.

We drove along the Alamein Road, which runs northwest out of Cairo toward the Mediterranean. A friend traveling through Egypt once asked me how hard it would be to drive to Libya from Cairo, and I answered: easy. Drive north and when you hit water turn left. There are so few roads through the Sahara that it is literally this simple. The Alamein Road is one of the prettiest and most surreal: it is surrounded by an empty wasteland, which continues uninterrupted until just south of the Med, where it becomes a stubbly plain of low brush and olive plantations. A portion of the road, the bit that runs through featureless desert, has an incongruous median of well-manicured baby palms and hibiscus. This two- or three-mile strip of civilized greenery is miles from the nearest town—not that there are really towns in that part of the Sahara, only dilapidated tea shops adjoining gas stations—and how it is maintained was long a mystery to me. As we drove to meet the *sheikha,* I found out: two men, barefoot and with long garden hoses attached to some unseen source of water, were out among the palms. There was no vehicle parked nearby, no obvious way they could arrive or leave. It was as if they'd sprung out of the earth when no one was looking. They stood straight and watched as we sped by. To me, the image was slightly unreal, but no one else in the car seemed to notice anything unusual.

We drove on without comment and the men receded in the distance, another Egyptian incident seemingly without cause or consequence.

After driving too far along the coast road, drinking tea, and turning back, we arrived at the house of Sheikha Sanaa. It was a flaking plaster building painted in faded pastels. The dignified decay, along with a sloping view down to the pale shoreline of the Mediterranean, lent the house a kind of poetry. I stood considering it, half-asleep from the motion of the car, when a middle-aged woman dressed in a brown scarf and robe approached me with a knowing smile. She was, like so many Middle Easterners, indulgent of reverie.

"*As-salaamu alaykum*," said the woman. "You are the writer?"

"*Alaykum salaam*—yes," I responded.

"You wear *hijab*."

"Yes."

"*Mash'allah*."

I smiled. *Mash'allah* literally means "by the grace of God," but is used to signify admiration. The woman introduced herself: she was one of Sheikha Sanaa's daughters—and, I gathered, the *khalifa* or presumptive heir to her mother's leadership position within their order. She led me into the house, where a woman with clear unlined skin and simple black robes sat at a plastic-sheeted table: it was Sheikha Sanaa. Though her face was remarkably youthful, her hands, which were pale and lined, suggested she was much older than she looked; I guessed her to be in her sixties.

I've never met a spiritual leader by whom I felt overwhelmed —I can't quite empathize with the stories other religious people tell about weeping at the feet of their sheikhs and pastors. I can't imagine giving a single person that much power over me, and losing my ability to be skeptical. So I felt no aura of sainthood or especial blessedness around the *sheikha,* but through her immediate and welcoming smile, she did give the impression of earnest goodness.

She rose to greet me and we exchanged the traditional kiss on each cheek. As Laila and the other women greeted her, I realized I had made something of a faux pas. They all kissed the *sheikha*'s hand instead, as a sign of deference; she in turn protested and tried to pull her hand away, to show that she felt unworthy of the honor. It was a game of courtesy I'd seen many times, but only among men and male sheikhs. Never before had I been in a religious situation mediated entirely by women.

During rounds of tea, coffee, and sweet and salty snacks, Sheikha Sanaa talked with us. I had come with a few prepared questions but let the conversation evolve organically, changing course to pursue interesting topics Laila and the others brought up. We spoke in Arabic, with sporadic bouts of English, French, and parenthetical translations by her daughters when she said things too complex or abstract for me to understand. I focused on what I knew would be most informative to a western audience: the tradition of female leadership in Islam. I asked her why this tradition was declining in the modern age.

"There are as many women sheikhs in the East today as there were in the past," she said. "In westernized countries like Egypt and Lebanon, people don't accept female religious leaders. But in Syria it's something natural."

"Westernization has made it *worse?*" This was the first time I had heard the suggestion that the relaxed western attitude toward gender was having a negative impact on Muslim women.

"It's true, in a way," Lamya, one of the women from Laila's Sufi order, chimed in. She was a cheerful, well-educated woman in her forties, and had led a spirited discussion about marriage on the drive up. "I used to live in Damascus. In Syria, men and women interact much less on a personal level. So if a woman wants spiritual knowledge, it makes more sense for her to seek it from a *sheikha* rather than a sheikh. She has better access to another woman. In westernized countries like this one, some people see female sheikhs as unnecessary, because it's more acceptable for women and men to be socially intimate. In places like Syria, they need more female sheikhs because male sheikhs have less personal access to female students."

I had learned by then that westernization is, at best, a game of unintended consequences: in the case of Islamic spiritual authority, it seemed to have eroded traditional opportunities for female leadership rather than created new ones. I questioned Sohair about this when we got back to Cairo and she confirmed what Sheikha Sanaa and Lamya suggested. "You used to hear about this *sheikha* and that *sheikha* all the time," she said, with a bitter expression she reserved for discussions about a former, better Egypt. "It was common, very common. Now they are all gone."

I wondered whether the decline in female sheikhs could have so pat an explanation—misogyny is an almost inevitable byproduct of political oppression, after all, as brutalized men turn around and brutalize the next most vulnerable population. The last fifty years of Egyptian history have been a steadily closing fist. It probably doesn't help that the sheikhs who now have free access to female students are almost all Wahhabi, and unlikely to promote ambition and leadership among women because of their puritanical beliefs. Still, it was interesting to know that Sheikha Sanaa and Lamya saw gender desegregation as a two-sided coin, one face of which had the potential to undermine authority.

As Laila chatted with Sheikha Sanaa, I drifted, and thought about women. It struck me that wherever I went, the subject was under discussion—whether it was about juggling careers and family in the West or modesty and public persona in the East, there seemed a universal lack of normalcy and solid ground. I could understand, now, why so many women in the Middle East were suspicious of women's rights movements and western feminism. Why push for rights when you have influence? A gutsy, intelligent woman in the Middle East can steer the fortunes of her entire family with a minimum of exposure and risk; giving her a full complement of western rights would limit the scope of her power by exposing her to the same public scrutiny as men. Rights would put the flaky and the idiotic on equal footing with the worthy and the able; what was the point? At a time of tremendous change and instability, why cause more disruption? You might end up with less than you started out with.

It was hot; there was a lull. The taste of tea—brackish here, where groundwater was drawn close to the sea—lingered on my tongue. Laila smiled at me.

"Do you think the best way for a woman to be a good Muslim is to take a traditional role—to be a typical wife and mother, and stay at home?" I asked Sheikha Sanaa, breaking the silence.

She shook her head. "Maryam umm Isa [Mary mother of Jesus] and Asia, wife of Pharaoh, were not typical," she said. "Asia disobeyed her husband. Maryam had no husband. They both took on great responsibilities and hardships to walk the straight path. It is said that 'one good woman is worth a thousand men.'"

I smiled ruefully—Sana'i, the twelfth-century poet to whom that saying is attributed, would be shouted down in most twenty-first-century mosques. I hesitated before asking my last question—it was not meant for a reading audience, but for myself.

"The world is so hostile now—there is so much anger between Muslims and non-Muslims and it's hard to know what to do, how to make things a little better, for yourself or for anybody else."

It didn't come out like a question, but the *sheikha* knew what I was asking. She leaned forward and took my hand, looking suddenly more focused. I had the odd feeling she had been waiting for me to bring this up.

"The Prophet was once asked this question," she said, "when the first Muslims were faced with many enemies and trials. He said 'When chaos enters the world, stick to the walls of your house like a saddle to a horse's back.' This means take care of your family and your neighbors and raise your children to be good. If everyone takes care of his own house, all troubles will end."

On some level, I knew she was right. It surprised me that after a single conversation, she could sense my need to communicate at all costs, and knew what that cost would be—perhaps better than I did. I loved being a wife; I felt I did more tangible good within my family and immediate community than I could do writing articles and books. Yet there was so much about Islam and the people who lived it that was left unsaid in the media and in public discussion, and I could do something about it. Staying silent when I saw news stories that were incomplete or religious issues that were poorly analyzed felt tantamount to lying. Beyond that, I had to relearn how to talk to my own people. The *New York Times* incident had left me shaken: I had lost touch with what people back home were thinking and feeling. I desperately wanted to get that connection back. I was still American, and I wanted to write for Americans.

That was the first time I started to think seriously about going home. Not for a few weeks or a month, but for years. The gap between the American experience and my experience was only going to get bigger. But I knew Omar had no desire to leave the Middle East. He was an idealist—better opportunities and a more comfortable life did not tempt him. His struggle was here, in Egypt, for an Islam that embraced intellect and art and spirituality. In Cairo, this war had only one front: the fight to regain control of the religious narrative by undermining fundamentalism. In the United States, there would be a second front. He would have to battle fundamentalism's mirror image, Islamophobia. He did not see this as his fight. Even the Christians and Baha'is and Jews were Arab in Egypt; fellow heirs of the language and history he loved. Western hostility toward Islam, with its mingled racial and xenophobic overtones, was alien to him.

Late in 2005, Hind el Hinnawy, a young upper-crust Cairene, claimed to be pregnant by actor Ahmad Fishawy and filed a pater-nity suit. Unremarkable by American standards, the case was shock-ing in Egypt. According to Hinnawy, she and Fishawy had an *orfi* or common-law marriage. Notoriously difficult to prove in court, these "marriages" are drawn up by private contract, and serve no other function than to legitimize mistresses and girlfriends in the eyes of Islamic law. When Hinnawy publicly announced plans to raise her daughter on her own and fight for the child's right to take Fishawy as her last name, all Cairo buzzed with scandal.

Everyone had an opinion: the papers published articles about Hinnawy's legal case in alternately tongue-in-cheek and outraged tones, while Fishawy's loyal fan base decried her as a slut. Fishawy himself refused to take a paternity test and denied any involvement with Hinnawy. The mufti, in turn, publicly admonished Fishawy, challenging him to take responsibility for his actions. In our family, opinions were split: I was surprised to find that many of the girls were fiercely critical of Hinnawy, while the uncles agreed with the mufti and thought Fishawy was setting a bad example.

"Why are people treating her as if she's a hero?" scolded Marwa, at whose wedding I had nearly tripped over Ali Gomaa's robe. "She's created *fitnah* [public controversy, unrest, or scandal] and had a child out of wedlock—"

"But it takes two people to make a baby," I said, irritated, translating the oft-quoted public health maxim into Arabic. "She's not the Virgin Mary."

"Exactly!" said Marwa. I felt my point had been lost.

"This is what happens when young men and women are out until two and three in the morning, going who knows where and doing who knows what," said Uncle Sherif, who had been listening. His expression was troubled. "This is what happens when the parents are too relaxed."

I sighed, pulling at the spot where my head scarf hugged my chin; it was too tight. "But," I struggled for the Arabic vocabulary to express what I wanted to say, "if he doesn't become the girl's father, men will think it is right to do as he has done."

By now everyone was used to the Zen-like pronouncements to which I was limited in abstract conversation.

"This is true," said Uncle Sherif, "and the way he is acting is wrong. But this situation should not have happened in the first place."

Among the Progressive Muslims in the West, opinions were less mixed. One of several articles penned in Hinnawy's defense was by Ginan Rauf, a Harvard PhD and staunch secular humanist. She had achieved notoriety with an article titled "Beer for Ramadan." Conservative Muslims loathed her; I admired her bravery if not her politics. But the article she wrote in response to a piece by Ahmad Fishawy's mother surprised me: she exhorted the woman to "appreciate the deep visionary wisdom of an Egyptian father who has courageously sought to de-link sexuality and honor, to stand firmly as an opponent of female infanticide, to resist oppression and to combat moral hypocrisy. That is how an honorable man conducts himself in the modern world. Surely these are all 'old' barbaric customs which I for one will not lament their passing away."

Alarm bells went off immediately in my head. She was setting up a misleading and dishonest straw man: no one, not even the most radical of cultural conservatives, had ever suggested Hinnawy's infant daughter should be killed. Egyptians are not sociopaths. I think even the most honor obsessed of family patriarchs would have been shocked to have this implicit accusation laid at his feet. Female infanticide, once common in the Arabian Peninsula, was strictly outlawed by Islam; there was even a chilling line in the Quran that spoke of infant girls rising from their graves on the Day of Judgment to confront their murderers. And even during the Arabian Dark Ages, female infanticide had nothing to do with extramarital affairs: girls born in lawful wedlock were killed for being female, for being a burden to a male-dominated warrior culture. I had never come across a single instance of female infanticide in modern Egypt. Rauf was creating a monster that didn't exist, and parading it in front of people too far removed from the real Egypt to question her.

Having seen what misinformation could do in this climate of fear, I was furious. It seemed so irresponsible, so unnecessary; there were other and better ways to make her point. In the discussion that ensued in the comments section following her online article, I said the worst thing you can say to a fellow Muslim, short of calling her a heretic: I called her an Orientalist.

To people unfamiliar with the last thirty years of post-colonial academics, this might seem a ridiculous word, without meaning or substance. They may be right. It's a fancy word for racist, but implies much more: an Orientalist is someone who invents exotic fictions about the East to prove a point about western superiority. Orientalism is a very serious charge to lay at the doorstep of a left-leaning academic.

It was a gross overreaction, and a very stupid one: I was white, she was Arab, and in leftist circles it was an unwritten rule that a white person couldn't criticize an Arab when it came to her depiction of the Middle East. It didn't matter who was right; it was an issue of race, tied up in centuries of misused privilege. The Muslim left was still governed by the ethnic identity politics of the seventies. But in the seventies, Arab leftists were using their new political voice to defeat myths about the Middle East, not spread them. Rauf and I were in a paradoxical position: as an Arab her opinions about the Middle East were considered more valid than mine, but she was promoting a false stereotype; as a white person my opinions were considered tainted by privilege, but I was trying to defeat that stereotype.

I had stumbled into the second war for the soul of Islam: the war being waged wholly within the West, where the Muslim community was struggling with problems arising from its unprecedented diversity. I had never set foot inside an American or British mosque and had no idea of the tensions that existed there: the deep-seated insecurities about race and religious legitimacy, the battles over tradition and identity. In public prayers, I had always been one of a tiny smattering of foreigners among uniformly Arab or Persian congregations. While the concept of foreignness loomed large in my experience as a Muslim, the concept of race did not.

It was clear there was more tension surrounding Islam in the West than I realized. Maybe that tension should have been obvious, but at the time I was only reading and watching Arab press, which was far less antagonistic and fear-mongering than its American counterpart. I thought I lived in a world that was learning from and moving past 9/11. But the reaction to my women's car essay and to the Hinnawy case—which proved not even Progressives were immune to propaganda—shook me out of my naïveté. I worried I would soon be forced to choose between two halves of myself. At one family gathering in Doqqi, my anxiety took on a particular clarity. After the stuffed grape leaves had been eaten and the tea had been poured, the talk turned to the war in Iraq.

"It's an occupation, no better than any other occupation," said one uncle. "You can't blame the Iraqis for fighting back. It's their land. You can't give someone freedom by pointing a gun at his head. The Americans want Iraqi oil—it's what they've always wanted. The Americans—"

I stayed silent, listening, thrown into fresh worry over this unusual use of "the Americans." To speak about America in such bitter generalities was not typical in Egypt, except perhaps among hard-line fundamentalists. I had never heard it used this way within Omar's family. I don't think this discretion was for my benefit, either—there seemed no great effort to stifle debate or anger when I entered the family. To most people, America was a half-wonderful, half-threatening political puzzle, and until very recently most Egyptians were as willing to separate the American people from the American government as they were to separate themselves from their own. No, this bitterness was new—it was fear.

Uncle Ahmad cleared his throat and I looked up. He was the ideal patriarch, pleasant and intelligent, with a deep authoritative voice and an unnervingly complete grasp of what was going on within the family at any given time. I argued with him exactly once, and for less than a minute; he simply restated his argument with a tone of finality and I fell silent in admiration.

"We must thank America," he said, in that same tone, "for Willow."

Two dozen faces turned fondly in my direction and assented. I put my head in my hands and made a sound that was half laugh and half something pained. Uncle Ahmad stared at me, bewildered. I was at a loss to explain what I felt. The responsibility of that unconditional affection was overwhelming. I could see what was coming: with angry rhetoric escalating in the press, and the possibility of war in Iran already on the table, I knew Uncle Ahmad's chivalrous, peace-making instincts would not be rewarded. There was no answering hand reaching out from the other shore of the Atlantic saying *We must thank Islam for Uncle Ahmad.* Even if there was, my country would still wage wars. Men would still blow themselves up in marketplaces and stone and mutilate in the name of Islam. Every day there would be something to erode that goodwill. I could not bear to see this family's faith and optimism stripped away.

My dreams turned violent: again and again I saw myself in a house with doors that didn't lock, trying desperately to barricade them against wolves or wild dogs that circled outside, seeking entry. It was as if my unconscious mind was trying and failing to take Sheikha Sanaa's advice: I was sticking to the walls of a house that was no longer under my control.

Fracture

The best lack all conviction, while the worst
Are full of passionate intensity.
                    —William Butler Yeats,
                    "The Second Coming"

THE MOVEMENT I HAD BEEN WATCHING WITH ANTICIPATION
from the other side of the world—the one that had given
me hope for middle ground—was falling apart, becoming a
parody of all the things it claimed to oppose. In Cairo, left
without support from liberal Muslims, Sheikh Ali Gomaa
began issuing fatwas designed to appease the hard-liners:
one was ambivalent toward wife beating, another forbade
the practice of yoga, a third discouraged the display of stat-
ues. The last blow came in a call from Ursula, my editor at
Cairo Magazine.

"You can stop working on anything due after next week,"
she said. "The next issue is going to be our last one."

"What?"

"We lost our funding."

"You had funding?"

"We estimated it would take about a year and a half for
the mag to become financially solvent—we needed another
six months of support. But the donors have pulled out."

It was the way of all independent media in the Middle East—in a climate of political pressure and economic disorganization, the pulling of funding was almost inevitable. It could be that the donors felt uneasy about supporting a paper so critical of the Mubarak regime in the repressive aftermath of the presidential elections. It could be they simply lost interest. Either way, it was over.

"This is *awful*," I said to Ursula.

"I know," she responded gloomily. "I feel worst for some of the young Egyptian journalists—about what this is going to do to their careers. Now they have to find somewhere else to go."

At home, Omar noticed the change in my mood. I was still functioning—I hate inactivity and don't tend to slow down even when I'm depressed. But though I went busily about my strangely parsed life, bartering for chickens in the souk in the morning and writing about politics and religion in the afternoon, Omar could tell I was not myself.

"I want to see you smile again," he said at one point, when we were driving to Madinat an Nasr to visit an aunt. "What's wrong with you? Is it just the magazine?"

I had been keeping my existential crisis more or less to myself. In Egypt, having an existential crisis is largely considered bad manners.

"I guess I've been feeling helpless," I said, after a long pause in which I discarded ten other ways to describe it. "And guilty. And like none of the positive things I've tried to do will make any difference."

"Guilty?" Omar looked incredulous. "Why?"

"I wonder a lot if I'm the best person to be saying and writing some of the stuff I say and write. I don't represent the majority of Muslims—I come from such a different background from the people I write about—I wonder if it's my place. I wonder if I should wait for someone else to say this stuff. Someone from here or Pakistan or something."

"I've learned something about westerners," said Omar, smiling a little. "The ones who feel guilty are the ones with the least reason to be. And the ones who should feel guilty never do."

"It doesn't matter, anyway." I rubbed my eyes. "No matter who tries to make things a little better, it always ends up the same—it's like trying to collect sand in a sieve. People *want* to hate each other."

"Who's put this in your head? What's going on?"

"Don't worry about it. It's a lot of little things all at once. I'll be fine."

The Oracle of Siwa

For thy kingdom is past not away,
Nor thy power from the place thereof hurled;
Out of heaven they shall cast not the day,
They shall cast not out song from the world.
—Algernon Charles Swinburne,
"The Last Oracle"

AFTER THE MAGAZINE FOLDED, I FOUND MYSELF AT LOOSE ends, with plenty of time for indulgent contemplation of my identity issues. Self-pity is hard work. When Omar's cousin Mohab suggested a trip to the remote oasis of Siwa, I didn't need much convincing. Mohab was a film student from Omar's father's side of the family. He was a couple of years older than me and had recently returned from a long stint studying in Italy. I liked him because he was a cultural intermediary. Raised in a staunchly socialist wing of the family, he could talk at length about European films and brands of cigarettes. At the same time, he maintained an avid interest in Sufism, reading and analyzing old texts of philosophy and jurisprudence with great enthusiasm. From Italy, he'd brought back a host of Region 2 DVDs and an accent. After a couple of weeks back in the smog and chaos of Cairo, he was eager to get out. Siwa, a mere forty kilometers from the Libyan border, was as far as one could get while still in Egypt.

Our route was simple but arduous: we drove north along the Alamein Road, skirting Alexandria, then took the coastal road to Mersa Matruh. After Mersa Matruh we left the coastline and crossed into the open desert. Between Matruh and Siwa are three hundred kilometers of indifferent road and no civilization of any kind—no way stations, gas stations, or even wells. Isolated as it is, Siwa vies with Central Africa as the birthplace of man: the oldest humanoid footprint on record, thought to date back three million years, was discovered there. Alexander the Great passed through, as did the Nazis, but neither stayed, and both left few traces of their presence. The oasis is too remote to be useful to imperial expansion. Today, the trek to Siwa is still daunting. If you don't take those three hundred kilometers at a good clip, armed with plenty of drinking water, a full tank of gas, and a spare tire, you can end up in trouble. I call it "the sprint." But even the sprint only provides so much insulation from the catalytic influences of tourism and westernization. In the face of modern technology, manifest in the air-conditioned buses from Cairo that roll through Siwa once a week, the Sahara is losing ground.

We originally planned to reach the oasis just after sunset, but a traffic jam outside Cairo had set us back a full three hours, and less than halfway through the sprint we found ourselves driving in total darkness. There was no moon, and the resulting black was like nothing I'd ever experienced. Our headlights reached out feebly in front of us, picking out a road blurred and faded by sand. Where the light petered out, the road seemed to drop off into nothing. The rippling earth around it, totally devoid of vegetation, caught the light we gave off in a strange way, and made shadows like massive trees; the illusion was so perfect that on several occasions I forgot there were no trees for a hundred miles in every direction, and several hundred in a few. There was no horizon, no city lights anywhere to distinguish the edge of the earth, and after half an hour we found ourselves in a state of semihallucinatory panic.

"Do you think we should pull over and wait—"

"Wait for what? *Dawn?*"

"How much water is there?"

"Four—wait, no, there's some—you count."

"Six bottles."

"That's it?"

"That's fine."

"Let's at least pull over, I have to rest my eyes." This last from Omar, who had insisted on doing all of the driving. We pulled off into the sand, the tires going silent as they met less resistance. I climbed out into purer air than any we had in Cairo. Taking deep breaths, I stepped off into space, and with a jerk found myself sliding down a small dune. I let out a shriek.

"Willow?" I heard Omar's anxious voice and saw the dancing beam of a flashlight.

"I'm fine." I started laughing almost uncontrollably, floundering ankle-deep in the sand. With effort, I climbed back up the dune, thinking of the vipers and scorpions that might be skittering around in the darkness.

"Are there snakes here?" I asked.

"Snakes? No, no!" Mohab's voice answered from some indeterminate point. "Snakes need to eat something. Out here there's nothing to eat." The Italian lilt to his Egyptian accent lent him a reassuring universality.

"Okay." I balanced on one foot, tapping sand out of the shoe belonging to the other foot. "I hope you're right."

We made our way back to the car, stumbling over rocks and giggling. An hour or so later, exhausted, dirty, and night-blind, we saw lights on the near horizon and found ourselves on the outskirts of the oasis. We pulled up to our hotel, an incongruous plaster building on a dirt road, and shedding our bags and sand-filled shoes, retreated to our rooms to sleep.

The next morning I woke up unsure of where I was. Going to the window, I looked out on a small town square circumscribed by roads that led off into dense blue-green palm groves. One corner of the square was dedicated to a fruit-and-vegetable souk; elsewhere there were open-air cafés lined with dusty plastic chairs and faded awnings. Beyond the square, rising on a prominent hill, was the Old City: a labyrinth of mud-brick houses and elevated streets, now in ruins. Before the Egyptian government extended its reach, and the rule of law, to its Libyan border towns, the Siwans used the Old City as a fortress to protect against Bedouin raids. In the early twentieth century, a hard rain—the first in three hundred years—destroyed much of the infrastructure and the Siwans built the modern buildings that make up the town today.

I felt the muscles in my shoulders relax. Cairo was so relentless and grimy that I had forgotten how good it is to have beautiful things to look at. The palm groves threw watery, inviting shadows in the morning sun, and the air smelled like wood smoke and warm earth. There were men moving in the streets below, driving donkey carts and carrying sacks of rice; the women, who were fewer, wore blue embroidered chadors and black face-veils, and slipped along with a ballerinalike, toe-first gait. I had an odd sense of déjà vu; I think I had constructed, unconsciously and with a kind of longing, a place that resembled this, where the stolen restful moments I had in the city were magnified and took physical form.

We met Mohab at a pleasantly shabby café called Abdu's for breakfast. As we tucked into bowls of cream and honey with hunks of flatbread, a man in a white robe and camel-wool cloak approached us, hailing Omar with an outstretched hand.

"Omar, my son," he said smiling, "your mother called to say you were coming. How are you?"

Omar rose to shake the man's hand, ducking his head respectfully.

"My wife, Willow." He put a hand on my shoulder. I lowered my eyes and smiled.

"Does she speak Arabic?" the man asked.

"I speak a little," I said.

"She speaks very well." Omar gave my shoulder a reassuring squeeze.

"Good," said the man in English. I looked up and met his eyes, and he smiled, approving. "That's very important."

His name was Abdullah, and he was a local tribal leader and education director. He was also the man responsible for the oasis's remarkably high literacy rate: 90 percent among men and nearly 98 percent among women, making Siwa the only place in Egypt where more women than men could read. Omar and Sohair had met him on a visit to Siwa a couple of years earlier, and had invited him to dinner when he was in Cairo for some governmental function; the old rules of hospitality meant that he was now a close friend of the family. Before that moment I had only vague ideas surrounding the term "tribal leader." No city dweller really understands how tribal societies function, study all she may. But seeing Abdullah, a lot of things fell into place.

He looked to be in his early fifties, and was bearded and sun-browned, with an athletic, erect posture that suggested a person used to leadership but familiar with difficult physical work. One of his hands was crippled, as if from polio or a poorly set break (it turned out to be the latter), but he was so able that I would forget about it until I saw him again several months later. What was most striking about Abdullah was his manner: without words, he commanded the attention of everyone around him. He provoked some inborn pack response in all of us, suggesting with the set of his shoulders and the tone of his voice that he was here to protect us, and in return confidently expected obedience. I saw no one, man or woman, Egyptian or European or American, who was immune to it.

Charisma is a silly word for this quality of Abdullah's. He didn't go out of his way to be charming or friendly, yet his presence was spellbinding. It was an aura of benign and formidable power, and of great intelligence. Meeting him, it became conceivable that an entire tribe could be organized around a single person. When we went back to Cairo, Sohair would ask me, with a twinkle in her eye, what I thought of Abdullah, and I could think of no reply but, "Talking with him, I understand how polygamy worked for all those years." She would laugh so hard she had to hold on to a chair to keep from falling over.

When Abdullah offered to take the four of us out into the desert to visit a hot spring, we said yes almost in unison. We left early the next morning, piling into a colossal, retrofitted Range Rover before the sun was high.

"Ready?" Abdullah asked when we were situated. "You'd better hold on." The Range Rover had no seat belts. We took off, winding through the palm groves until we reached the open sand. This was the Sahara as it is most often envisioned: the "sea into which no oar is dipped," dune after dune of vanilla-colored sand stretching a thousand miles into the distance. Even with the rise of modern technology and sophisticated satellite locating devices, it is one of the least-explored places on earth. I watched Omar as we went bumping over the dunes: he was watching the horizon, turning every so often to grin at us in silent glee. Mohab leaned precariously out one window with his video camera, filming, using his free hand to keep the incongruous newsboy cap he wore from flying off his head.

"You'll fall out!" I said as the nose of the truck went up and came down with a jaw-rattling thud.

"No, I won't!" Mohab smiled, gripping his hat, and I caught my breath as we tipped down a thirty- or forty-foot dune toward a tiny oasis sheltering in a broad ditch below.

The oasis—a stand of palm trees, some brush, and a few flowering plants—veiled a deep spring around which the Siwans had built a circular retaining wall. Nearby was a bamboo shelter where I went to change—not into a bathing suit, but into a cheap galibayya I didn't mind ruining. The path to the shelter went through a dense patch of brush. Abdullah told me, in an offhand unconcerned way, to watch for snakes, and I shrieked and ran the rest of the short way. When I had changed I came back out and joined the men by the spring, which sent little eddies of vapor up into the morning air.

I sat on the retaining wall and dipped one foot in the water: it was the perfect temperature, very warm but not hot. One by one we all slid in, taking seats on the bathing steps that led down from the wall. The palms made dry whispering sounds as they moved overhead and beyond the oasis the sand rose up yellow-white in the sun. When we went back to Siwa proper there would be an e-mail from the State Department waiting in my inbox, asking very politely whether I was registered at the local embassy (I was), but for now I was happy without reservation—the happiest, I think, that I have ever been. I knew then what Heaven must look like: a garden in a desert, all unapologetic and sudden green, where there were friends to talk to and springs to bathe in. You couldn't think about war there, or injustice, or sacrifice, only wonderful simple things. It was un-Babel —everyone present spoke at least three languages, but for a few reverent minutes we didn't need to use a single one of them.

Omar and Abdullah broke the spell, speaking quietly in Arabic. I didn't listen until I heard my name.

"Willow is a writer," Omar was saying. "She has written about Egypt for western magazines." Like so many educated Egyptians I knew, Abdullah was trying hard to believe that the banality and misinformation western media spread about his culture were the product of ignorance, not conspiracy. Earlier he had voiced quiet concern that western outrage over Arab attitudes toward homosexuality was being used as a smoke screen to divert attention from the exploitative gay sex tourism perpetrated by western travelers.

"I'm not an ignorant man," he had said, "I know there is homosexuality in every culture. But these boys who are involved are all very young and very poor, and willing to do anything for money—it's child abuse."

Apparently they had returned to the same subject: Abdullah was talking about the way women's society functioned in Siwa and how it was difficult to describe to outsiders because it was hard even for other women to participate in it. Omar told him about the profile of Sheikha Sanaa I had written, which had recently been published in Canada's *National Post*.

"Really?" Abdullah looked at me with a more frank, appraising expression than his former reserved one—it was a shift I was used to by now; among men I was often very quiet, much more quiet than most Egyptian women. Silence, the apex of modesty, was my best weapon against common male assumptions about my availability. With women it was different—I could talk and laugh and be more open about my opinions. My female friends accepted my unusual profession almost without question, but most men were surprised to learn that a woman who spoke so little in person addressed an audience in print. Abdullah's surprise was brief.

"What do people say to what you write?" he asked.

I thought of the reaction to the women's car piece.

"Awful things, sometimes," I said, smiling without conviction. "It's hard to help people understand something they've never seen—ideas they've never heard of. Everybody's scared. I don't really think it's possible to make a dent in this—" I waved my hand vaguely; the clash of civilizations was implicit.

"We yet may," said Abdullah. His tone was quiet and confident, not patronizing. It surprised me. Most people seemed to encourage me out of fondness, or, like Sheikha Sanaa, told me to pray and be good and not worry about other people.

"And if not," Abdullah continued after a pause, "we have our own lives." He looked out past the foliage at the sand, and I wondered if he, too, saw this place as evidence of divine mercy. He turned back and smiled at me. No doubt shadowed his face.

Flood Season

I am a part of all that I have met
Yet all experience is an arch wherethro
Gleams that untravelld world whose
    margin fades
Forever and forever when I move
    —Alfred Lord Tennyson, "Ulysses"

FOR THREE YEARS, MY FATHER-IN-LAW HAD BEEN ASKING me to visit the Mahmoud Khalil Museum of Art with him. I was the only member of the family who had not heard his theories about Picasso and the French School a dozen times, and I still enjoyed listening to these little lectures. Talking with him, I discovered I'd absorbed a dismal amount of information through years of public school French, and did my best to be a good conversation partner. But something or other always came up to postpone our trip to this museum, which, according to Amu Fakhry, housed the largest number of Impressionist paintings in North Africa. It did not have much competition.

A day came in the summer of 2006 when the weather was too hot to do anything but browse in an air-conditioned building. We drove down the Nile in middling levels of smog, and I pulled at my head scarf, letting gritty air pour over my face. The museum was a white villa flanked by lawns: beautiful in the jaunty, out-of-place way that all colonial architecture was beautiful. I waited in the shade as Amu Fakhry argued with the ticket taker, insisting that I should count as an Egyptian, and not have to pay the tourist price. I began to feel depressed.

"*Yalla,*" said Amu Fakhry, holding the counts-as-an-Egyptian ticket over his head triumphantly. I smiled and took his arm as we went through the front door.

I felt as though I was back in Boston. Everything was cool and quiet; there was a marble staircase with a red runner, rooms with large windows, vases of flowers, and paintings arranged in a way that demonstrated an articulate understanding of what they represented. The paintings themselves were plentiful—works of Degas, Pissarro, Toulouse-Lautrec, Monet, Manet, and the odd John Singer Sargent from an earlier age. Gathered around them were groups of fine-art students, quartets of veiled girls murmuring to each other over their drawing boards, charcoals flying, sketching windmills and nudes.

Their quiet engagement was striking. There is usually such noise when Egypt and Europe encounter each other. In the Valley of the Kings the tourists bark and laugh in echoing tunnels, and at French or American movies Egyptian mothers admonish their children to look away during kissing scenes that have escaped the censors, as if each culture must defend itself against the beauty of the other. If the art is beautiful then the ideas are beautiful, and this cannot be if the opposing culture is strange and backward. We decide what is civil in ourselves by deciding what is uncivil in others.

We wandered into a room whose centerpiece was an enormous rectangular canvas. It had been painted over a hundred years ago by a Frenchman, and depicted a group of Nubian women carrying their washing to the banks of the Nile at flood, somewhere in what is now Sudan.

"See," said Amu Fakhry, gesturing a circle around the canvas with his hand, "the artist was a master, he draws your eye down the right side, past the women, to the brightness of the water, then up again past the temple on the other side of the river, back to the women." He laughed with delight. "It is marvelous. Here we have found something."

I looked more closely at the canvas. There was a spot that troubled me—from far away it was nothing, but up close it exposed itself as a dark place in the water at the edge of the river, disguised as a stray eddy over a rock. But it had once been something else. I stepped back in surprise.

"This was a man. There was a man here, and the artist painted over him," I said, pointing to the spot.

Amu Fakhry bent toward it. "Perhaps," he said.

I looked at the spot again. Sure enough, crouched in the water, swirling something in a sieve, was a man. The women were all looking at him impassively and his head was tilted toward them as if he was about to speak. Why had he been omitted?

I stepped back again to look at the painting as a whole. The artist had captured the heaviness of the river and the weight it imparts to everyone around it. The women had that drowsy-alert look that announces summer along its banks, when the heat is so intense that the middle hours of the day are spent in thick, tropical sleep, the body's only defense against the season. The artist knew all this; the heat seemed to hang in the air of the painting, shimmering on the bare limbs of the women.

I thought, *The women are unveiled. Their arms are showing.* Of course he couldn't have included the man. To do so would have destroyed the authenticity of the painting. The artist had given up his original vision so that the painting told the truth. It was beautiful, and it was true, and it was painted by a westerner. The women were left alone in the space sacred to them; they stared not at a man, but at a river, *the* river, swollen with flood.

"What are you thinking about?" asked Amu Fakhry.

"Home," I said.

Omar and I had discussed moving to the United States off and on throughout our married life, but only in the abstract. He was uneasy with the idea. And as long as he didn't have a green card, it would be difficult for us to visit my family together. When Omar picked up a tourist visa packet—half an inch thick—from the American Embassy downtown one winter, the consular official who handed it to him gave him a strange look. If Omar was married to an American, why didn't he just apply for permanent residency? Omar told him he didn't intend to live permanently in the United States. The official said it would look very strange for the spouse of an American to apply for a tourist visa. When we opened the application at home, we discovered that it required Omar to have more money in the bank than both our savings accounts put together—proof that he did not intend to immigrate illegally. I put my head down on the table.

"This is too complicated," I muttered. When I had gone to renew my Egyptian residence visa at Mugamma several months earlier, a government employee in a blue head scarf called me her beloved and asked me how long I wanted to stay.

Omar petted my head. "Don't be upset," he said. "Please."

"What if we just did it?" I asked, "The whole thing? Lived in the U.S. for a few years so you could get citizenship, and we wouldn't have to deal with all this visa crap anymore?"

My husband took a breath and smiled. "Okay. Let's think about it."

I wanted to spend at least part of my adult life in my own country. By leaving the United States right out of college and promptly getting married, I skipped the extended adolescence that is such an important part of American life. I could not define how I was different: in some ways I felt much older than friends my age, but in others I felt almost naive. At an age when most women were still dating, I was married, caught up in establishing a household and settling down. But because I was a woman, I was sheltered in Egypt in a way I wouldn't have been in America. I had no idea how to operate a car beyond turning the key in the ignition; I couldn't change a tire or even check fluid levels. I didn't know how insurance worked. In Egypt it would be unthinkable to ask a woman to move something heavy, or perform a mechanical task more complex than changing a lightbulb; even today I have to remind myself to attempt these things on my own before asking for help.

What I could do is barter. Using herbs, I could cure a mild case of dysentery without antibiotics. I could tell if the live duck I was about to buy was overfed to make it look healthier. I could argue with a man holding a semiautomatic rifle without feeling afraid. I could write a thousand words a day while fasting. These were the things I knew. All the strengths I had developed as an adult were Egyptian strengths. Yet I was not Egyptian, and barely a day went by when I did not feel an eddy of restlessness.

Omar had never traveled west of Morocco, and never lived anywhere but Cairo. When I met him, he did not have a bank account—having grown up in an African cash economy, he'd never needed one. Like most Egyptian lives, his had very little paper attached to it. There was no orderly proof of his education beyond a certificate made of cheap copy paper proclaiming him a Bachelor of Science; there was no certified trail of letters to describe his self-directed study of history and linguistics, equal at least to an MA.

"I don't want to be one of those immigrants who's treated badly because they can't prove anything about themselves," he fretted.

"We won't let that happen," I said, though I was afraid of the same thing. As we began the green card application process, I was surprised to find I felt more restless instead of less so. Our lives, from this point onward, would be unwieldy and nomadic; going home would always mean leaving another home behind. By this time, we owned an apartment in a suburb of Cairo, filled with arabesque wooden furniture from one of the last traditional workshops in the city. Even when my life in Egypt frustrated me—which was often—I felt anchored to it. It was reassuring. It was something I had created from the ground up, on my own. Homesick as I was, I would return to the United States as something of a stranger, without a credit history, a rental history, or professional roots in any particular place. Something Ahmad told me in Iran—at some tea shop or other—haunted me: "If you want to leave your country, leave before you're thirty." He never mentioned how best to return.

I watched Omar closely during trips to the American Embassy, looking for signs of anxiety or fear. I knew he was doing this for me. The material comforts of the first world didn't tempt him much; he was satisfied with the spiritual comforts he had at home. He had mastered his environment. As Omar leaned back in a plastic chair outside the intake area of the embassy—containing more Americans than I'd seen in nearly four years—I felt a little eddy of guilt. Being Cairene is not like being American; Cairenes are specialists, with skills and instincts unique to their unforgiving city. Americans live in broader strokes, taught to paint over whatever cultural surfaces they encounter. Both are immune to assimilation, but for very different reasons.

"*Bitfakari fi eh?*" Omar asked me; *What are you thinking?*

"Nothing." I smiled and touched his hand. We were an island in a sea made up of damp official forms, dimpled along the edges where their owners clutched them. This was a waiting room in every sense. Around us were middle-class Cairenes in their best suits, listening for their numbers to be called. A delegation of Coptic monks sat in a row. Anxious eyes told me that for many of these people, America meant an escape—from political oppression, chaos, social upheaval, economic strife, or fundamentalism, any one of a hundred things. But not for Omar. He sat with a sad half-smile, his long fingers folded in his lap. For Omar, America meant exile.

I knew I was risking my marriage by taking it across the Atlantic. New York, Boulder, Boston; these places would never be to Omar what Cairo was to me. But the United States was my home, and I couldn't go the rest of my life with my back turned to it. I might begin to forget what I was. But would we forget what our marriage was, once we uprooted it? I wondered. Omar wondered, too. When we began filling out his visa application, he asked me whether I would love him in America the way I loved him in Egypt. Yes, of course, I insisted. The third party in our marriage—geography —said nothing, but waited in the background to be recognized. Omar could hate America. If he did, I might never be able to live in my country again. There was no certainty. Then again, there never had been—all love is risk. We would go forward and hope. The rest was written on our palms, an inscrutable poem known only to God.

Early that May, Omar's green card came through. We made plans to leave Egypt in late June. In the interim, we unknit our Cairene lives, pulling out the stitches that bound us to people and things. Our car we left in Ibrahim's capable hands. My house plants went to cousins who lived down the street. Spare keys went to Sohair, who promised to check on our apartment twice a month.

Since moving to the far side of Cairo, we had only been in the habit of visiting Sohair, Fakhry, and Ibrahim in Tura twice a month or so. Once we set the date of our departure, we started going once or twice a week. The drive became a ritual: we crossed a short interim of desert to meet the Ring Road, followed that for a while, then went south along the Corniche, hugging the Nile. That stretch of road and river are perfect in my memory. I can close my eyes and see a succession of minarets: as you exit Tura Bridge there is one directly ahead of you and one on your left; then comes another, smaller, nestled in a slum; then there is a beige stretch of wire-topped wall, patrolled by policemen half-asleep on matched horses; and behind that wall is the butterfly mosque. Still in prison, but not imprisoned, it sits patiently, stone on stone, as if it has folded its wings and come to rest at the bottom of the jar, waiting for the inevitable day when the jar will crack. The prison may be gone in ten years, destroyed in one of Egypt's intermittent coups and revolutions. Or it may stand another hundred. It doesn't matter; the mosque will outlive it. On the day the dissidents inside those walls are freed, the mosque will be free also. It will unfurl; it will catch the light as the sun goes down across the river, and proclaim that it, too, has a destiny.

Since we would be separated from *molokheya* (a spinach-like soup) and stuffed doves and real baklava, Omar's relatives wanted to feed us. There was a rush of family lunches. Aunties made their signature dishes, the desserts they knew I liked, and the twenty or thirty of us who were closest in our vast tribe sat together for hours, each one unwilling to be the first to leave. I was reminded, with pain whose intensity I did not expect, of the strange, limping last weeks I had spent in the United States before moving to Cairo. It was a burden to be so loved. I felt unworthy of it.

"I honestly don't know what I will do on Monday and Wednesday afternoons," said Sameh the last time I saw him. It was a thick evening, the air clogged with the perspiration of the Nile and the filth of human industry. He sat in his office at the language center, talking to one of his students from the Delta—who, just as Sameh predicted, stared at me slack-jawed and unspeaking for the entire duration of my visit. Sameh gave me a morose, sympathetic smile.

"To think—at our first lesson you could barely put four words together," he said. "*Wa delwa'ti bititkellimi wa betif'hami. Enti misrayya ba'a, khalas.*" ("And now you speak and understand. You're Egyptian, it's over.")

"*Hashoofak b'khayr,*" I told him; *I'll see you well.* It's something you say when you're only leaving for a little while.

Sameh nodded. "*In sha'allah.*"

During the last couple of weeks before our departure, I took to wandering the city by myself. It was an odd thing for a man to do, and unheard of for a woman. Cairo is not conducive to wandering. It presses on you like a dirty hand, and with a stinking mouth shouts in your ear. If you're wise, you take a cab or a car or the subway from point to point, and shut out as much of the in-between as you can. But I was leaving. I could afford to spend myself on the city. I walked through the alleys behind the Mosque of Imam Husayn, dense with the smells of fat and cumin, and was amazed to remember a time when these things were unfamiliar. Sometimes I took a book with me and sat at a café alone. During the day, Fishawi's—the famous *ahua* (café)at the heart of Khan al Khalili, where Omar and I had one of our first conversations—was almost quiet. I could drink black tea with mint and watch the sunlight bake the carved wooden doorways, undisturbed, under the bemused, oddly tender watch of a handful of day waiters.

When I could, I visited Husayn itself. The mosque is not as grand as Sultan Hassan or as whimsical as Al Rifa'i, where the last shah of Iran is entombed. But the presence of the shrine—the gilt house of unseen remains, the last physical traces of the last imam holy to both Sunnis and Shi'ites— makes its atmosphere unforgettable. The imam was among the last people to whom I said good-bye before we left. It was a day in June when the heat was tempered by a wind off the Mediterranean: you could tilt your head up and catch a water-drenched breath of oxygen, proof of some more rarified existence in some other place, beyond the city. I took off my shoes at the door of the mosque and walked inside on bare feet. The women's side was crowded: girls, young boys, and their mothers and grandmothers sat in bunches and rows, praying or talking quietly. I threaded my way toward the shrine. Picked out in silver and marble, it stood at the center of the mosque, accessible from either side. Men and women, hushed or reciting Quran under their breath, pressed against the railing that protected the imam from too much adoration. I found an empty spot next to a woman in a dust-spattered abaya. She gave me a little smile and patted my hand. I lost my composure. Standing there, in the damp human crush of my religion, I began to cry. Not for the things I was leaving, but for the things I was taking with me—all I had fought for, all I had lost, and a joy so potent it felt like pain.